SPEECHES THAT CHANGED
Canada

DENNIS GRUENDING

Fitzhenry & Whiteside

Published in Canada by Fitzhenry & Whiteside,
195 Allstate Parkway, Markham, ON   L3R 4T8

Published in the United States by Fitzhenry & Whiteside,
311 Washington Street, Brighton, MA 02135

10 9 8 7 6 5 4 3 2 1

Fitzhenry & Whiteside acknowledges with thanks the Canada Council for the Arts
and the Ontario Arts Council for their support of our publishing program.

Library and Archives Canada Cataloguing in Publication
Speeches that changed Canada / [selected and edited by] Dennis Gruending.

ISBN 978-1-55455-112-5 (paperback)

1. Speeches, addresses, etc., Canadian. 2. Canada--History--Sources.
I. Gruending, Dennis, 1948-, compiler, editor

PN4055.C3S64 2017   C815'.008   C2017-904593-8

Publisher Cataloging-in-Publication Data (U.S.)
Names: Gruending, Dennis, 1948-, author.
Title: Speeches That Changed Canada / Dennis Gruending.
Description: Markham, Ontario : Fitzhenry & Whiteside, 2018. | Includes index. | Summary:
"On Canada's 150th anniversary this book brings together speeches on contemporary issues that produced great
oratory. Each speech is introduced and placed in historical perspective" – Provided by publisher.
Identifiers: ISBN 978-1-55455-112-5 (paperback)
Subjects: LCSH: Canada -- History. | Speeches, addresses, etc., Canadian. |
BISAC: HISTORY / Canada / General.
Classification: LCC F1026.6G784 | DDC 971 – dc23

Cover image courtesy of Shutterstock
Interior and cover design by Tanya Montini
Printed in Canada by Houghton Boston

DEDICATION

To Maria, Matt & Solomon
To Anna & Salim
And, always, to Martha

ALSO BY DENNIS GRUENDING

Gringo: Poems and Journals from Latin America

Emmett Hall: Establishment Radical

Promises to Keep: A Political Biography of Allan Blakeney

The Middle of Nowhere: Rediscovering Saskatchewan

Great Canadian Speeches

Truth to Power: The Journalism of a Benedictine Monk (ed)

*Pulpit and Politics: Competing Religious Ideologies
in Canadian Pubic Life*

ACKNOWLEDGMENTS

This book has had a long period of gestation. I proposed it to Fitzhenry & Whiteside in 2008 and they agreed to publish it. I began work on the manuscript but withdrew later that year when I took on a busy full-time job. In a conversation several years later, Sharon Fitzhenry asked if I was still interested in the project. Indeed, I was. My research files were still awaiting attention and I had added to them over the years. I want to thank Sharon, who has published several of my books, for her continued interest in my work and support for my ideas. Thanks also to Charlene Dobmeier, a consummate editor and literary counsellor.

A number of discerning friends and acquaintances agreed to read chapters of the manuscript and I have benefitted from their observations and comments. They include David Blaikie, Jennifer Ditchburn, Graham Fraser, William Knight, Julianne Labreche, Kate Malloy, George Melnyk, Margaret Robbins, Maggie Siggins, Alma Wiebe, Frieda Wiebe, Barry Wilson, and Ian E. Wilson. My wife and life partner, Martha Wiebe, reads everything that I write and always provides wise advice, not to mention her enduring love and support. I am especially grateful to her.

A READING NOTE

I have written this book as a narrative uninterrupted by textual notes, but it has been thoroughly researched. For those who are interested in sources, I provide them in the Notes section near the back of the book.

CONTENTS

INTRODUCTION

A good speech is a literary work but it also aims at
persuading an audience to do something.

There is something basic and enduring about the relationship between a speaker and an audience, and the best orators continue to move us for better or worse. While arts such as literature, music, painting, and dance are food for the soul, rhetoric is by its nature public and activist. A good speech is a literary work but it also aims at persuading an audience to do something. Great orators have been able to convince others to wage war or to make peace, to commit acts of generosity and sacrifice or turn to hatred and violence. Adolph Hitler's speeches were rambling and incoherent but he was mesmerizing in his ability to stoke resentment through his appeals to racial nationalism. Other orators appealed to our better angels. Many of us know at least something of Abraham Lincoln's Gettysburg Address, Winston Churchill's defiant wartime speeches, Franklin Delano Roosevelt's fireside chats, and the inspiring speeches of Martin Luther King, Jr., John F. Kennedy, Nelson Mandela, and Vaclav Havel. The enthusiasm generated by Barack Obama's speech-making in the United States in this decade proves there is still a receptive audience for well-crafted messages that offer hope and vision. Canadians have been just as eager to be moved and persuaded, and this book provides examples of such oratory drawn from our history.

In Athens and other Greek city states in the fourth and fifth centuries BCE, a citizen's prowess and prestige were judged in great measure by the eloquence that person displayed in public meetings or courts of law. Important community decisions were made only after a debate in which all (male) citizens could speak. Rhetoric, the art of public persuasion, was in this way closely tied to the development of democracy. Unfortunately, eloquence has been employed for authoritarian and totalitarian purposes as well.

The art of public speaking was studied and rehearsed in ancient Greece. Aristotle's book *On Rhetoric* became a classic for the ages. He wanted to instruct about effective public speaking but he wanted, as well, to teach his students how to judge and analyze the speeches of others. He outlined three forms of persuasion an orator could use in a speech or other discourse. They are: *logos*, the presentation of a logical argument; *ethos*, the projection of the speaker as sympathetic and trustworthy; and *pathos*, the speaker's emotional appeal to the beliefs, values, and feelings of an audience. Aristotle's categories of analysis have been used for centuries, although they have of necessity been adapted and extended. Aristotle was less informed than we are about psychology and biography, so he had fewer tools to probe a speaker's character and motives. The ability to influence, and, yes, to manipulate audiences has also changed dramatically. It now depends to a great extent upon the efforts of speech writers, the machinations of spin doctors, and most significantly the audio and visual impact of television and social media transmitted instantaneously and everywhere.

Our story in Canada is not as dramatic as that of nations born in revolution or those in which violence reigns in the streets, but it is if anything more admirable. We were once a group of vulnerable British colonies but through circumstance and acts of genius we have become a democratic, prosperous, and diverse nation. Where others have used bullets and bombs, our projectiles have been words. They are the essence of all politics and negotiation. Words are an incomparably better tool than artillery or marching armies.

It is too simple to say that Confederation occurred because John A. Macdonald crafted fine speeches at Charlottetown and later at Quebec City. There were many forces at play, including a British Colonial Office eager to forego the expense of protecting colonies it believed to be indefensible. Yet Macdonald was the main architect of Confederation. He used his considerable powers of speech and persuasion to bring others along once he had belatedly become convinced of its need. In this book I analyze his speech to the Legislative Assembly of the United Province of Canada in 1865 and the circumstances that surrounded its preparation and delivery. In Macdonald's case and others, I examine the impact of their speeches upon audiences of the day; but I also scrutinize their continuing impact upon contemporary Canada.

Wilfrid Laurier's masterful speech on political liberalism in 1877 disarmed his critics, both clerical and lay, and succeeded in winning political space for his ideology and his party. Based in large measure upon his skills and popularity, the Liberals came to dominate Quebec, and hence Canadian politics, for decades to come. Louis Riel attempted valiantly in his speech to the jury in 1885 to plead for the Métis and Indigenous peoples suffering the onslaught of European settlement. Riel could not convince that jury to spare his life but his words have resonated through the decades. His execution created a major fault line in Canada—between French and English, Quebec and Ontario, Catholic and Protestant, Indigenous and European, which in some ways persists to this day. Nellie McClung made a brilliant mock speech at a theatre in Winnipeg in 1914. She lampooned Manitoba Premier Rodmond Roblin, who was stubbornly opposed to women having the vote. McClung's speech was pivotal in achieving the change she and so many others desired.

Arthur Meighen understood public debate as a form of combat and used his commanding rhetoric and sarcastic wit to drive a conscription bill through Parliament in 1917. Agnes Macphail, Canada's first female member of Parliament, was so skilled and audacious in her oratory that during summer recesses she was invited to perform on a Chautauqua speech-making circuit in the United States. Her speech in the House of Commons in 1928 about the need for political reform provides a trenchant example of her wit and charisma. In 1961 Tommy Douglas used his prowess as an orator to convince people that the time was right for publicly financed health care. He faced hostile opposition from his political opponents and the medical establishment. Lester Pearson's speeches in 1964 calling for a new Canadian flag met intense opposition, but his firm resolution helped change the way Canadians see themselves—not as a vestigial colony but as a proud and independent nation making its own way in the world.

We who write about these speeches have a problem. Some of us are old enough to remember Lester Pearson, and if we aren't, we can watch old news clips and documentaries. They display the Pearsonian lisp and stammer, the frequent roll of his head, and his impish smile. He appears almost embarrassed to be delivering a speech; but those same traits were part of his diplomat's persona and he used them to neutralize both friends and adversaries. However, we have never heard and cannot retrieve the sound of John A. Macdonald's voice nor that of Laurier or Riel because in their day, technology did not exist to record and store the human voice. We have to make do with references scattered throughout the considerable literature about those individuals and by examining the texts they left behind.

One could say that reading such texts without actually seeing or hearing the speech is like reading Shakespeare without ever having experienced his plays in the theatre. We miss the rise and fall of the voice, the smile, the wink, the proffered arm or pointed finger, and the shouts of encouragement or heckling from the audience. To continue this analogy, or to use that of reading a novel, familiarity with context and character does allow us to use our imagination to set the scene. That is what we happily do in literature all of the time and it is rich in its reward. We should, at least, be grateful that the textual record endures: Macdonald speaking on Confederation, Laurier addressing the Club Canadien in Quebec City, Riel pleading to the jury, and McClung playing the part of Premier Roblin in a mock parliament. I encourage you to read aloud the speeches presented here to get a better sense of how they were created and delivered.

Radio was coming into its own when Richard Bedford Bennett took to the airwaves in 1935 to talk about the need for economic reform. There was no national network in Canada so he paid forty radio stations to carry his message. Bennett was clearly more accustomed to delivering a leather-lunged stump speech than he was with the intimacy of radio. But millions of people heard his addresses, rather than just the few hundred who would have attended an event. It was Bennett's brother-in-law, W. D. Herridge, who convinced him that he should follow the lead of Franklin Delano Roosevelt. The American president had introduced the New Deal in the United States to get the economy moving again. In his fireside chats he used radio to great effect in convincing citizens to follow and support him. In Canada, Bennett's speeches were unique in another way. He was likely the first prime minister to use speech writers. He had Herridge and another aide write the radio addresses for him. In that way also he imitated Roosevelt, who relied so thoroughly upon trusted writers that they sometimes lived in the White House and accompanied him on presidential trips and holidays. Unfortunately, it appears any audio recordings that may have been made of Bennett's 1935 radio addresses have been lost.

There is one piece of jumpy silent film footage showing Laurier, and several of Bennett, but the moving image really came into its own with the advent of Canadian television in the early 1950s. Pearson was not a riveting television personality by any means, and even Tommy Douglas, so adept in debate and so comfortable on radio, appeared oddly angular and too formal in his diction for the new medium. Pierre Trudeau and René Lévesque were among the first Canadian leaders to master the use of television. Both men had charisma. Trudeau's friend, the media guru Marshall McLuhan, told him that his face was perfect for television. Trudeau understood the theatrical dimension of the medium, which explains his playing to the cameras with a pirouette behind Queen Elizabeth or his sliding down staircase railings. It is difficult to imagine Diefenbaker, Pearson, or Tommy Douglas doing that. René Lévesque was as rumpled as Trudeau was regal but he also had impressive television presence. Trudeau and Lévesque often faced off but never so dramatically as during the 1980 referendum on Quebec sovereignty. Trudeau's famous "No" speech is in this book.

I do not believe there was in the past some gilded age of Canadian oratory. However, the political speeches selected for this book are generally of a better quality than almost anything that we are likely to hear today.

There is one significant limitation to the excellence of several speeches in this collection. They interpret the creation of Canada as a project of two founding peoples—the French and English—and later extend that list to other immigrants as well. The Indigenous peoples who have lived here for tens of thousands of years are almost completely overlooked. It is as if they did not exist in the minds of most of our political leaders. But Indigenous leaders and peoples have increasingly been making their own case for justice. Witness the powerful speech in this book by Chief Joseph Gosnell in favour of the Nisga'a treaty.

My intention in *Speeches that Changed Canada* is to examine, in an accessible fashion, some of Canada's most outstanding oratory. In a previous book, *Great Canadian Speeches*, I anthologized sixty-eight speeches. This time I have chosen a much smaller number of orators and go into considerable detail about a speech given by each of them. I explore the historical context, the facts surrounding the preparation and delivery of the speech, the persona chosen by the speaker, and the speech's lasting impact upon Canada and Canadians. Also, I pay close attention to the speech itself and analyze the rhetorical techniques employed by the speaker to win over his or her audience.

This book will be of interest to those who love Canadian history, to those attentive to the role of rhetoric in that history, and to those who write and deliver speeches. The book is also meant for anyone who, in the tradition of Aristotle, wants to become more skilled at analyzing the words spoken by others, and to recognize the rhetorical tricks of the trade being used by those asking for our vote or our money. A skill at deconstructing rhetoric is an important one for any citizen to possess; acquiring and honing this ability is a pleasure in itself.

JOHN A. MACDONALD ON CONFEDERATION

FEBRUARY 6, 1865

"We should feel also sincerely grateful to beneficent Providence that we have had the opportunity vouchsafed us of calmly considering this great constitutional change, this peaceful revolution—that we have not been hurried into it, like the United States by the exigencies of war ... "

John A. Macdonald's appearance, disposition, family circumstances, and his personal weaknesses combined to produce the image of a man whose reputation has endured as a likeable scoundrel in Canadian politics. He was a pre-Confederation lawyer and politician representing Kingston in a legislative assembly that contained Upper Canada (Ontario) and Lower Canada (Quebec). Initially, he did not support a wider confederation that would include the Maritime provinces but, once invested, he became the chief draftsman and promoter of the idea. He spoke convincingly in 1864 at the Charlottetown conference that pondered Confederation, but there is no complete public record of that event. Politicians from Canada and the Maritime provinces met again in Quebec City later in the year and agreed to continue with the project, but each jurisdiction had to make its own decision about whether to join. So, early in 1865, representatives from the United Province of Canada met in Quebec City to decide if they were ready to proceed. Macdonald spoke convincingly on behalf of a federation that was to form the original basis of Canada as we know it.

◆

John Alexander Macdonald was born in Glasgow, Scotland, in 1815, and came to Canada at age five with his parents, Hugh and Helen Macdonald, and his two sisters. Hugh had owned several small businesses in Scotland that failed due to his inattention and probably to his drinking. That made immigration to Canada, where the family had well-connected relatives, an attractive option. In Canada, young Macdonald attended local schools between the ages of nine and fourteen, then studied in grammar schools run by clerics, one of them a graduate of Oxford University. Macdonald studied English and mathematics as well as Latin and French. He was never able to attend university because there were none in Upper Canada at the time, and only three in all of British North America—in Montreal, Quebec; Windsor, Nova Scotia; and Fredericton, New Brunswick. His family's modest means ruled out his being sent back to Britain to study, as did some of those who later became his supporters and opponents in politics. At age fifteen, he became an apprentice clerk with an established Kingston law firm, which was how young men in that day found their way into the profession. It was a good opportunity and he made the most of it.

As a youth, Macdonald was spindly, blue-eyed, and pale. He had a shock of dark curly hair and a full mouth with tucks at the corners, but his most distinguishing feature was a large nose. Girls teased him at school and called him "ugly John Macdonald." He grew to be six feet tall and cut an imposing figure, but he was "no beauty" as one author describes him. As an adult, Macdonald was always clean-shaven in contrast to many of his contemporaries, who wore thick beards or bushy mutton-chopped sideburns. He was something of a dandy in his manner of dressing, given to frock coats, starchy collars, and cravats. He was courtly and flirtatious with women and he seemed comfortable with them, perhaps due to a close relationship with his strong mother and his two sisters.

There was tragedy enough in Macdonald's family. A drunken servant killed his younger brother James when Macdonald was just seven years old. His marriage in 1843 to his second cousin Isabella Clark was a difficult one. She came to spend most of her time in a sickbed where she made liberal use of a prescription for liquid opium. She often sought cures on extended visits elsewhere in Canada and the United States, with her husband accompanying her on at least some of those occasions. Their infant son, John Alexander, died in 1848. A second son, Hugh John, often lived with relatives during his mother's illnesses and his father's long absences attending to his political career. Isabella died in 1857 without ever having a clear diagnosis of her condition. Macdonald married again in London in 1867 to Susan Agnes Bernard, a sister to his private secretary Hewitt Bernard. Macdonald was fifty-two and she was thirty. Strong willed and devoted, she savoured her role as the spouse of a leading politician. She was a loyal partner and an intellectual companion who read widely and spoke French. They had one daughter, Margaret Mary, who was born with fluid on her brain. She was never able to walk or to look after herself. Macdonald was inordinately fond of her.

Macdonald drank heavily, particularly during the later years of his first marriage and during his time as a widower between 1857 and 1867. A compulsive worker, he was a binge drinker whose benders often followed periods of intense and protracted activity. When the pressure became too intense, he would take to his bed for days accompanied by a decanter of brandy. He would at other times be drunk while speaking in the assembly and later in Parliament. The *Toronto Globe* reported that during one all-night debate Macdonald "was simply drunk in the plain ordinary sense of that word." It is worth noting, however, that many men in public life drank heavily in nineteenth century Canada. Macdonald's drinking and the shadow of personal tragedy that lay behind his sociable public persona made him more likeable to political friends and even to foes. They may have seen in him a man who was as broken and imperfect as many of them were. There was no doubt a tactical element in Macdonald's bonhomie as well. He knew well how unstable the political situation was in the United Province of Canada. He needed the goodwill and votes of his colleagues from both sides of the House.

◆

John A. Macdonald was a capable orator but not a great one, particularly when compared to his eminent contemporaries, such as the British prime ministers Benjamin Disraeli and William Gladstone, or American president Abraham Lincoln. Macdonald was sceptical about flights of oratory and was not impressed when on a visit to Georgia he heard an American senator give a two-hour speech. He described the man as "too theatrical in his manner and turgid in style." By the mid-nineteenth century, when Macdonald was coming into his own as a political leader, the florid and lofty style of public address was giving way to a simpler and more colloquial form of speech. American historian Garry Wills argues that all modern political prose descends from Lincoln's 272-word Gettysburg Address in 1863. Wills writes that Lincoln's rhetoric, at Gettysburg and elsewhere, was carefully honed prose that gave the appearance of being artless and plain. Macdonald did not cultivate Lincoln's economy of words even though he tended to keep his parliamentary speeches relatively brief at a time when others were in the habit of speaking for hours. Macdonald's manners and speech always had about them something of the "urbanity, tolerance, and sense of humour" of regency England in the early 1800s. His oratory was not florid but rather a jocular and backslapping style suited to the legislatures he served in for so many years. He seldom drafted text for his speeches, other than to make brief notes on scraps of paper or an envelope, and it was only occasionally that he asked for assistance in research.

One might expect that Macdonald spoke with a brogue because he emigrated from Scotland and was raised in a Scots family. Yet, while his speech contained "some muted legacy of his family background," he had lived in Canada from the age of five and retained only a trace of an accent. Alexander Campbell, his former law partner, described Macdonald's accent as typical to Upper Canada of the time: "He was in tone of voice and manner as thoroughly a Bay of Quinte boy as if he had been born there." Macdonald's use of language likely changed significantly with his formal education and his profession. He would have spoken in a certain manner in the legislative assembly while choosing a different tone and vocabulary in other locations. Campbell recounted how once, at a trial, Macdonald said colloquially of the defendant that, "he took and went and hit him with a brick." The writer Wallace Stegner talks in his book *Wolf Willow* about how easy it is in adulthood to "fall back into the corrupted lingo that is your native tongue." Adults can slip into the familiar language of their youth as soon as they cross the threshold of the family home, and so it may have been with Macdonald. He had also adopted the quintessential Canadian habit of ending his sentences with a rising inflection and the interrogative "eh?" Even British prime minister Benjamin Disraeli was to note that Macdonald ended his sentences with "a little sing song."

Tall and erect, with his shock of crinkly dark hair and his frock coats, Macdonald presented an impressive figure when he rose to speak in public. Often, he talked with his hands in his pockets. He seldom gesticulated with his arms, unless it was to point a finger at an opponent. His voice was soft but highly pitched when he was younger. Later it grew to be somewhat hoarse due to his many years of speaking and perhaps to his drinking. At times, there were complaints from his contemporaries and journalists covering his speeches that he did not speak loudly enough or enunciate clearly. He did not own a pipe-organ sound, so useful at the time for speakers who had to project to audiences in large halls or outdoor venues in an era prior to electronic magnification of the voice. Macdonald was at his most effective in the cut and thrust of debate in a legislative assembly and later in Parliament.

◆

At first, Macdonald was a sceptic about the Confederation of the British North American provinces, as indeed, he was a sceptic about most everything. He was a classic conservative who didn't believe in the perfectibility of either individuals or institutions; he tended to accept both as he found them, and thought that too much vision could be a bad thing. Macdonald's political star rose—a cabinet position in 1847, attorney general in 1854, and prime minister of the United Province of Canada in 1857. Throughout those years, he was consumed more by the mundane but necessary tasks of getting himself and his colleagues re-elected than he was in any grander vision.

The political situation in which he practised his art in the 1850s and '60s was inherently unstable. In the Constitution Act of 1791, Great Britain had created the provinces of Upper and Lower Canada, but there was agitation for self-government and economic reform in both jurisdictions that led to separate rebellions in 1837. Lord Durham was sent from

England to make recommendations following those troubles. He reported that he had found "two nations warring in the bosom of a single state … " He insisted that Upper and Lower Canada should be united for economic reasons. He also believed that the assimilation of francophones, an inferior race in his mind, was inevitable. Following his recommendation, the Act of Union in 1840 created one united province. It was a situation destined for frustration and deadlock.

There was widespread distrust between the French and English and each group jealously guarded its own prerogatives. Governments came and went with regularity and there were three general elections held between 1858 and 1864. Upper and Lower Canada had the same number of votes in the assembly but the population of the former was growing more rapidly. George Brown, publisher of *The Globe* in Toronto and Macdonald's bitter political rival, led the Reformers from Upper Canada and promoted representation by population. The idea was politically logical but Reformers believed that it would have the added advantage of weakening the power and influence of Lower Canada.

For their part, the French Canadians insisted on continued equal representation between the two jurisdictions. There were two political formations in Lower Canada—the Parti bleu, a conservative movement founded in the 1850s and led by George-Étienne Cartier; and the Parti rouge, a radical liberal party founded in the 1840s. Cartier and the bleus came to be allied with Macdonald in what was then known as the Liberal-Conservative Party. They were able to form a durable political partnership. When in 1858 Macdonald became leader of the Liberal-Conservatives, he showed little enthusiasm for the idea of Confederation. In that year, however, he lured Alexander Galt away from the Parti rouge. Galt became Macdonald's finance minister and was passionate about Confederation so Macdonald professed to be at least open to it, a price that he was willing to pay in his wooing of Galt. Someone else who was passionate about Confederation was Thomas D'Arcy McGee, an Irish patriot who immigrated to Montreal via New York in 1857 and was pleasantly surprised to discover peace and freedom flourishing under the auspices of the British Crown. McGee was an oratorical spellbinder and was frequently delivering an eloquent set speech as early as 1860, promoting his vision for "a northern nation" and "a new Canadian nationality." McGee made these speeches at a time when there was no Pan-Canadian consciousness, and when the focus was almost exclusively upon local concerns.

The British Colonial Office was at first unenthused about talk of Confederation. They did not think the Canadians could manage it and they believed the Maritime provinces would not want it. There was, however, a sentiment in Britain that the cost of protecting its colonies was a burden and many had come to believe that Canada was not defensible against the Americans. The outbreak of the American Civil War in 1861 had a sobering effect on British diplomats and on politicians in the Canadian provinces. They feared that when the war ended, Northern armies might set their sights upon Canada because the British had been openly sympathetic to the South during the conflict.

Macdonald began to take Confederation seriously only when these events and other political players forced him into it. That happened in March 1864 when his nemesis George Brown tabled a motion in the assembly requesting that a special constitutional committee look at alternative proposals for some form of federation. Macdonald sat on the committee but he opposed the idea. When a report was issued on June 14, proposing "changes in the direction of a federative system," he voted against it. He may have done so out of conviction, but more likely he was suspicious of Brown and did not want to give him any advantage. The Macdonald-Cartier government fell and it appeared that yet another election was imminent. Then something remarkable happened. Brown sent a message to Macdonald, asking if the political crisis could be used to address the nagging question of Confederation. Within days they had negotiated the terms of a coalition government with this new project in mind.

Macdonald, who had now become engaged, wanted Confederation to include both the Canadian and Maritime provinces. His abrupt transformation from grudging opponent to visionary nation builder may have been based mainly on political considerations. As historian P. B. Waite described it, "Any government that found a tangible, realistic proposal that would satisfy Canada West [Upper Canada] without alienating Canada

East [Lower Canada] would obtain a satisfying and firm hold on power." Macdonald, of course, was always interested in power.

Fortuitously, Nova Scotia, New Brunswick, Prince Edward Island, and Newfoundland were already planning to meet in Charlottetown in September 1864 to discuss a union among the Maritime provinces. Macdonald, Brown, and other representatives from Canada invited themselves to the meeting and arrived by steamship. It was Macdonald who prepared much of the Canadian material outlining the details for a new and broader union. He spoke to the delegates on September 3, 1864, in the small red sandstone building that housed Prince Edward Island's Parliament. The sessions were held behind closed doors and the remarks of Macdonald and the others were not captured verbatim. Macdonald spoke again when the joint Canadian and Maritime delegations met in Quebec City in October 1864 to continue the discussion. His motion in favour of a British North American federation was carried unanimously. Following that meeting, the assembly of each participating province was required to debate and ratify the agreement. For the United Province of Canada, that occurred in Quebec City where the legislative assembly was called to order on January 19, 1865.

It was a cold day and the ice was thick on the St. Lawrence River. Governor General Monck was driven to the assembly in a four-horse sleigh. Once inside the chamber he read the Speech from the Throne to the packed galleries. It contained the Confederation motion as its most prominent item of business. Macdonald had arrived in Quebec City on January 22, late for the opening session and pleading illness. On February 5, the day before he was to speak, Macdonald secluded himself in his room at a boarding house and the concerned proprietor heard him talking to himself for hours. Macdonald was preparing and rehearsing what was to be one of the most important speeches of his career. On the cold evening of February 6, he arose, his voice still weak, to move that the United Province of Canada adopt the resolutions agreed to in October 1864. If the Confederation proposal did not pass here, the whole project was doomed to failure. It is to the assembly that we turn now, as Macdonald describes the merits of Confederation.

MACDONALD'S SPEECH

Mr. Speaker, I have had the honour of being charged, on behalf of the Government, to submit a scheme for the Confederation of all the British North American provinces—a scheme which has been received, I am glad to say, with general, if not universal approbation, in Canada. The scheme, as so propounded through the press, has received almost no opposition. While there may be occasionally, here and there, expressions of dissent from some of the details, yet the scheme as a whole has met with almost universal approval, and the Government has the greatest satisfaction in presenting it to this House. This subject, which now absorbs the attention of the people of Canada, and of the whole of British North America, is not a new one. For years, it has more or less attracted the attention of every statesman and politician in these provinces, and has been looked upon by many far-seeing politicians as being eventually the means of deciding and settling very many of the vexed questions which have retarded the prosperity of the colonies as a whole, and particularly the prosperity of Canada ...

The subject was pressed upon the public attention by a great many writers and politicians; but I believe the attention of the Legislature was first formally called to it by my honourable friend [Alexander Tilloch Galt] the Minister of Finance. Some years ago, in an elaborate speech, my hon. friend, while an independent member of Parliament, before being connected with any Government, pressed his views on the Legislature at great length and with his usual force. But the subject was not taken up by any party as a branch of their policy, until the formation of the Cartier-Macdonald administration in 1858, when the Confederation of the colonies was announced as one of the measures which they pledged themselves to attempt, if possible, to bring to a satisfactory conclusion ...

Macdonald leads off the Confederation debate as befits his role as attorney general and drafter of the resolutions. His tone is easy and familiar. He provides an overview of the Confederation proposal and the main arguments for it. Others, including Brown and Galt, will later speak to the financial implications and D'Arcy McGee will provide a rousing and poetic call to nationhood. Macdonald begins by claiming there is near universal support for, and little opposition to, Confederation. That is not quite so. Prince Edward Island and Newfoundland will back away from the deal. In New Brunswick, Leonard Tilley will soon lose an election on the issue and there is also opposition in Nova Scotia led by the respected Joseph Howe. In Lower Canada, there is significant resistance among francophone members. Macdonald will offer his own chronology of events leading to this debate but cannot claim that the idea for Confederation originated with him. He correctly attributes its origin to Alexander Galt but he hastens to add that Macdonald's administration embraced the idea.

The subject, however, though looked upon with favour by the country, and though there were no distinct expressions of opposition to it from any party, did not begin to assume its present proportions until last session. Then men of all parties and all shades of politics became alarmed at the aspect of affairs. They found that such was the opposition between the two sections of the province, and such was the danger of impending anarchy, in consequence of the irreconcilable differences of opinion, with respect to representation by population, between Upper and Lower Canada, that unless some solution of the difficulty was arrived at, we would suffer under a succession of weak governments—weak in numerical support, weak in force, and weak in power of doing good. All were alarmed at this state of affairs …

A committee was struck, composed of gentlemen of both sides of the House, of all shades of political opinion, without any reference as to whether they were supporters of the Administration of the day or belonged to the Opposition, for the purposes of taking into calm and full deliberation the evils which threatened the future of Canada … The committee, by a wise provision, and in order that each member of the committee might have an opportunity of expressing his opinions without being in any way compromised before the public, or with his party, in regard either to his political friends, or to his political foes, agreed that the discussion should be freely entered upon without reference to the political antecedents of any of them, and that they should sit with closed doors, so that they might be able to approach the subject frankly and in a spirit of compromise. The committee included most of the leading members of the House—I had the honour myself to be one of the number—and the result was that there was found an ardent desire, a creditable desire, I must say, displayed by all members of the committee to approach the subject honestly, and to attempt to work out some solution which might relieve Canada from the evils under which she laboured.

Macdonald describes the legislative committee that Brown initiated in 1864 to investigate Confederation. He praises the statesmanship and calm deliberation of the committee members drawn from both government and opposition, most of them sitting in the chamber as he speaks. Conveniently, he avoids mentioning that as a member of the committee he had initially voted against the motion to pursue negotiations for Confederation. He exaggerates when he says that the country faced "impending anarchy" and then he blames that state of affairs upon the campaign for representation by population. Brown and the Reformers had demanded that. Macdonald resisted as had politicians in Lower Canada, who feared their rights and influence would be diminished. But George-Étienne Cartier was now ready to gamble that representation by population was acceptable to the French in a decentralized federation where the autonomy of Lower Canada would be protected. It was on those terms that Cartier had formed an alliance with Macdonald.

Macdonald's idea of popular democracy is a limited one. He opposes universal suffrage, equating it with an excess of democracy and mob rule. It is worth remembering that even with representation by population, only male property owners would be allowed to vote. That would, or course, exclude any male who did not own property and all women. It would exclude as well the original Indigenous inhabitants of Canada. They did not receive the right to vote until 1961, more than one hundred years after this Confederation debate.

By a fortunate coincidence the desire for union existed in the Lower Provinces, and a feeling of the necessity of strengthening themselves by collecting together the scattered colonies of the seaboard, had induced them to form a convention of their own the purpose of effecting a union of the Maritime Provinces ... knowing this, we availed ourselves of the opportunity, and asked if they would receive a deputation from Canada, who would go out to meet them at Charlottetown, for the purpose of laying before them the advantages of a larger and more extensive union, by the junction of all provinces in one great government under our common sovereign. They at once kindly consented to receive and hear us. They did receive us cordially and generously, and asked us to lay our views before them. We did so at some length, and so satisfactory to them were the reasons we gave; so clearly, in their opinion, did we show the advantages of the greater union over the lesser, that they at once set aside their own project and joined heart and hand with us in entering into the larger scheme, and trying to form, as far as they and we could, a great nation and a strong government ...

The result was that when we met here on the 10th of October [1864], on the first day on which we assembled after the full and free discussions which had taken place at Charlottetown, the first resolution now before this House was passed unanimously, being received with acclamation as, in the opinion of everyone who heard it, a proposition which ought to receive, and would receive, the sanction of each government and each people. The resolution is: "That the best interests and present and future prosperity of British North America will be promoted by a federal union under the Crown of Great Britain, provided such union can be effected on principles just to the several provinces."

It seemed to all the statesmen assembled—and there are great statesmen in the lower provinces, men who would do honour to any government and to any legislature of any free country enjoying representative institutions—it was clear to them all that the best interests and present and future prosperity of British North America would be promoted by a federal union under the Crown of Great Britain. And it seems to me, as to them, and I think it will so appear to the people of this country that, if we wish to be a great people; if we wish to form ... a great nationality, commanding the respect of the world, able to hold our own against all opponents, and to defend those institutions we prize; if we wish to have one system of government, and to establish a commercial union with unrestricted free trade between people of the five provinces, belonging, as they do, to the same nation, obeying the same sovereign, owning the same allegiance, and being, for the most part, of the same blood and lineage; if we wish to be able to afford to each other the means of mutual defence and support against aggression and attack, this can only be obtained by a union of some kind between the scattered and weak boundaries composing the British North American provinces (Cheers) ...

Macdonald continues with his chronology but begins to talk with increasing passion about the desire to become a "great people" and a "great nationality." He believes that Confederation is the vehicle that will enable that to happen. He describes the aspirations succinctly: mutual defence, liberty, and prosperity for all under the British sovereign. These are what today we might call his applause lines, and the members reward him with cheers. Macdonald is fond of using a rhetorical device known as metanoia, which is the insertion of a parenthetical structure in a way that both interrupts the flow of his remarks and amplifies them. Metanoia allows him in a carefully prepared speech to adopt an informal and familiar tone, mimicking everyday conversation, in which speakers correct themselves or augment their points. Macdonald uses it here to describe "the statesmen assembled." In his amplification, he says that they are not only statesmen, but statesmen of a high calibre. He is heaping praise on his audience, some of whom are sceptical of his proposal for Confederation.

Now, as regards the comparative advantages of a legislative or a federal union, I have never hesitated to state my own opinions. I have again and again stated in the House that, if practicable, I thought a legislative union would be preferable. I have always contended that if we could agree to have one government and one Parliament legislating for the whole of these peoples, it would be the best, the cheapest, the most vigorous, and the strongest system of government we could adopt. But, on looking at the subject in the [Quebec City] conference, and discussing the matter as we did, most unreservedly, and with a desire to arrive at a satisfactory conclusion, we found that such a system was impracticable. In the first place, it would not meet the assent of the people of Lower Canada, because they felt that in their peculiar position—being in a minority, with a different language, nationality, and religion from the majority—in case of a junction with the provinces, their institutions and their laws might be assailed, and their ancestral associations, on which they prided themselves, attacked and prejudiced; it was found that any proposition which involved the absorption of the individuality of Lower Canada, if I may use the expression, would not be received with favour by her people. We found too, that though their people speak the same language and enjoy the same system of law as the people of Upper Canada, a system founded on the common law of England, there was as great a disinclination on the part of the various Maritime provinces to lose their individuality, as separate political organizations, as we observed in the case of Lower Canada herself. Therefore, we were forced to the conclusion that we must either abandon the idea of union altogether, or devise a system of union in which the separate provincial organizations would be in some degree preserved. So that those who were, like myself, in favour of a legislative union, were obliged to modify their views and accept the project of a federal union as the only scheme practicable, even for the Maritime provinces ...

Macdonald signals a shift from loftier rhetoric to the more practical matter of the division of powers. He states his preference for a strong central government, much as in Britain where one parliament rules over England, Scotland, Wales, and Ireland. He believes the American constitution is defective in that it grants too much power to individual states. Yet he admits that a highly centralized system is "impracticable" in British North America. The French in Lower Canada fiercely guard their language and nationality, their legal system, and religion. Interestingly, he concedes that they constitute "a nationality," something that later generations of politicians have frequently argued about. He knows that the Maritime colonies, too, are on guard to maintain their individuality and existing political institutions. There has been an enduring debate about whether Macdonald and the other founders meant for Canada to be a centralized state or a decentralized federation. Macdonald in Quebec City wants as much centralization as his political peers will allow. For him, Canada should be more than the sum of its parts. But he is also attempting to show by his example what he expects of others. He had to modify his views to reflect not his ideal but rather to achieve what was possible, and he is asking the others assembled to take a similar practical approach.

He proposes, as well, that a Confederation adopting the Westminster style of democracy will protect the right of political minorities—French and English, Catholic and Protestant—because no one party could easily dominate. He wants to assure Lower Canada and the Maritime colonies that their distinctiveness and jurisdiction will be preserved. However, in describing the considerable powers retained by a central government he is attempting to reassure anglophone members who fear the power of Lower Canada in Confederation. The debate focuses solely on the rights of the English and French in Confederation. Macdonald makes no mention of the Indigenous peoples who had lived upon the land for thousands of years.

I say to this House, if you do not believe that the union of the colonies is for the advantage of the country, that the joining of these five peoples into one nation under one sovereign, is for the benefit of all, then reject the scheme. Reject it if you do not believe it to be for the present advantage and future prosperity of yourselves and your children. But if, after a calm and full consideration of this scheme, it is believed, as a whole, to be for the advantage of this province—if this House and country believe this union to be one which will ensure for us British laws, British connection, and British freedom—and increase and develop the social, political, and material prosperity of the country, then I implore this House and the country to lay aside all prejudices, and accept the scheme which we offer. I ask this House to meet the question in the same spirit in which the delegates [to the earlier Quebec conference] met it. I ask each member of this House to lay aside his own opinions as to particular details, and to accept the scheme as a whole if he think it beneficial as a whole. As I stated in the preliminary discussion, we must consider this scheme in the light of a treaty ...

Here Macdonald employs the rhetorical device of antithesis, the contrasting of ideas in a balanced or parallel construction, something he would have learned from his avid reading and his familiarity with British statesmen. He describes the positive attributes of Confederation—prosperity for all in a unified Canada under the British sovereign. He challenges others in the room to reject his proposal if they do not support those positives. The inference is that they would be mean-spirited and unreasonable if they oppose; visionary and generous if they support. He sets up the comparison using a string of negatives, contrasted with a series of positives, and he uses parallel constructions to sustain and build his rhythm.

I trust the scheme will be assented to as a whole. I am sure this House will not seek to alter it in its unimportant details; and, if altered in any important provisions, the result must be that the whole will be set aside, and we must begin de novo. If any important changes are made, every one of the colonies will feel itself absolved from the implied obligation to deal with it as a treaty, each province will feel itself at liberty to amend it ad libitum so as to suit its own views and interests; in fact, the whole of our labours will have been for naught, and we will have to renew our negotiations with all the colonies for the purpose of establishing some new scheme. I hope the House will not adopt any such a course as will postpone, perhaps forever, or at all events for a long period, all chances of union. All the statesmen and public men who have written or spoken on the subject admit the advantages of a union, if it were practicable, and now when it is proved to be practicable, if we do not embrace this opportunity the present favourable time will pass away, and we may never have it again ...

Macdonald drops two Latin terms into his speech here: *de novo* means starting anew, and *ad libitum* means at one's pleasure. He is saying that if legislators for the United Province of Canada make changes at will to what had been proposed at Quebec some months earlier, they will create a legislative free-for-all in which the whole exercise will have to begin anew. In that case, it will founder. He is a sly fox. He wants the House to pass all seventy-two of the Quebec Resolutions in their entirety; he says that the package is akin to a treaty and cannot be divided. Actually, it is not a treaty for a number of reasons. The four Maritime provinces and that of Canada are not yet united; they do not have a common legislature or parliament; they lack the power to declare or even to negotiate Confederation. They can merely petition the Parliament of Great Britain to grant that status. The earlier meetings at Charlottetown and Quebec City had no official standing, although the British Colonial Office was pleased to see them occur. Macdonald is right in saying that debating and amending individual clauses would be time consuming and potentially divisive, but parliamentarians everywhere are accustomed to clause-by-clause analysis of proposed legislation. Macdonald wants to get the deal done and one cannot blame him for that. But he employs a sleight of hand in his argument. In fact, he and others do later amend some of the Confederation clauses amid acrimonious negotiations that occur behind closed doors in London before the British Parliament finally passes the British North America Bill in March 1867.

If we are not blind to our present position, we must see the hazardous situation in which all the great interests of Canada stand in respect to the United States. I am no alarmist. I do not believe in the prospect of immediate war. I believe that the common sense of the two nations will prevent a war; still we cannot trust to probabilities. The government and legislature would be wanting in their duty to the people if they ran any risk. We know that the United States at this moment are engaged in a war of enormous dimensions, that the occasion of a war with Great Britain has again and again arisen, and may at any time in the future again arise. We cannot foresee what may be the result; we cannot say but that the two nations may drift into a war as other nations have done before. It would then be too late when war had commenced to think of measures for strengthening ourselves, or to begin negotiations for a union with the sister provinces …

Fear of the Americans is a major reason why Macdonald and others want Confederation. The brutal civil war is in its final throes even as the Confederation debate is occurring in Quebec City early in 1865. The Union armies under General Ulysses S. Grant are engaged in a scorched earth campaign in the American south. Macdonald and the other legislators have observed the war on their doorstep. They fear that when it ends, the Americans might march northward. Macdonald uses another rhetorical device to make his point, somewhat along the lines of Shakespeare having Mark Anthony say that Brutus is an honourable man. Those words say one thing but mean another. Here Macdonald tells the legislators that he is not an "alarmist" and does not believe in the likelihood of "immediate war" with the Americans. Note his use of the word "immediate." In fact, he is warning that there may be a war and he uses parallel constructions to good effect in making his points. The obvious conclusion is that there is much to fear from the Americans.

The conference having come to the conclusion that a legislative union, pure and simple, was impracticable, our next attempt was to form a government upon federal principles, which would give to the general government the strength of a legislative and administrative union, while at the same time it preserved that liberty of action for the different sections which is allowed by a federal union. And I am strong in the belief that we have hit upon the happy medium in those resolutions, and that we have formed a scheme of government which unites the advantages of both, giving us the strength of a legislative union and the sectional freedom of a federal union, with protection to local interests. In doing so we had the advantage of the experience of the United States …

I shall not go over the (other) powers that are conferred on the general parliament. Most of them refer to matters of financial and commercial interest, and I leave those subjects in other and better hands. Besides all the powers that are specifically given in the 37th and last item of this portion of the Constitution, it confers on the General

Legislature the general mass of sovereign legislation, the power to legislate on "all matters of a general character, not specifically and exclusively reserved for the local governments and legislatures." This is precisely the provision that is wanting in the constitution of the United States. It is here that we find the weakness of the American system—the point where the American constitution breaks down. (Hear, hear.) It is in itself a wise and necessary provision. We thereby strengthen the central parliament, and make the Confederation one people and one government, instead of five peoples and five governments, with merely a point of authority connecting us to a limited and insufficient extent ...

Macdonald clearly believes the British parliamentary system is superior to the Republican model in the United States. He has a strong aversion to the American Revolution and to the liberal ideas that inspired it. He believes also that the Civil War was made possible because too much power was vested in individual states. He claims that the proposals the Canadians are debating have achieved a "happy medium" in the division of powers between the central government and the provinces. He says that he will not describe the allocation of those powers but will rather leave that to Cartier, Brown, and Galt, who are to speak later. He believes, however, that the central government will retain the major power; citizens and their local governments will give up a degree of their freedom in the interests of the protection offered by a central government. This is essentially the thinking of British political philosopher John Locke. Macdonald lives in a time of small government and he sees a limited, albeit important role for the state. He clearly does not foresee the role that government was later to assume; nor does he anticipate how significant the provincial power over health, education, and other matters was to become.

Let me again before I sit down, impress upon the House the necessity of meeting this question in a spirit of compromise, with a disposition to judge the matter as a whole, to consider whether it is really for the benefit and advantage of the country to form a Confederation of all the provinces; and if honourable gentlemen, whatever may have been their preconceived ideas as to the merits of the details of this measure, whatever may still be their opinions as to these details, if they really believe that the scheme is one by which the prosperity of the country will be increased, and its future progress secured, I ask them to yield their own views, and to deal with the scheme according to its own merits as one great whole. (Hear, hear.)

One argument, but not a strong one, has been used against Confederation, that it is an advance towards independence. Some are apprehensive that the very fact of our forming this union will hasten the time when we shall be severed from the mother country. I have no apprehension of that kind. I believe it will have the contrary effect. I believe that as we grow stronger, that, as it is felt in England we have become a people, able from our union, our strength, our population, and the development of our resources, to take our position among the nations of the world, she will be less willing to part with us than she would be now, when we are broken up into a number of insignificant colonies, subject to attack piece-meal without any concerted action or common organization of defence ...

Macdonald signals to his audience that he is approaching the end of his speech. That will relieve those who thought he had gone on for too long. It also is a way to retrieve their attention should it have wandered. He appeals to the politicians in the assembly to put aside any "preconceived ideas" and to judge the plan on its merit "as one great whole." In other words, he does not want them to nitpick or to change anything in the clauses that he has drafted. Then he uses another rhetorical trick—the straw man argument with an unidentified foe—when he says that some fear that Confederation will lead to severed ties with Great Britain. That was certainly not the most common criticism made of the proposal, although some few, particularly in the Maritime provinces, may have believed that. Macdonald punctures his own balloon. He says that Confederation will actually strengthen ties with Britain. He does not normally wear his heart on his sleeve and is often criticized for possessing more guile than vision; but as Macdonald reaches the end of his speech he predicts that Canada will use its union, its strength, its population and resources to take its place among the world's great nations. He is using pathos, a vision statement meant to appeal to the beliefs and values of his audience.

When this union takes place, we will be at the outset no inconsiderable people. We find ourselves with a population approaching four millions of souls. Such a population, in

Europe, would make a second, or at least, a third rate power. And with a rapidly increasing population—for I am satisfied that under this union our population will increase in a still greater ratio than ever before—with increased credit—with a higher position in the eyes of Europe—with the increased security we can offer to immigrants, who would naturally prefer to seek a new home in what is known to them as a great country, than in any one little colony or another—with all this I am satisfied that, great as has been our increase in the last twenty-five years since the union between Upper and Lower Canada, our future progress, during the next quarter of a century, will be vastly greater. (Cheers) And when, by means of this rapid increase, we become a nation of eight or nine millions of inhabitants, sought by the great nations of the earth. (Hear, hear.) I am proud to believe that our desire for a permanent alliance will be reciprocated in England ...

In this younger country one great advantage of our connection with Great Britain will be, that, under her auspices, inspired by her example, a portion of her empire, our public men will be actuated by principles similar to those which actuate the statesmen at home. These although not material, physical benefits, of which you can make an arithmetical calculation, are of such overwhelming advantage to our future interests and standing as a nation, that to obtain them is well worthy of any sacrifices that we may be called upon to make, and the people of this country are ready to make them. (Cheers)

We should feel also sincerely grateful to beneficent Providence that we have had the opportunity vouchsafed us of calmly considering this great constitutional change, this peaceful revolution—that we have not been hurried into it, like the United States, by the exigencies of war—that we have not had a violent revolutionary period forced on us, as in other nations, by hostile action from without, or by domestic dissension within. Here we are in peace and prosperity, under the fostering government of Great Britain—a dependent people, with a government having only a limited and a delegated authority, and yet allowed, without restriction, and without jealousy on the part of the Mother Country, to legislate for ourselves, and peacefully and deliberately to consider and determine the future of Canada and of British North America ... It is our privilege and happiness to be in such a position, and we cannot be too grateful for the blessing thus conferred upon us. (Hear, hear.)

This is what those who study rhetoric call the peroration, Macdonald's visionary summing up of what the new country can become. But in best Canadian fashion he cannot resist using understatement. He says that

Canadians, post-Confederation, will be "no inconsiderable people." With that nod to modesty, he goes on to predict greatness for the new country that he envisions. Canada will offer security for immigrants; the population will grow; the land will be prosperous and occupy an elevated position in the eyes of Europe. In Canada, public men will be inspired "by principles similar to those which actuate the statesmen at home." Note Macdonald's use of the phrase "at home," which implies that he considers Britain his political home. In his final crescendo, he talks of the great advantage of achieving Confederation without violent revolution—another reference to the United States.

I must apologize for having detained you so long—for having gone too much perhaps into tedious details with reference to questions bearing on the Constitution, now submitted to this House (cries of "no, no" and "go on.") In conclusion, I would again implore the House not to let this opportunity pass. It is an opportunity that may never recur. At the risk of repeating myself, I would say, it was only by a happy concurrence of circumstances that we were enabled to bring this great question to its present position. If we do not take advantage of the time, if we show ourselves unequal to the occasion, it may never return, and we shall hereafter bitterly and unavailingly regret having failed to embrace the happy opportunity now offered of founding a great nation under the fostering care of Great Britain, and our sovereign lady, Queen Victoria.

As he nears the end, Macdonald apologizes to the members for having gone on too long. That is another rhetorician's device to maintain the sympathy of an audience and to show deference. Then he returns to his point of most pressing concern—members must seize the day and vote in favour of the constitutional proposal before them. At no point does he refer to the fact this is not a constitution but rather a petition to the Parliament of the United Kingdom. No matter. If legislators do not act now, the opportunity may never come again and they will regret their failure. It is now or never and everything is at stake. Macdonald ends by wrapping himself in the British flag. He never doubts Canada's connection to England and its sovereign. He could not have known that within fifty years the United States would begin to eclipse Britain as the world's greatest military and industrial power.

THE IMPACT OF MACDONALD'S SPEECH

William Safire, the American writer and anthologist, cautions that great speeches are not always good speeches—that is to say, speeches with the greatest impact may not be the most rhetorically polished. George Brown, Macdonald's long-time rival (but his temporary ally from 1864 to 1867), wrote to his wife that day to say that Macdonald's address was "a very poor speech for such an occasion." Biographer Donald Creighton pleaded illness on behalf of Macdonald then described the speech as informative but not one of Macdonald's best. It may well be that Macdonald's speech at Charlottetown, or the earlier one at Quebec City in September 1864, were more impressive, but there is no complete record of either. Fortunately, in February 1865 the legislative assembly decided that the debates would be transcribed. More than nine hundred thousand words were delivered during the five-week debate on the Quebec Resolutions. They were published in the same year in a tome of more than one thousand pages, longer even than the King James Version of the Bible. There were seventy-five hundred copies printed in English and four thousand in French, with each member allowed fifty copies of his speeches in the language of his choice.

Members of the legislative assembly were Macdonald's immediate audience. When the Confederation resolution came to a vote in the early morning hours of Saturday, March 11, it was not even close. The division on the main motion was ninety-one to thirty-three, with all but six of the 130 members casting a vote. The members from Upper Canada voted heavily in favour. However, of the sixty-two members from Lower Canada, which consisted of French and some English members, only thirty-seven voted yes; and of the forty-eight French Canadian members present, twenty-seven voted for and twenty-one against. Macdonald won the vote, but despite his best efforts at conciliation, the racial, linguistic, and religious differences persisted, and to some extent they remain today.

A second audience consisted of newspaper reporters and through them the reading public. The previous debates in Charlottetown and Quebec City occurred behind closed doors, although there was some newspaper reportage gleaned from interviews with various members and officials. But the January to March 1865 sessions were legislative debates open to the press. They were covered widely by newspapers of the day in both Upper and Lower Canada and the Maritime provinces. By one count there were 380 newspapers being published weekly or more often in British North America in 1865. There were eleven papers in Halifax alone. The reach of at least the largest of those papers was extended by the development of railways in the years leading to Confederation. Many of those newspapers were partisan in an unabashed way, and a number of them were actually owned by people in public life. George Brown, the Reform leader and publisher of *The Globe*, was among the prominent public figures debating Confederation at Quebec. Some reporters became frustrated over the lack of excitement generated by what they considered the interminable Confederation debates. They even complained that no fights had broken out during the session, although at least one eventually did.

The voters of Upper and Lower Canada were obviously an important audience for Macdonald, but only indirectly. He scoffed at suggestions made during the debate that the Confederation question should be placed before the people in either a general election or plebiscite. He believed that would subvert the principles of British parliamentary tradition and its reliance upon elected representatives to make decisions. His philosophy followed the representative democracy ideals of Edmund Burke, who believed that once elected a representative had to follow his own conscience and good judgment rather than being led by his constituents. Macdonald associates direct democracy with mob rule, where unscrupulous leaders can exploit the passions of the people.

The politicians in the Maritime colonies were another audience. Macdonald was frustrated when Leonard Tilley called an election in New Brunswick with Confederation as its major issue for March 1865, just as the topic was being debated in the Canadian Assembly. Tilley lost that election but Macdonald refused to accept it as a repudiation of Confederation. He maintained contact with Tilley and when another election was engineered with the help of British colonial officials, Macdonald procured tens of thousands of dollars for Tilley's side from railway magnates in an election which the pro-Confederation side won. The railways saw in Confederation their opportunity to build a government-subsidized rail line from the central provinces to the Maritimes.

British officialdom and the political class were yet another of Macdonald's audiences. The Colonial Office had decided to support Confederation and Macdonald was seen as the undisputed leader of that cause. He remained in close contact with Governor General Monck, who described Macdonald as "the ablest man in the province." Late in 1866 Macdonald led a delegation to London, where the Confederation resolutions were refined and additional closed-door negotiations were conducted among the Canadians. The Maritime colonies, in particular, attempted to reopen the agreement to improve its terms in their favour. The Canadian delegates named Macdonald as the conference chair in London. It was he who steered the discussions, wrote the resolutions, and managed the consensus. Macdonald received a knighthood for his efforts, an award that excited the bitter envy of his Canadian colleagues, including Cartier.

On December 24, 1866, the Confederation resolutions were sent to the Colonial Office. Throughout February the British North America Act made its way through the British Parliament and finally passed on March 8, 1867. By then Macdonald had taken time out to get married to Agnes Bernard, whom he had met again while in London. Most British politicians showed little enthusiasm for the founding of this new nation. Macdonald was to complain to a friend years later, "This remarkable event in the history of the British Empire passed almost without notice ..."

The Confederation debates in Canada were an extraordinary moment in history. The politicians in Quebec City in 1865 were debating the very purposes of government and the forms that their democracy might take. The debates ranged through the best choices available for responsible government and constitutional liberty, for economic prosperity and minority rights; they included passionate disagreements regarding the merits of direct versus representational democracy. The most knowledgeable politicians among the group—and that certainly included Macdonald—exhibited a wide knowledge and understanding of law, history, and political thought.

They were familiar with British and American constitutional history. Macdonald at least was also familiar with what was occurring in other colonies such as Australia and New Zealand. The Canadian politicians seldom named the great political philosophers of the British and European traditions—Burke, Locke, Mill, Hobbes, and Rousseau—but many were clearly steeped in their thought. Those meeting in Quebec City were at times boastful, mocking, and angry or confused—but they were debating the creation of a self-governing and democratic state, which was to become a model for other British colonies throughout the world. The creation of modern Canada occurred without marching armies, menacing warships, the firing of canons, or even musket fire. Canadian democracy today continues to be guided by what was being debated then, and in 1865 John A. Macdonald was the first among equals.

WILFRID LAURIER ON LIBERALISM AND THE CHURCH

JUNE 26, 1877

*"You wish to organize all Catholics into a single party
without other tie, without other basis than that
of religion ... you will bring on war, religious war,
the most frightful of all wars ..."*

*Wilfrid Laurier was among Canada's finest political orators and was equally adept
in two languages, an achievement that few legislators in any country could match.
Gratton O'Leary, an iconic Ottawa journalist who was a confidante of Conservative
prime ministers and eventually a senator, described Laurier as "the greatest [orator] I
was privileged to hear in sixty years of observing Parliament." It is only rarely that a
single speech can be said to have changed history but Laurier's address to an audience
of two thousand at Le Club Canadien in Quebec City on June 26, 1877, was one
of those moments. The Catholic hierarchy and clergy were adamantly opposed to the
Liberals and had forbidden Catholics to vote for the party. They even talked about
creating their own Catholic political party. Laurier decided to challenge them and he
delivered a speech that disarmed his critics. His eloquence helped to create a space for
Liberals that led to their becoming the dominant political force in Quebec and Canada
for more than a century.*

◆

Wilfrid Laurier was born in 1841 in the parish of Saint-Lin, a
predominantly agricultural community of about two thousand people,
situated in the forested Laurentian Mountains north of Montreal. His was

the seventh generation of Lauriers in New France. His father, Carolus, and his grandfather, Charles, were staunch supporters of Louis-Joseph Papineau, who had led a brief and ill-fated insurrection in 1837 against the authority of the British governor and his unelected advisors. The thinking of Papineau and other leaders was suffused with liberal revolutionary ideas drawn from the United States and Europe, particularly from France.

In 1847 Laurier began to attend the Catholic parish school at Saint-Lin. Tragically, his mother, Marcelle Martineau, died of tuberculosis the following year. Three years later his father enrolled him in another school ten kilometres away in the predominantly Scottish Presbyterian settlement of New Glasgow. Laurier stayed initially with an Irish family and later with the Murrays, who were Scots and owned a general store in the village. During his two years in New Glasgow, he learned to speak English and did so with a slightly Scottish accent. He was also exposed at an impressionable age to the world outlook of his English-speaking hosts. He voluntarily attended family worship with the Presbyterian Murrays each evening.

Few students in this era went beyond grade school, but Carolus Laurier was determined his son would be one of them. That would mean years in secondary school followed by professional study, most likely in law, medicine, or the church—and it was in church schools that New France's elite were trained. At age twelve, Laurier went off to spend seven years at a college called L'Assomption, in a town of the same name about thirty kilometres from his home. There he received a classical education, with an emphasis on Latin, the masterpieces of Roman and French literature, and other courses in Greek, English, mathematics, philosophy, geography, and history, as well as studies in rhetoric and style. He brought with him to the Catholic college his family's support of liberalism as it had been enunciated by Papineau and others. The instructing priests, however, were vigilant about preventing the introduction of revolutionary or even liberal ideas into the school.

Laurier was never physically robust and there was a fear on numerous occasions that he was developing tuberculosis. Eventually his condition was diagnosed as chronic bronchitis, an affliction that confined him to bed on occasion throughout his adult life and that often sapped his physical energy. His favourite recreation as a student took the form of extra reading, particularly of Roman, French, and English literature, and of discussion and debate.

When he left L'Assomption in 1861, Laurier enrolled in law studies at McGill University, an anglophone bastion in Montreal, where, nevertheless, students were able to take their classes in either English or French. Law students were expected to work in a firm while taking their studies. Laurier found a place in the office of a prominent supporter of the Parti rouge, a precursor to the Liberal party in Quebec. The rouges were proponents of political reform but their opponents called them reds, which had a revolutionary connotation. Laurier did well at McGill and was even chosen as the class valedictorian. He was admitted to the bar in 1864 and began to practise law in Montreal. The first two firms with which he engaged became business failures. To make matters worse, he was also suffering from throat and lung infections and serious haemorrhaging. Antoine Dorion, the rouge leader, had become a trusted friend and advised the young man to move to the Eastern Townships, where the air was less polluted than in Montreal.

In 1867, the year of Confederation, Laurier opened a law practice in Arthabaska, a rural area near Victoriaville in the Eastern Townships. In 1868 he married Zoé Lafontaine, a young piano teacher of modest means who had been a fellow boarder in the home where Laurier lived when he was studying law in Montreal. Theirs was to be a long marriage although Laurier also had a "passionate attachment" to Émilie Barthe, the wife of one of his law partners. Their liaison continued for decades and copies of their correspondence still survive. It was rumoured, but never certain, that Laurier was the father to one of Émilie's sons.

Laurier always had about him a somewhat physically fragile air, which lent credence to his reputation as an intellectual and even a dreamer. He was slim and more than six feet tall, with wavy brown hair that turned prematurely grey, and he cut a dashing figure, particularly when he wore a waist coat and top hat. He was at once intelligent and affable but more ambitious than his demeanour implied. Oscar Douglas Skelton, an academic turned senior civil servant who later became one of Laurier's sympathetic biographers, described him as "the noblest and most unselfish man, it has ever been my good fortune to know." J. W. Dafoe, editor of the *Winnipeg Free Press*, and often an informal advisor to Laurier, had a saltier view, describing him as "a man who had affinities with Machiavelli as well as Sir Galahad."

◆

Laurier was an unrepentant rouge and later a Liberal and that put him into direct conflict with the powerful Catholic hierarchy. The Catholic Church had deep roots in New France. After General Wolfe defeated Montcalm and the French by taking Quebec City in 1760, the British shrewdly left the church's authority and most of its property intact. The church continued to be a dominant force in what was a semi-feudal society—controlling education and health care and collecting tithes from its parishioners. The bishops and clergy were in a sense more Catholic than the pope and attempted to inoculate people against revolutionary and liberal ideas.

By the late 1700s those ideas and revolutions were sweeping through Europe. The Roman Catholic Church, long accustomed to being both the spiritual and temporal authority, came under increasing attack. It pushed back with a robust movement that, in France, came to be called ultramontanism. That word described an unerring allegiance to the pope, described as the "man beyond the mountains" in Italy. Adherents supported papal authority in all matters of faith and temporal life. The ultramontanes insisted that political rulers had either to submit to the pope's will or face condemnation.

The liberal revolutions led to an attempt by other Catholics to reconcile the church's authority with modernity and liberalism, which emphasized liberty of conscience and the separation of church and state. What came to be known as Catholic Liberalism originated in France and was strongest there and in Belgium. It was more of a humanistic philosophy than a political movement; nonetheless it was considered a threat and heartily condemned by the Vatican. In 1864 Rome decided that Catholic Liberalism was in error and pronounced against it. In 1869 the First Vatican Council was to declare that the pope was infallible in matters of faith and morals.

When Laurier began to attend McGill University in 1862, he was introduced to the L'Institut Canadien, an intellectual and literary society and a centre of rouge activity. Its library contained books banned by the church; its ideas were liberal and the club was also open to Protestants. Bishop Ignace Bourget of Montreal warned that Catholics who participated in the institute would be excommunicated. Laurier served as the organization's vice-president for several years and was once a member of a delegation that met with the bishop in an attempt to work through the disagreements. The young men were rebuffed. Eventually the institute was forced to fold in the face of the church's hostility.

Nor was Laurier able to escape the bitter conflict between Liberals and the church when in 1867 he moved to rural Arthabaska. He soon became editor of the rouge newspaper called *Le Défricheur*, in which he denounced the Confederation of provinces that had occurred in that year. The local bishop, Monseigneur Louis-Francois-Richer Lafleche, in turn denounced Laurier, not because of his stand on Confederation but rather because Lafleche believed him to be a revolutionary and a traitor. The bishop placed a ban on the newspaper and it was forced to stop publishing. Despite those admonitions, it was just a matter of time until Laurier ran for political office. He did so in Arthabaska for the provincial Liberals in 1871 in a bitterly contested election. A group of Conservative politicians, editors, and lawyers had devised a so-called Catholic Programme that had been approved in advance by Bishops Bourget and Lafleche. Ultramontanes among the Conservatives promised that their party would support the church's claim of primacy over any legislature. That stance concerned some other Conservatives as well as a few bishops, notably Archbishop Elzéar-Alexandre Taschereau of Quebec City. He believed that his fellow bishops were going too far.

Laurier won in the provincial election in 1871 but the Liberals fared poorly. Despite making some impressive speeches in the National Assembly, he appeared not to enjoy his work. Meanwhile, in Ottawa, the scandal-plagued government of John A. Macdonald fell in 1873. By this time, Liberals in Quebec had merged with a group in Ontario called the Clear Grits to create the Liberal Party of Canada. Laurier ran in the 1873 federal election and won. By this time he had trimmed his more radical and nationalist inclinations and he did an about-face on Confederation, which he and other rouges had once denounced. This represented both a calculation and an evolution in his thinking. He was impressed in his reading about the Liberalism of the British Whigs under leaders such as Sir William Gladstone. Laurier decided that the future of French Canadians would be best protected within the new Canadian state rather than in isolation, a conviction that he was to hold for the rest of his life. Laurier may have been one of the most intellectual MPs in Ottawa, but not the most energetic. He could often be found reading in the alcoves of the parliamentary library. When he did speak in the House, he was conspicuous by his eloquence.

In Quebec, the Catholic Programme featured significantly again in the provincial election campaign of 1875 which hurt the Liberals. The bishops issued a pastoral message in that year and another in 1876 attacking Catholic Liberalism. Bishop Bourget offered the following advice to loyal Catholics: "Let each say this in his heart: 'I hear my curé, my curé hears the bishop, the bishop hears the pope and the pope hears our Lord Jesus Christ.'" In a federal by-election in Charlevoix in 1876, priests again attacked Liberals from the pulpit, saying that those Catholics who voted Liberal would be committing a mortal sin. Some clerics told parishioners that heaven was blue and hell was red, in obvious reference to bleus and rouges, the Conservatives and Liberals respectively. The Liberals lost and then went to court arguing that the church had overstepped its bounds. They also contested results of an election in the Bonaventure riding. The courts ruled in their favour in both cases, which only added to the bitter tone. There was even a court case over the church's refusal to bury a former member of the L'Institut Canadien in a consecrated part of the cemetery when he died. Again, an appeal was made to the courts and eventually the church was ordered to conduct the burial, which had to be done under armed guard. One historian has described what happened at the time as a holy war.

Both liberal and ultramontane Catholics in Quebec took their case to Rome in 1876. The continuing feud was divisive within Quebec, and it was becoming a public embarrassment for the international church. In May 1877 the Vatican sent Irish bishop George Conroy to investigate and make recommendations. He was based in Quebec City and made his rounds to talk discretely to all sides in the internecine feud. It was at about the same time that a group of young Liberals invited Laurier to speak in Quebec City on June 26, 1877. One is left to wonder if the timing was accidental. Laurier and those who looked to him for leadership knew that Conroy's recommendations would be crucial. The Liberals had been deeply wounded by the clergy's intervention against them, and their future prospects were dim in the face of such hostility. Laurier had decided to confront his critics directly, and to do it before Bishop Conroy made his report to Rome. The speech would provide a platform to define and put the best face upon the Liberal Party and its ideas. Laurier would also confront the claim that Liberalism was a heresy condemned by the head of the church and that a Catholic could not be a Liberal.

He began to write his speech at home in Arthabaska in late May and sent a summary to Prime Minister Alexander Mackenzie on June 21. The stakes were high, so much so that Mackenzie, after conferring with other Liberals, advised Laurier not to make the speech. Mackenzie had met with Bishop Conroy, who had been told by others that Quebec's Liberals were extremists linked closely to revolutionaries in France and Italy. However, Mackenzie concluded that Conroy appeared open to Liberal arguments and warned Laurier to avoid stirring up any controversy before the bishop had completed his mission. If Laurier chose to deliver the speech, there was a chance that he would offend Conroy and further alienate Quebec's bishops; that he would fail to sway his critics; and that he might frustrate his ambitions and destroy his career. Despite those risks, Laurier sidestepped Mackenzie, telling him in a return letter that he almost regretted having accepted the invitation but that his speech would be a prudent one. He mailed the letter to his leader on June 22, too late for Mackenzie to receive it and respond before the speaking engagement. On Sunday, June 25, Laurier took the train to Quebec City.

The location for the Club Canadien speech was a music hall. As Laurier arrived on the evening of June 26 there was a crush of horse-drawn carriages in the street. He was accompanied by a number of young Liberals and once in the hall he met briefly in an ante-room with other party members, some from as far away as Montreal and Ottawa. There were many journalists in the audience, some friendly and others not, since most newspapers of the day were partisans. Many members of Quebec's assembly, Liberals and other, were there as was the Anglican archbishop of Quebec, Catholic priests, and professors—both clerical and lay—from nearby Laval University. The hall was built to accommodate about twelve hundred but this night it was overflowing with more than two thousand. Many of them were in the aisles, on the steps, and even on the platform. The wide front doors were left open for those who spilled out into the street. For the crowd, this was a form of entertainment as well as engagement.

Journalists who were present that evening described how, when the time came to speak, Laurier was so pale they believed he might be ill. He was introduced, and then, in the words of one reporter, there were several moments of absolute stillness as the orator pondered his audience and they scrutinized him. Then Laurier began to speak, in French.

LAURIER'S SPEECH

I cannot conceal that it is with a certain feeling of pleasure I have accepted the invitation to come here to explain the doctrines of the Liberal Party, and what is the exact meaning of the word "Liberalism," as understood by the Liberals of Quebec.

I may say that it is not without a certain sentiment of pleasure that I have accepted the invitation; but if I had taken into consideration the difficulties of the task, I would, certainly, have refused. Nevertheless, if those difficulties were numerous and delicate, on the other hand I am so impressed with the importance to the Liberal Party, of clearly defining its position before public opinion in this province that I found that this consideration outweighed with me all the rest; I do not deceive myself as to the standing of the Liberal Party in the province of Quebec; and I, at once, declare that it occupies a false position in the eyes of public opinion.

I know that for a great many of my fellow citizens, the Liberal Party is a party composed of men holding perverse doctrines, with dangerous tendencies, and knowingly and deliberately progressing towards revolution. I know that in the opinion of a portion of our fellow countrymen, the Liberal Party is made up of men of good intentions, perhaps, but not the less dupes and victims of their principles, by which they are unconsciously but fatally led to revolution. I know that for yet another portion, not the least numerous, Liberalism is a new form of evil, in other words a heresy, carrying with it its own condemnation. I know all this, and it is because I do so that I consented to appear before you ...

Laurier states his intentions to the audience within the first phrase of his address; he will explain the meaning and doctrines of Liberalism in Quebec. However, he clothes that intention with a few niceties. One can sense that Laurier is surveying his audience—the clerics, the politicians, and the press—using his honed sensibility and intuition as a measurement of how best to proceed. He expresses a "certain" feeling of pleasure and sentiment, deliberately understating his real feelings and reducing expectations, a stylistic device known as meiosis. He engages in some false modesty, saying that had he known how difficult his task would be, he would surely have refused it. He does not mention that he may have orchestrated his own invitation and that he refused the prime minister's entreaties to avoid giving the speech. In his perceived modesty and deference, Laurier is also engaging in ethos by presenting himself sympathetically to members of his audience as he begins the speech. He is subtly asking that they look favourably both upon him and his argument. He presents himself as a most reasonable person but in politics it is always good to have an enemy. He takes the liberty of summarizing the criticisms that have been made by his as yet unnamed adversaries. Those criticisms are that Liberals are perverse and dangerous revolutionaries, or they are well intentioned, but naive dupes—but in either event they are (Catholic) heretics. These are the charges that Bishop Conroy has been sent to investigate. He is one of the intended recipients of Laurier's message even though he is not in the room. It is also clear from Laurier's reference to "public opinion" that he knows his audience extends well beyond the two thousand people packed into the hall.

I know that Catholic Liberalism is condemned by the head of the Church; and I may be asked, what is Catholic Liberalism? At the threshold of the question, I refrain. The question is not included in my subject and, moreover, is beyond my power to elucidate. But I may also say that Catholic Liberalism is not political Liberalism. If it were true that ecclesiastical censure against Catholic Liberalism should apply to political Liberalism, this fact would constitute for us, French in origin and Catholic in religion, a state of things the consequence of which would be as strange as sad. The fact is we French Canadians are a conquered race. This is a sad truth to tell, but it is nevertheless the truth. But if we are a conquered race, we have also made a conquest, the conquest of liberty. We are a free people. We are in the minority; but we have preserved all our rights and privileges. But what is it that guarantees us this liberty? It is the constitution that was won for us by our fathers and which we, today, enjoy. We have a constitution that places the government in the hands of the people. We have a constitution that has been granted to us for our own defence. We have no more rights nor greater privileges, but we have as many rights and privileges as the other races which, with us, constitute the Canadian family. Again, it must not be forgotten that the other members of the Canadian family are divided into two parties, the Liberal and the Conservative.

Now, if we who are Catholics had no right of choice, if we had not the right of belonging to the Liberal Party, one of two things must occur: either we would be obliged to completely abstain from taking part in the direction of public affairs, and then the constitution, which was granted to us for our protection, would be but a dead letter, or we should have to take part in the administration of state affairs under the direction and for the benefit of the Conservative Party; thus, our action being no longer free, the constitution would be a dead letter in our hands, and we would, moreover, have to suffer the disgrace of being, for the other members of the Canadian family who make up the Conservative Party, mere tools or supernumeraries. Do not these absurd consequences, but of which no one can deny the strict correctness, show, in the most undoubted manner, how utterly false the assertion is that a Catholic cannot belong to the Liberal Party?

As for myself, I belong to the Liberal Party. If to be a Liberal is a term of reproach, that reproach I accept. If it is a crime to be a Liberal, then I am guilty. One thing only I claim, that is that we be judged according to our principles ... It behooves, however, before all things to understand the meaning, the value and the bearing of the word "liberal" and the word "conservative" ...

The Vatican has condemned Catholic Liberalism and in Quebec the bishops have applied that sanction to the Liberal Party. It is critical to Laurier's purpose that he separates the two forms of Liberalism. He does not want to get sidetracked by defining or defending Catholic Liberalism, which has been condemned, so he deftly avoids the issue.

Laurier then presents a tautological argument describing why it does not make sense for the Catholic hierarchy to denounce Quebec Liberalism. This is an appeal to logic or what students of rhetoric call logos. Laurier's arguments are as follows: French Canadians are a "conquered race" but despite that, they have the same rights as all other Canadians. If Catholics are forbidden to support Liberals, they must, by definition, either abstain from political affairs or support Conservatives. However, in that case French Canadians would have less freedom than other Canadians and would be forced into the hands of the Conservative Party. Is this not absurd, he asks, using the rhetorical device of hypophora to pose a question which has only one logical answer? Having made that extended argument, Laurier says defiantly that he is a Liberal. He then explains Liberal principles by comparing and contrasting them to those of the opposing Conservatives. This is a subtle shift away from his earlier stated intentions for the speech.

I now ask whether between these two ideas which form the basis of these parties there can exist a moral difference; is one radically good and the other radically bad? Is it not manifest that both are, what are called in morals indifferent, that is to say, that both are susceptible of appreciation, of thought and choice. Would it not be as unjust as it is absurd to condemn or approve either one or the other, absolutely good or bad?

Both are susceptible of great good and great evil. The Conservative, who defends the old institutions of his country, can do much good while he may perpetrate a great evil if he persists in perpetuating intolerable abuses. The Liberal who fights against those abuses, and who after unceasing efforts eradicates them, may be a public benefactor, while the Liberal who would raise a profane hand against its sacred institutions, would prove a scourge not only of his country, but of humanity ...

In fact Liberalism appears to me on all points to be superior to the other principle. The Liberal principle is in the very essence of our nature, in that thirst for happiness which we all feel in this life, which follows us everywhere, to be, however, never completely satisfied on this side of the grave. Our souls are immortal, but our means are limited. We unceasingly approach toward an ideal which we never reach. We dream of the highest good, but secure only the better. Hardly have we reached the limits we have yearned to alter, when we discover new horizons, which we have never dreamed of. We rush towards them, and when they have been reached in their turn, we find others which lead us on further and further.

Thus shall it be as long as man is what he is, as long as the immortal soul dwells in the mortal body, so long shall its desires be beyond its means, its actions can never equal its conceptions. He is the true Sisyphus of the fable, its completed work has ever to be recommenced.

This condition of our nature is exactly what constitutes the greatness of man; for it urges him ceaselessly to push forward to progress; our means are finite but our nature can be improved, and we have the infinite as our field of labor. There is then always room to improve our condition, to perfect our nature, and to render an easier life to a greater number. This it is, in my opinion, which constitutes the superiority of Liberalism ...

Laurier reverts again to logical appeal in comparing Liberals and Conservatives. But he refers as well to the term "morals indifferent," a theory that had been developed by Catholic philosophers and theologians. Laurier was always cautious and circumspect about his religious sensibilities but he is obviously aware of theological arguments. Morals indifferent describes an act that is neither intrinsically good nor evil but rather is amenable to choice. Laurier applies the concept to Liberals and Conservatives. Both political options, he says, are worthy of consideration and neither can be declared evil out of hand. Conservatives can practise evil by defending "old institutions" and "intolerable abuses." Liberals, if they become too aggressive, can become a "scourge." He is referring here, without naming them, to the French and other European revolutions in which the power and wealth of the church were greatly diminished. He wants to put the prelates in the front row at their ease; they have nothing to fear from the Liberals.

He then shifts from his earlier tautologies to an emotional appeal on behalf of Liberalism. Having briefly compared the two philosophies, he insists that Liberalism is superior on all points. He uses repetition, parallel linguistic structure, and antithesis to contrast the gap between yearning and achievement, a characteristic that he obviously believes is central to Liberalism. Reach exceeds grasp. Striving but never quite achieving, he says, is the human condition and to anchor his point he uses an allusion to Sisyphus. In that Greek myth a king is condemned to rolling a boulder uphill only to have it roll down and then to begin again. Laurier says that these constant although frustrated efforts toward progress and improvement are the essence of Liberalism; and which explains why Liberalism is superior to Conservatism. He has, in this part of the speech, performed another sleight of hand: a shift from describing the choice between Conservatives and Liberals as "indifferent" to one of arguing that Liberalism is clearly the better choice.

The highest art in governing is to guide and to direct by controlling these aspirations of humanity. The English possess this art in the highest degree. Look at the work of the great English Liberal party. The reforms they have carried out, the abuses they have suppressed, without violence, without commotion, without disturbance. They understood the longings of the oppressed, they comprehended the new wants created by new conditions of society, and under the authority of the law, and without anything else than the law, they have carried out a series of reforms which have made the English the freest of peoples, the most prosperous, and the happiest in Europe ... Members of the Club Canadien! Liberals of the Province of Quebec, these are our principles; behold our models; such a party is ours.

It is true that there exists, in Europe, in France, in Italy and in Germany, a class of men who call themselves liberals, but who are liberal but in name, and who are the most dangerous of men. They are not Liberals, they are Revolutionists. Their principles carry them so far that they aspire to nothing less than the destruction of modern society. With these men we have no connection, but it is the tactics of our adversaries incessantly to compare us to them. Those accusations are beneath us, and the only reply worthy of us is to state our true principles and to always act in a manner conformable to them ...

Having compared the philosophies of Conservatives and Liberals in Quebec and preferring the latter, Laurier sings the praises of Liberalism in Great Britain. He is an admirer of seventeenth and eighteenth century Whigs such as Charles James Fox, William Gladstone, and Daniel

O'Connell, often called the Irish liberator. Gladstone was, like Laurier, a durable politician, who served as prime minister for fourteen years, a time that was interspersed with several periods in Opposition. He was a dynamic and popular speaker and had a record of educational, political, and judicial reform. Laurier builds his argument on behalf of British Liberalism through the use of parallel structures and in one case through the use of asyndeton—removing conjunctions between phrases: "without violence, without commotion, without disturbance." These are Laurier's principles and British Liberalism is his model.

Laurier, however, has a motive beyond mere admiration of British Liberalism. The liberal revolutions in Europe had been accompanied by violence and destruction. The Catholic hierarchy and clergy in Quebec, not to mention the Conservatives, have accused local Liberals of harbouring similar revolutionary motives. Laurier must draw a clear distinction between Liberalism in Britain and that on the continent, between Liberals and "revolutionists." He disavows any connection with continental European liberals. But that does not quite solve his problem. He has also to immunize contemporary Liberals in Quebec from the legacy of Louis Joseph Papineau and the young militants who supported his armed revolt in 1837. Some of those who were young men then are now mature Liberals and are in the audience on this evening.

The only excuse for these Liberals was their youth; the oldest among them not being twenty-two years of age. Gentlemen I state facts, I do not intend to reproach anyone. Talent and sincerity of conviction ever command respect. Which of us now, who, living in that age, can flatter himself that he would have been wiser, and would not have fallen into the same errors? Everything then led to such exaggerations, the state of affairs both in this country and in Europe. This state of things acted powerfully on the imaginations of the ardent and inexperienced youth; and our young reformers not contented with revolutionizing their own country greeted joyfully each new revolution in Europe ...

However, scarcely had they lived a few years when they perceived the great error into which they had fallen. As early as 1852 they published a new paper. They left L'Avenir *to hot headed madmen and endeavoured in their new paper the* Pays *without always succeeding, it is true, to point out the new path which the friends of liberty under the new constitution should follow ... However the evil was done. The clergy alarmed by measures which reminded them only too vividly of European revolutions, immediately declared merciless war against the new party ...*

Laurier was born in 1841. Had he been of age in 1837 he might well have been carrying a musket among Papineau's supporters. Laurier rationalizes the radical commitments of those young men as exuberance. They soon recognized their error but it was too late and the clergy declared "merciless war" against them. Even worse, some Conservatives backed by ultramontane bishops are talking about organizing a political party to represent Catholics only.

You wish to organize all Catholics into a single party without other tie, without other basis than that of religion, but you have not reflected that by that fact alone you organize the Protestant population as a single party, and that then instead of peace and harmony which now exists amongst the elements of our Canadian populations, you will bring on war—religious war, the most frightful of all wars ...

But our adversaries, in reproaching us with being the friends of liberty, still further reproach us with a charge which would be very serious—were it well founded, that is—with refusing the Church the liberty to which it is entitled. They reproach us with endeavouring to silence the administrative body of the Church, the clergy, with wishing to prevent them from educating the people in their duties, as citizens as well as electors. They reproach us, if I may use a hackneyed saying, with wishing to prevent the clergy from meddling in politics and sending them back to their vestries.

In the name of the Liberal Party, in the name of the liberal principle, I deny the assertion. I assert that there is not a single Canadian Liberal who wishes to hinder the clergy from taking part in political affairs if they wish to take part therein; under what principle would the friends of liberty refuse the priests the right of taking part in public affairs? ... This is everyone's right; there is no reason why the priest should not have it. I am here to say what I think and I add that I am far from finding the intervention of the clergy in politics opportune as exercised during the last few years. On the contrary, I think that the priest has everything to lose as regards the respect due to his station by meddling with the ordinary questions of politics. However, his right is incontestable, and if he chose to avail himself of it, our duty as Liberals is to secure it to him against every opponent.

This right, however, is not unlimited. We have, amongst us, no absolute rights. The rights of each man in our state of society cease to exist when he trespasses on the rights of others. The right of intervening in politics ends when it trespasses on the independence of the elector ...

Laurier's intention in his speech is to create a political opening for the Liberal Party. But it is equally important to dissuade Catholics from promoting a political party composed of and representing only themselves. His warning here contains the harshest words spoken that evening. The message could well apply to situations today where political and clerical powers have merged with sometimes catastrophic results. "You will bring on war," he warns, "religious war, the most frightful of all wars."

Laurier and the Liberals were also under attack for supposedly attempting to prevent priests from participating in politics or educating their parishioners. Laurier denies that, saying that the Liberals support the right of anyone, including clergy, to participate in politics. However, he twice describes the clergy's "meddling" in politics, softening the description the first time by describing it as a "hackneyed expression" used by others. His language may be subtle but his intent is direct. He repeats that clergy has the right to be involved in politics but he adds a caveat that also has resonance in today's debates about religious versus other freedoms—one person's rights end when they trespass on the rights of others. Laurier's remarks would by now have reached forty or forty-five minutes. An audience, even in those more leisurely days, might have begun to shift uncomfortably anticipating a conclusion. Having made his logical and emotional arguments, he begins to build toward his crescendo.

Now to fully appreciate the value of our present institutions let us compare our condition with what it was before they were granted to us. Forty years ago, the country was in a state of feverish excitement and agitation which in a few months later, culminated in rebellion. The British Crown was upheld in the country, but by powder and shot. And yet what did our forefathers demand? Nothing else than our present institutions; these institutions were granted and loyally applied, and behold the consequences: the English flag floats from the ancient Citadel of Quebec.

It floats this evening above our heads and yet there is not a single English soldier in the country to defend it; its sole defence is the consciousness that we owe to it the liberty and security we find under it.

What Canadian is there who, comparing his own with even the freest of other countries, but feels proud of its institutions?

What Canadian is there who, in going through the streets of this old city, and seeing the monument a few feet from this place, erected to the memory of two brave men who fell on the same field of battle in fighting for the possession of this country, but feels proud of his country? In what country under the sun could you find a similar monument, erected to the memory of the conqueror and the conquered? In what country under the sun could you find the names of the victor and vanquished honored in the same degree, occupying the same place in the sentiments of the population?

Gentlemen, when in this last battle, commemorated by the monument erected to Wolfe and Montcalm, the cannon spread death among the French ranks; when the old heroes, whom victory had so often followed, saw her at last deserting them; when reclining on the sod, feeling their hearts' blood flowing and life departing they saw, as a consequence of their defeat, Quebec in the hands of the enemy and their country forever lost, no doubt their last thoughts turned towards their children, towards those whom they left without protection and without defence; doubtless they saw them persecuted, enslaved, humiliated; and then we may imagine their last breath to have been a cry of despair.

But if, on the other hand, heaven had permitted the veil of the future to be raised before their expiring vision; if heaven permitted them, before their eyes closed forever, to penetrate the unknown; if they could have seen their children free and happy, walking proudly in every rank of society; if they could have seen in the ancient cathedral the seat of honor of the French governors occupied by a French governor; if they could have seen the spires of churches piercing the azure in every valley from the waters of Gaspé to the plains of Red River; if they could have seen this old flag which reminds us of our greatest victory triumphantly borne in all our public ceremonies; finally, if they could have seen our free institutions, may we not believe that their last breath was softened to a murmur of thanks to heaven, and that they found consolation as they died.

If the shades of those heroes yet move about this old city for which they died, and if they are on this evening in this hall, we Liberals may believe, at least we have the dear illusion, that their sympathies are entirely with us.

DENNIS GRUENDING

Every grand speech has a climax or peroration and Laurier's is a poetic and an emotional appeal praising the peace and good governance that exists for a people who had been conquered but are now free. He begins with contrasting comparisons, extending and drawing them out. The age of agitation and rebellion that existed in 1837 has been replaced by a calm symbolized by the English flag floating peacefully over Quebec City's old citadel. Laurier uses the city where his speech is occurring as an emotional set piece for his climax. He continues with the contrasts: Wolfe and Montcalm, conqueror and conquered, victor and vanquished—in Quebec City all are "honored in the same degree." In the city, the two generals share a monument constructed in 1827. Laurier goes on to paint a picture of French soldiers on the historic battlefield, "old heroes" who, as they lay dying, feared that all was lost and that only humiliation and persecution lay ahead for their descendants. Here he employs the funeral oration to fallen soldiers, a rhetorical genre at least as old as Pericles and the Greeks. In this style or oration, the fallen heroes are praised as brave and noble and the living are exhorted to prove worthy of those who have sacrificed their lives for an ideal.

Laurier, however, adapts the oration to his own purposes, turning a potentially sombre reality into a sunny one. He describes what those old heroes would have been able to observe had they lived. He does so by employing a series of repetitions and parallel structures, each using the phrase "if they could have seen ... " In the Quebec of 1877 the children are happy, the spires of Catholic churches pierce the blue skies, and all enjoy life under free and democratic institutions. Following this climax, Laurier's denouement is brief, but in it he states his belief that the ghosts of those grand old heroes, if they were in the hall on this evening, would surely be in full sympathy with the Liberals. That is cheeky.

THE IMPACT OF LAURIER'S SPEECH

Laurier's audacious speech in Quebec City established him as the pre-eminent spokesperson for French Canadian Liberals. The speech also played a key role in undercutting the dominance of the church in political affairs, although this process would take some time. Arguably, none of

Laurier's future career accomplishments would have been possible without this address. As well, the creation of a religiously based political party would have been a turn away from the inclusion that Laurier promoted and represented.

Laurier's biographers, sympathetic to a fault, described the ovation he received after he had finished his speech: deafening applause, striking ovation, unequivocal triumph are just some of the descriptions used. The speech was widely covered by Quebec's newspapers, most of them highly partisan. *Le Nouveau Monde*, a Conservative paper, said that despite Laurier's protestations Quebec's Liberals were "revolutionists" similar to those in continental Europe. The newspaper also wrote that Laurier and his ilk placed parliamentary authority above that of the church, which proclaimed immutable truths. Another Conservative paper, *Le Courier de St. Hyacinthe*, wrote that Laurier would have been better advised not to show up for the speech and that he had done himself and the Liberals great harm.

However, the *Montreal Herald*, a paper supporting the Liberals, wrote that Laurier's speech was a masterpiece of diction worthy of his growing national reputation as an orator. *The Montreal Witness*, another Liberal-friendly paper, said the speech indicated that a new master had arrived on the scene but tweaked Laurier for his implied criticism of those Liberals who had previously been young radicals.

Laurier may well have been less concerned with the judgments rendered by those in the hall and by newspapers than he was with that of Bishop Conroy. He was in the city and observing closely via his clerical helpers in the room. It was Conroy's task to recommend what approach the Vatican should take toward Canadian Liberalism. He had to decide if there was any difference between it and the Catholic Liberalism denounced by the pope. He had also to recommend what, if any, limits there should be on clerical interference in elections. Laurier dealt with both of those issues in his speech.

Either Laurier was utterly convincing or the legate had already come to his own conclusions. The Vatican passed word along to Quebec's bishops. They issued two pastoral letters in October 1877 in which they instructed that whatever the Holy See said against Catholic Liberalism was not to be applied to any political party in Quebec. Priests were not to tell their parishioners that it was a sin to vote for a particular candidate or party. The bishops did not withdraw anything they had said in earlier pastorals but they had in reality changed their position based upon Conroy's recommendations.

Laurier was a young man on the move. His speech helped to consolidate his position as the leading spokesperson for Quebec Liberals and to gain for him wider attention. In the following year, more than three hundred pages of Hansard were devoted to what Laurier had said in Quebec City. He had also been talking privately with Prime Minister Mackenzie about being appointed to the cabinet. But he attached a bold condition to his acceptance: Joseph Cauchon, an older Quebec Liberal who had changed parties on several occasions, must first be removed from cabinet. That decision had been delayed because Cauchon was instrumental in having the Vatican send Bishop Conroy to Quebec; and he acted as an intermediary while the bishop was in the country. By October, however, Bishop Conroy had reported to Rome and Cauchon was expendable. Mackenzie appointed him as the lieutenant-governor of Manitoba. That cleared the way for Laurier, at age thirty-six, to become the principal Liberal spokesperson for Quebec. On October 8, 1877, he was sworn in as the minister of inland revenue.

Laurier was to serve a long apprenticeship plagued by disappointments as well as triumphs. According to existing political convention, he had to resign his seat upon being appointed to the cabinet and to run in a by-election. Despite Bishop Conroy's recent orders to the bishops and clergy, the church took sides in this election. Once again the campaign was a bitter one and Laurier lost by five votes. He and Mackenzie were both shaken by the loss, but they convinced a sitting member to give up his seat in the constituency of Quebec East. Laurier was soon running in another by-election in November 1877. This time he won and he was to represent that seat for the next forty-two years.

His first tenure in cabinet was to be short-lived. In 1878 the Liberals lost power to the aging John A. Macdonald and the Conservatives, who also won a majority of the seats in Quebec. The years in opposition were difficult ones for both the Liberals and Laurier. He was often ill and at times appeared unengaged. However, he came to national prominence in 1885–86 with his attacks on Macdonald and the Conservatives following the hanging of Métis leader Louis Riel. By then Alexander Mackenzie had given way to Edward Blake as Liberal leader, but after the Conservatives won again in 1891 Blake resigned. Laurier replaced him. It was to be another five years before he became prime minister in 1896.

By that time the tide had turned in Quebec and the Liberals were to supplant the Conservatives as the party of choice. In the elections of 1891 and 1896, and thereafter, a majority of Quebec MPs were Liberals. Their hold on power was largely unchallenged for decades. In all but one of twenty-six federal elections held between 1891 and 1984, Quebecers provided the Liberals with a majority of seats. The battle for political supremacy in Quebec was a tribal feud. Nothing was more important to Laurier's success and that of the Liberals than his breaking the lock that the Conservatives held with the help of the church. Laurier's speech in June 1877 set the stage for much of what was to come in Canada's twentieth century.

LOUIS RIEL'S SPEECH TO THE JURY

JULY 31, 1885

"Even if I was going to be sentenced by you,
gentlemen of the jury, I have this satisfaction
if I die—that if I die I will not be reputed
by all men as insane, as a lunatic ... "

Louis Riel is one of the most controversial figures in Canadian history. A Métis from Red River, he had been educated in a seminary school in Montreal. Upon his return he led a resistance against the newly federated Canadian government, which was sending surveyors into a region where the Métis occupied land but had no official title to it. Riel set up a provisional government and the province of Manitoba was born amid the turmoil; but as the Canadian militia approached, he feared for his life and fled to the United States. After years in exile, the Métis in the Saskatchewan River country farther west called upon Riel. Once again the surveyors had appeared and the Métis hoped Riel could do for them what he had done in Red River. It turned out badly. There was violence and the government sent troops to crush the Métis at Batoche in 1885. Riel surrendered and was put on trial for treason. His speech to the jury was at once powerful and erratic and it echoes still.

◆

Louis Riel was born in 1844 in the Red River settlement of the North-West Territories, which is the area in and around present-day Winnipeg. He was the eldest of eleven children born into the mixed-descent family of Jean-Louis Riel and Marie-Anne Lagimodière. Louis Riel's ancestors were francophones from Quebec but with a great-grandmother on his father's side who was Chipewyan. Jean-Louis, the father of Louis, had been born in Île-à-la-Crosse on the Upper Churchill River where his father worked for the North West Company as a middleman between Indian trappers and Montreal fur merchants. The family later moved back to Quebec. Jean-Louis received an adequate education and acquired a trade as a wool carder. As a young man in Quebec he became an admirer of Papineau, who led the 1837 insurrection in Lower Canada. Jean-Louis was later to return to the northwest where he took land along the Red River and also established a mill. It was at Red River where he met Julie Lagimodière and they were married in January 1841. Jean-Louis was a community leader among the French and Métis inhabitants of Red River and was passionate about the abuses perpetrated by the monopolistic Hudson's Bay Company. The Riels were also devout Catholics. Jean-Louis had spent a brief time as an Oblate novitiate considering the priesthood and Julie had planned to become a nun before consenting to marry him.

Their eldest son, Louis, was a gifted student. In 1858, when he was fourteen years old, the local bishop, Alexandre Taché, sent him on full scholarship to Montreal where he was to study for the priesthood at the Collège de Montréal. The school, operated by the Sulpician order, existed to produce priests but it also was a training ground for Quebec's male elite. The education Riel received would have had much in common with that provided to Wilfrid Laurier at L'Assomption College. It was a classical education based on philosophy, rhetoric, and the literature of Greece, Rome, and France. Riel consistently ranked near the top of his class in an environment where the workload was heavy and the discipline strict.

He was a handsome young man, tall and slender with flashing eyes and dark, wavy hair. He was popular with his classmates, but he could also be moody, quick-tempered, and stubborn. In Montreal he made many friends who would come to his aid throughout a turbulent life. It was also at the Collège de Montréal that he began writing poetry and keeping a diary, activities that he was to maintain for life. In 1864, when Riel was twenty, he received the devastating news that his father had died. Lingering sadness over that event, in addition to his falling in love with a young woman whose family opposed their relationship, led him to drop out of seminary studies in 1865 just a few months short of his graduation. He found a job in Montreal as a law clerk but he did not like the work. He left the city in 1866 and spent the next two years doing odd jobs first in Chicago and later in St. Paul, Minnesota. When he returned to Red River in 1868, he found that much had changed in ten years. The old settlement, populated in earlier times mainly by French-speaking Métis and people of mixed descent, had attracted Canadians and some Americans, almost all of them Protestants and unsympathetic to both Roman Catholicism and the Métis.

In 1869 the newly confederated government of Canada purchased the vast reaches of Rupert's Land from the Hudson's Bay Company, but there was no provision made for the rights of the existing Indian, Métis, and other mixed-descent residents. There was much talk among the recently arrived whites in the Red River settlement of annexation to Canada or even the United States. Then the surveyors arrived and the Métis feared they would lose the lands on which they had built their farms, pastures, and woodlots. When young Louis Riel returned to Red River, most of the buffalo-hunting Métis welcomed his leadership, believing his education and life experience among the whites would accomplish in political terms what their traditional skills could not.

In 1869 the Métis turned back the surveyors and set up a provisional government to fill the political vacuum that existed in the interval between the sale of Rupert's Land and its legal annexation to Canada. Riel led the Métis campaign and did much to draft the terms of Manitoba's entry into Confederation in 1870. Tragically, however, the provisional government executed Thomas Scott for treason. Scott was a racist troublemaker who had threatened violence against the Métis. The decision to execute him was to ruin Riel's life as well as taking Scott's. In May 1870 John A. Macdonald's government sent Colonel Garnet Joseph Wolseley on a military expedition toward Red River. Riel was still at the head of the provisional government, but he heard that Ontario militiamen among Wolseley's men were planning to lynch him. One of those volunteers was Hugh John Macdonald, the prime minister's son. Riel fled to St. Joseph Mission just across the border in the United States. John A. Macdonald promised an amnesty to Riel and others as part of the negotiations that created Manitoba, but he later reneged on that pledge. Riel had a price placed on his head by Edward Blake, leader of the Ontario Liberal Party. Rather than becoming a Manitoba statesman, Riel was forced into a lengthy exile in the United States. That banishment took its toll upon his mind and spirit. Even so, he was elected three times as an MP for the new province of Manitoba. He was not allowed to take his seat and ultimately politicians in the House of Commons voted to expel him.

As he wandered in the American states, Riel became increasingly convinced that God had chosen him to be a religious prophet who would usher a new form of Christianity into the Canadian northwest. His intense religious visions were accompanied by increasingly erratic behaviour that frightened even the fondest of his hosts. In March 1876 his uncle in Montreal had him confined to an asylum. Riel was soon moved from there to the Beauport Asylum near Quebec City. Upon his release in January 1878 he was spirited away to the United States and once again he moved from place to place. In 1881 he married a young Métis woman named Marguerite Monet. He became an American citizen and in 1883 accepted an offer from Jesuit priests to teach children in a remote mission school in Montana. While he was attending mass there one morning in June 1884, a woman whispered to him that guests had arrived to see him. The group waiting when Riel emerged from the church included Gabriel Dumont, a Métis leader from the banks of the Saskatchewan River ninety kilometres to the north of what is now the city of Saskatoon.

Following Manitoba's entry into Confederation, the Métis were largely marginalized and disenfranchised within their homeland. They faced racism and many of them remained landless. The Manitoba Act provided that they receive what was called land scrip—certificates worth a certain amount of money, which would allow them to purchase small plots of land at a later date. The scrip was meant to extinguish any rights they might claim to the larger land mass of Western Canada. It was left to the government to determine the location of the farm plots. The process was complex and bureaucratic and as a result, families were often unable to obtain any land. A black market quickly arose in which poor Métis families

DENNIS GRUENDING

took cash in return for their scrip and speculators came to own the land.

Many of the Métis simply chose to move farther west to escape encroaching white settlement. In 1884 they became alarmed at the appearance of federal land surveyors near their homes on the South Saskatchewan River. As it had in Red River, the Macdonald government ignored their requests, so the Métis sent Dumont and the others on a dusty seventeen-day trek to Montana where they asked Riel to return and help them secure and defend their rights. The Métis hoped that Riel could do for them what he had done in Manitoba. Within a day he agreed to return with their party. The delegation had arrived with three wagons and now they packed up Riel, his wife Marguerite, and their two young children, along with their few belongings, and made the slow journey northward.

After they arrived, Riel and others drafted a ten-point bill of rights that requested, among other things, that all mixed-descent and white settlers be provided with patents guaranteeing the possession of their farms. The document also asked that provinces called Saskatchewan and Alberta be created with legislatures organized on the basis of representation by population. That petition was also ignored by Macdonald. By the early winter months of 1885 the Métis were beginning to talk of armed resistance if their demands were not acknowledged. Then in March they encountered a group of nearby police and government supporters who fired upon them. In the ensuing skirmish, twelve members of the police and government side were killed and eleven wounded while the Métis lost five men. The point of peaceful resolution had passed. Macdonald was determined not to have a repetition of the Manitoba experience. He would crush the Métis and several Indian bands that had risen in armed resistance. Major-General Frederick Middleton, who commanded the militia, was in charge of the Canadian forces that travelled west by train and then marched on the Métis village of Batoche. Hugh John Macdonald volunteered for service in that campaign as well. The resistance was short-lived and after a siege of several days in May 1885, Middleton defeated the Métis. Dumont evaded the dragnet and slipped away to the United States. Riel chose not to leave. He hid in the woods near Batoche for several days before surrendering to Middleton.

Riel was taken to Regina, a small and makeshift village on the plains, which had become the territorial capital in 1882. He was immediately confined to a dingy three-by-two-metre prison cell and shackled with a ball and chain, which he was forced to wear constantly, even during his brief periods of exercise. Prison authorities read all of Riel's incoming and outgoing mail and he was allowed no visitors, except by the prime minister's written consent. Riel's jailer, however, allowed him to use an office where he wrote many letters and petitions in the period leading up to his trial, which began on July 20.

◆

Much has been said and written about Riel's trial. Beverley McLachlin, chief justice of the Supreme Court of Canada, spoke about it in a lecture delivered in Manitoba. "Judged from the perspective of 2010," she said, "Riel's trial, while minimally legal, suffered from many imperfections." The chief justice also reviewed the political context in which the trial occurred. She added: "The Prime Minister attempted to satisfy both of his constituencies [Ontario and Quebec] as well as his desire (admitted on more than one occasion) to be rid of Riel. The result was a process that was arguably lawful but unquestionably harsh and unwise."

First, there was the location chosen for the trial. General Middleton's orders were to transfer Riel to Winnipeg under guard, but Macdonald changed the instructions and Riel was sent instead to Regina. Winnipeg was a more established civic and legal centre. Regina was a raw frontier town where passions ran high against Métis and Indians involved in the resistance. In Manitoba, Riel would have been entitled to a twelve-person jury but in Regina he had to settle for six. In Manitoba, he would likely have been judged by some French-speaking, perhaps even Métis and Catholic jury members. The six men in Regina were all English-speaking Protestants, although one did understand French. In Manitoba, Riel would have been tried by a Superior Court judge with tenure. In Regina, his case was heard by Hugh Richardson, a unilingual magistrate who held office at the pleasure of the federal government and who could be dismissed at any time. Richardson was also a member of the Council of the North-West Territories and an occasional advisor to Lieutenant-Governor Edgar Dewdney. Richardson had participated in a March 1885 meeting where a decision was made to send extra police from Regina to crush the Métis resistance. Then there was the charge itself. Of the seventy-two people charged in the resistance, only Riel was accused of high treason under a statute from fourteenth-century England that carried a mandatory penalty of death.

Riel would have been desperately anxious. Following his return to Canada in 1884 there had been months of constant political activity and agitation prior to the outbreak of violence. There was a military campaign that saw his side crushed and many of his people killed. During all of this time his young wife was pregnant with their third child and ill with tuberculosis. The Riels were destitute and dependent upon the generosity of their family, friends, and supporters.

As the July 20 trial date approached, old friends from Riel's school days in Quebec raised money to hire four defence lawyers. Riel had hoped for a political trial and wanted above all to defend his actions as the just response to the government's ignoring the Métis petitions. He wanted to show as well that it was the government's forces that attacked the Métis, who he believed were acting in self defence. However, his lawyers Charles Fitzpatrick and François-Xavier Lemieux, without consulting Riel, chose not to contest the merits of his case but rather to plead insanity on his behalf.

When the trial began on July 21, the lawyers did challenge the jurisdiction of Judge Richardson and of the jury as it was constituted to hear the case in Regina. But they were abruptly overruled and made no further objection. In fact, they were later to say in court that the Métis resistance could not be justified. The defence lawyers also asked the court to order the provision of all documents related to the petitions and representations that had been made to the government by the Métis and to subpoena various officials, including those from Indian Affairs. The Crown's lawyers were contemptuous of the request and Judge Richardson refused it. Again Riel's lawyers chose not to argue the point further and thus his hopes of showing that the resistance was justified were lost. The defence lawyers had arrived in Regina only eight days before the trial began and they asked for a month's postponement to prepare their case. Judge Richardson granted them a week.

When the trial resumed on July 28, Riel was distraught by the insanity plea being advanced, and by his lawyers' failure to undertake vigorous cross-examinations of the Crown's witnesses about the events that had occurred. Riel attempted in the courtroom to intervene on various occasions. He was silenced by the judge upon the insistence of his lawyers. Charles Fitzpatrick even told Richardson that Riel was obstructing the proper management of the case and that he must be told that he was not allowed to interfere. Fitzpatrick and the others threatened to cease acting for Riel, which would have left him entirely on his own against a battery of experienced Crown lawyers. Faced with that frightening prospect, Riel reluctantly agreed to be silenced.

Paul Groake, a Canadian lawyer and academic, writes that the refusal by Riel's lawyers to act on their client's wishes and their co-operation with the judge in having him silenced were the most shocking aspects of the trial. Groake says this should have been grounds for a mistrial and the case should not have gone to the jury. Groake says further that Riel's lawyers should have pressed his case and forced the hand of Judge Richardson so that the unfairness of the trial was on record and could have been used as the basis of a later appeal.

The heart of the trial occurred in just a few days between July 28 and July 31 when Riel, following a summation by his defence counsel, was allowed to address the jury. Even then his lawyers told the court that they did not want to be held responsible for anything he said. The courtroom was located on the ground floor of a two-storey brick building with unpainted walls. The space was far too small for all of the people crammed into it. The room contained Riel in the prisoner's box, the judge and six-person jury, five Crown and four defence lawyers, a number of red-coated mounted police, newspaper reporters, and the wives of Judge Richardson, General Middleton, and other spectators who wanted to enjoy the proceedings. A black and white photo taken at the time leaves one feeling claustrophobic even now.

Riel was dressed in a frock coat and white shirt as he arose to address the jury. His hair was thick and dark and he wore a full beard. One court spectator wrote that on that day Riel resembled John the Baptist. He waved his arms as he spoke, particularly when he became agitated. He had many things he wanted to say; in fact, there were far too many. He was fighting for his life. He wanted to salvage his personal reputation as someone who had acted on behalf of his people and not for personal gain. He also wanted to convince the jury that he was a religious prophet and to lay out his elaborate plans for a province or territory in the northwest. There he believed various races and cultures could coexist in peace and harmony under a divine and Catholic guidance. While these arguments were important to him, they had no little real relevance to the charges levelled against him. They were unlikely to impress any jury, particularly one composed of six local Protestants. The insanity plea put forward by his lawyers undercut Riel's political argument that it was the government's irresponsibility that had led to the resistance. He was forced to argue on two fronts—against the substantive case of treason put forward by the Crown, but also against the defence of insanity argued by his lawyers. He faced a terrible dilemma. If he was successful in convincing the jury that he was sane, he would almost surely be found guilty and executed. However, if the jury accepted the insanity argument, then the Métis resistance would be seen as the work of a madman.

Riel had written some brief notes in preparation for his trial speech but they amounted to only a few hundred words. There was a torrent of information presented and accusations made against him during the trial. He was forced to improvise, often reacting to arguments and testimony that his lawyers had ignored. Of necessity, most of what he had to say was extemporaneous. His classical education in Quebec meant that he was familiar with rhetoric. During his involvement in the struggle for Métis rights he had proven to be a capable, even accomplished orator; but on this day, as he began to speak in his second language, the dice were loaded against him.

RIEL'S SPEECH

Your Honours, gentlemen of the jury: It would be easy for me today to play insanity, because the circumstances are such as to excite any man, and under the natural excitement of what is taking place today (I cannot speak English very well, but am to do so, because most of those here speak English), under the excitement which my trial causes me would justify me not to appear as usual, but with my mind out of its ordinary condition. I hope with the help of God I will maintain calmness and decorum as suits this honourable court, this honourable jury.

You have seen by the papers in the hands of the Crown that I am naturally inclined to think of God at the beginning of my actions. I wish if I do it you won't take it as a mark of insanity, that you won't take it as part of a play of insanity.

Oh, my God, help me through Thy grace and the divine influence of Jesus Christ. Oh, my God, bless me, bless this honourable court, bless this honourable jury, bless my good lawyers who have come seven hundred leagues to try to save my life, bless also the lawyers for the Crown, because they have done, I am sure, what they thought their duty. They have shown me fairness which at first I did not expect from them. Oh, my God, bless all those who are around me through the grace and influence of Jesus Christ our Saviour. Change the curiosity of those who are paying attention to me, change that curiosity into sympathy with me.

Riel wants desperately to convince the judge and jurors that he is sane and not mad as his lawyers have presented him. He deals immediately with that concern. He wants also to maintain control of his emotions even in these trying circumstances because some witnesses and his lawyers had talked about his volatility when under pressure. His tone is one of respect toward all involved. His words have a ring of sincerity, although it is likely also his rhetorician's way of winning sympathy for the speech to come. Riel is a devout man who prays multiple times a day and he breaks into prayer early in his speech. He asks a blessing not only for himself but for the judge and jury, his lawyers, and even the Crown's lawyers to whom he pays a somewhat backhanded compliment. He even calls for God's blessing upon the court's spectators. For some of them, he is an object of voyeuristic curiousity. He attempts to parry any belief that his calling upon the Almighty is a sign of insanity. Indeed, many people, then as now, resort to prayer at difficult times although usually not from the prisoner's box in a courtroom. Riel also asks those in the courtroom to excuse the fact that he does not speak English well. He is doing so "because most of those here speak English." Actually, he does speak English quite well but it is not his first language. This could be seen as an attempt to gain sympathy from the judge and jurors but as used here it appears transparently honest. It hardly seems just that he is forced to communicate in a second language while pleading for his life and defending his reputation.

The day of my birth I was helpless and my mother took care of me although she was not able to do it alone; there was someone to help her to take care of me and I lived. Today, although a man I am as helpless before this court, in the Dominion of Canada and in this world, as I was helpless on the knees of my mother the day of my birth. The North-West is also my mother; it is my mother country and although my mother country is sick and confirmed in a certain way, there are some from Lower Canada who came to help her to take care of me during her sickness and I am sure that my mother country will not kill me more than my mother did forty years ago when I came into the world, because a mother is always a mother, and even if I have my faults, if she can see I am true, she will be full of love for me.

When I came into the North-West in July, the 1st of July 1884, I found the Indians suffering. I found the half-breeds eating the rotten pork of the Hudson Bay Company and getting sick and weak every day. Although a half-breed, and having no pretension to help the whites, I also paid attention to them. I saw they were deprived of responsible government, I saw that they were deprived of their public liberties. I remembered that half-breed meant white and Indian and while I paid attention to the suffering Indians and the half-breeds I remembered that the greatest part of my heart and blood was white and I have directed my attention to help the Indians, help the half-breeds and to help the whites to the best of my ability.

We have made petitions, I have made petitions with others to the Canadian government asking to relieve the condition of this country. We have taken time; we have tried to unite all classes, even if I may speak, all parties. Those who have been in close communication with me know I have suffered, that I have waited for months to bring some of the people of the Saskatchewan to an understanding of certain important points in our petition to the Canadian government and I have done my duty ...

In these remarks Riel combines in his arguments logos (rational appeal), ethos (sympathy for the speaker), and pathos (an emotional appeal to decency and values). He describes his helplessness at birth and the protection he received from his mother. He says he is equally helpless before the court. He then extends the motherhood image, saying that the North-West is also his mother but that she is sick, a reference to the injustice inflicted on the Métis and others. This is what he wants to have talked about during the trial. His reference to people coming to help refers to the lawyers who have taken on his case. He describes the deplorable conditions that he found among the Indians and half-breeds when he returned to Canada in 1884. Those people and the whites, too, Riel says, were deprived of responsible government and this is his justification for the petitions and other actions that he led. This is the factual, logical explanation for his leading the resistance and is an articulate description of the issues. It was this argument on which he wanted to be tried by the court but one in which his lawyers largely refused to engage.

Finally, Riel argues that he is a person of good character who acted honourably. However, neither his appeal for sympathy nor his description of his own integrity can save him. There is only one sentence for the crime of high treason with which he has been charged, and that is death. The court has shown that it is not prepared to acknowledge the government's culpability in triggering the North-West resistance.

Were all of these arguments rolling naturally off of Riel's tongue? Or were they rhetorical devices that he had learned during his classical studies in Quebec and honed during campaigns on behalf of the Métis in Red River and Batoche? We do not know, but in making these arguments as cogently as he does, Riel undercuts the plea of insanity put forward by his lawyers. This is of great importance to him but it will also seal his fate if he convinces the jury that he is sane.

It has been said in this box that I have been egotistic. Perhaps I am egotistic. A man cannot be individuality without paying attention to himself. He cannot generalize himself, though he may be general. I have done all I could to make good petitions with others, and we sent them to the Canadian Government, and when the Canadian Government did answer, through the Under Secretary of State, to the secretary of the joint committee of the Saskatchewan, then I began to speak of myself, not before; so my particular interests passed after the public interests.

DENNIS GRUENDING

A good deal has been said about the settlement and division of lands; a good deal has been said about that. I do not think my dignity today here would allow me to mention the foreign policy, but if I was to explain to you or if I had been allowed to make the questions to witnesses, those questions would have appeared in an altogether different light before the court and jury. I do not say that my lawyers did not put the right questions. The observations I had the honour to make to the court the day before yesterday were good, they [the lawyers] *were absent of the situation, they did not know all the small circumstances as I did. I could mention a point, but that point was leading to so many that I could not have been all the time suggesting …*

Riel wanted to put the government on trial for its lack of attention to real grievances, but he ends up using much of his speech to defend his character from statements made by the Crown lawyers and their witnesses. He feels obligated to respond to trial testimony that he is a selfish egotist who could be bought off and that he was prepared to return to the United States if the government would settle his personal grievances. When General Wolseley marched upon Red River in 1870, Riel feared for his life. He accepted a deal proffered by Macdonald and brokered by Bishop Taché. Riel agreed to leave Canada for five years and he was provided with a modest amount of money with which to do it. He always believed, however, that additional money was owed to him for establishing and leading the provisional government in Manitoba. He also believed that the government owed him for land he had owned when he was forced to leave Manitoba. In his trial speech, Riel tacitly agrees that he had some of his own business to conduct, but says that he did so only after he had made petitions on behalf of the collective. The Crown lawyers, in attacking his integrity, attempt to show that he was calculating and self-serving and that those are not the actions of someone who is insane.

Riel clearly believes that his lawyers have not defended him as well as they might have. He was particularly upset when his Métis cousin Charles Nolin appeared for the prosecution and testified about what he saw as Riel's violent intentions. Riel attempted to intervene in the questioning but he was shut down. Now in his speech he says in frustration that he cannot follow the threads of all of the accusations made against him.

No one can say that the North-West was not suffering last year particularly the Saskatchewan, for the other parts of the North-West I cannot say so much; but what I have done, and risked, and to which I have exposed myself, rested certainly on the conviction, I had to do, was called upon to do something for my country.

It is true, gentlemen, I believed for years I had a mission, and when I speak of a mission you will understand me not as trying to play the role of insane before the grand jury so as to have a verdict of acquittal upon that ground. I believe that I have a mission, I believe I had a mission at this very time. What encourages me to speak to you with more confidence in all the imperfections of my English way of speaking, it is that I have yet and still that mission, and with the help of God, who is in this box with me, and He is on the side of my lawyers, even with the honourable court, the Crown and the jury, to help me, and to prove by the extraordinary help that there is a providence today in my trial, as there was a Providence in the battles of the Saskatchewan ...

Today when I saw the glorious General Middleton bearing testimony that he thought I was not insane, and when Captain Young proved that I am not insane, I felt that God was blessing me, and blotting away from my name the blot resting upon my reputation on account of having been in the lunatic asylum of my good friend Dr. Roy. I have been in an asylum, but I thank the lawyers for the Crown who destroyed the testimony of my good friend Dr. Roy, because I have always believed that I was put in the asylum without reason. Today my pretension is guaranteed, and that is a blessing too in that way. I have also been in the lunatic asylum at Longue Pointe, and I wonder that my friend Dr. Lachapelle, who took care of me charitably, and Dr. Howard are not here. I was there perhaps under my own name.

Even if I was going to be sentenced by you, gentlemen of the jury, I have this satisfaction if I die—that if I die I will not be reputed by all men as insane, as a lunatic ...

Riel returns to his preferred theme, the irresponsibility of the government and his honest attempt to do something for the people, but he soon veers off again. He believes he has been chosen by God for a divine mission to be a religious prophet in the North-West. This is so important to him that he returns to the point numerous times in his address. This obsession arose from a series of religious experiences—in contemporary parlance we might call them charismatic experiences—that occurred prior to and following his internment in asylums in Quebec in 1876. Thomas Flanagan, who has made something of a reputation as a Riel scholar and never a sympathetic one, says Riel's focusing on his prophetic mission shows that he was "trapped in a private world of imagined revelations."

Riel is aware it is dangerous for him to continue speaking of his self-assigned prophetic role. He is running the risk of convincing his Protestant jurors that he is not sane. He attempts to counteract that by using the trial testimony of General Middleton and of Captain Young, who had been his guard on the journey from Batoche to the prison in Regina. Not surprisingly, both Young and Middleton testified on behalf of the Crown that they believed Riel to be rational and sane. Riel uses an indirect approach to assert his sanity, quoting others regarding his state of mind, a device that rhetoricians call praeterito. Today's political parties and public relations firms call it third party validation.

Riel says that testimony about his soundness of mind is another blessing from God. It removes the blot on his reputation arising from being confined in an asylum. He says he believes he was placed there without reason, although it was his own uncle who had him committed following what can only be described as erratic behaviour. Conspicuously, he thanks the Crown lawyers who "destroyed the testimony" of Dr. Roy who had been his asylum keeper and who testified at the trial. This is a further and indirect rebuke by Riel to his lawyers who were pleading insanity on his behalf. He then speaks directly to members of the jury in one of the trial's most dramatic statements: "Even if I was going to be sentenced by you, gentlemen of the jury, I have this satisfaction if I die—that if I die I will not be reputed by all men as insane, as a lunatic … "

You have given me your attention, Your Honours; you have given me your attention, gentlemen of the jury, and this great audience. I see that if I go any further on that point I will lose the favor you have granted me up to this time, and as I am aiming all the time at practical results, I will stop here, master of myself, through the help of God. I have only a few more words to say, Your Honours, Gentlemen of the jury, my reputation, my liberty, my life, are at your discretion. So confident am I, that I have not the slightest anxiety, not even the slightest doubt, as to your verdict. The calmness of my mind concerning the favorable decision which I expect, does not come from any unjustifiable presumption upon my part. I simply trust, that through God's help, you will balance everything in a conscientious manner, and that, having heard what I had to say, that you will acquit me. I do respect you, although you are only half a jury, but your number of six does not prevent you from being just and conscientious; your number of six does not prevent me giving you my confidence, which I would grant to another six men. Your Honour, because you appointed these men, do not believe that I disrespect you. It is not by your own choice, you were authorized by those above you, by the authorities in the North-West; you have acted according to your duty, and while it is, in our view, against the guarantees of liberty, I trust the Providence of God will bring out good of what you have done conscientiously.

Although this court has been in existence for the last fifteen years, I thought I had a right to be tried in another court. I do not disrespect this court. I do respect it, and what is called by my learned and good lawyers, the incompetency of the court must not be called in disrespect, because I have all respect.

The only things I would like to call your attention to before you retire to deliberate are: first, that the House of Commons, Senate, and ministers of the Dominion, and who make laws for this land and govern it, are no representation whatever of the people of the North-West.

Second, that the North-West Council generated by the federal government has the great defect of its parent.

Third, the number of members elected for the council by the people make it only a sham representative legislature and no representative government at all …

If you take the plea of the defence that I am not responsible for my acts, acquit me completely since I have been quarrelling with an insane and irresponsible government. If you pronounce in favor of the Crown, which contends that I am responsible, acquit me all the same. You are perfectly justified in declaring that having my reason and sound mind I have acted reasonably and in self-defence, while the government, my accuser, being irresponsible, and consequently insane, cannot but have acted wrong, and if high treason there is, it must be on its side and not on my part.

All good orators have an intuitive sense of their audience and despite his anxious intensity, Riel is aware that he has gone on for long enough in the crowded and stifling courtroom. He signals his intention to conclude his remarks, which is a common rhetorical device, and he asks for just a few more minutes of the court's time. He comments once again on the calmness of his demeanour, which would negate any claim that he is not sane. He expresses his confidence in the jury and, with God's help, the verdict they will render.

It is at this moment that his frustration provides him with exceptional clarity. He deals with some of the salient points that his lawyers had made, too meekly, at the beginning of the trial. The jury of six men is "only half a jury," Riel says, and Judge Richardson in appointing them was acting on the instructions of his political masters. Riel adds that he had a right to be tried in another court, which is a challenge to the validity of this one. It is common in political trials for the accused to defy the court in this way, whether it is nineteenth century Irish patriot Robert Emmett, or Fidel Castro speaking to the trial judge after his attack on Cuba's Moncada barracks had failed in 1953. Riel couches his negatives in a positive light, saying that despite the court's shortcomings, he believes that by the providence of God the judge and jury will do the right thing. He is using the rhetorical device of antithesis, placing opposing or contrasting ideas in close proximity: "I do respect you, although you are only half a jury."

Riel extends his criticism to describe the irresponsibility of both the federal government and the North-West Council, most of whose members were appointed by the government and have virtually no independent authority. The federal politicians do not represent the North-West; the appointed North-West Council is a sham. He then engages in an extended and somewhat cumbersome metaphor that plays off of the insanity plea put forward by his lawyers. He reverses the description by saying that it is the government that is insane. These are mostly cogent arguments and ones that Riel had hoped to use in a political trial, but his lawyers prevented him from doing so. Yet he commits an error when he spends more time defending his character and his religious mission than in challenging the legitimacy of the court and the lack of response by the government. Given the nature of the trial, however, it would likely have made little difference to the outcome.

HIS HONOUR: Are you done?

RIEL: Not yet, if you have the kindness to permit me your attention for a while.

HIS HONOUR: Well, proceed …

RIEL: For fifteen years I have been neglecting myself. Even one of the most hard witnesses on me said that with all my vanity, I never was particular to my clothing; yes, because I never had much to buy any clothing. The Rev. Father Andre has often had the kindness to feed my family with a sack of flour, and Father Fourmand. My wife and children are without means, while I am working more than any representative in the North-West. Although I am simply a guest of this country [—] a guest of the half-breeds of the Saskatchewan [—] although as a simple guest, I worked to better the condition of the people of the Saskatchewan at the risk of my life, to better the condition of the people of the North-West, I have never had any pay. It has always been my hope to have a fair living one day. It will be for you to pronounce if you say I was right, you can conscientiously acquit me, as I hope through the help of God you will. You will console those who have been fifteen years around me only partaking in my sufferings. What you will do in justice to me, in justice to my family, in justice to my friends, in justice to the North-West, will be rendered a hundred times to you in this world, and to use a sacred expression, life everlasting in the other.

I thank Your Honour for the favor you have granted me in speaking; I thank you for the attention you have given me, gentlemen of the jury, and I thank those who have had the kindness to encourage my imperfect way of speaking the English language by your good attention. I put my speech under the protection of my God, my Saviour, He is the only one who can make it effective. It is possible it should become effective, as it is proposed to good men, to good people, and to good ladies also.

The judge, clearly showing his impatience, interrupts Riel, asking if he is done. Riel has already had his peroration, the ringing crescendo of his address in which he described the government as irresponsible and his own case as just. After the judge's interruption, Riel turns briefly to pathos, describing his poverty and that of his family, which must rely on a priest to provide them with a sack of flour. He says he worked to better the condition of people of the Saskatchewan River and in the North-West. He asks the jury to acquit him and says it will win them everlasting life in eternity if they do. His harsh and direct rhetoric of a few moments earlier has been replaced by serenity and he ends graciously, thanking the judge and jury for their attention and even thanks the ladies in the audience who have been enjoying the trial as a spectacle. He offers a reminder that he has been defending himself in the English language, and finally he places his speech "under the protection of God my Saviour." Riel is placing his future in the hands of a deity who he believes has an authority beyond that of any temporal court.

THE IMPACT OF RIEL'S SPEECH

Riel's speech to the jury was both a success and a failure. The six men returned within about ninety minutes to announce that they had found him guilty as charged of high treason. Riel had failed to convince them that his actions were justified. Nor did he convince them that the Métis had acted in self-defence after the police fired the first shot leading to the uprising. His lawyers, though, did not seriously attempt to pursue a defence that would have justified his actions or highlighted the government's negligence. Riel's loss in court was profound; it would cost him his life. On the other hand, it is likely that nothing he said in his defence could have saved him.

Riel did succeed in convincing the jury that he was sane, which was even more important to him than saving his life. Significantly, the foreman of the jury told the judge that while they found Riel guilty of treason, they were recommending clemency. So it might be said that the jury responded positively to two of Riel's points: he had convinced them that he was sane and that he was worthy of mercy. There was no chance of clemency, of course, because the charge of high treason meant an automatic sentence of death. It was that sentence that Judge Richardson pronounced and which the government had intended all along in charging Riel as it did.

Riel's lawyers immediately appealed the sentence but ultimately all appeals were denied. While they were pending, the trial and its aftermath were playing out in the court of public opinion. The trial was widely covered by newspapers in both English and French Canada. Francophones, particularly those in Quebec, were convinced that the trial had been a travesty and that Riel was being executed because he was French and

Catholic. Their case was bolstered by the fact that Will Jackson, Riel's anglophone secretary during the resistance, was tried immediately after Riel and found to be insane. He was to be transferred to a lunatic asylum in Manitoba, but once in the province he escaped, or was perhaps allowed to escape, to the United States. There he became, among other things, a union organizer and the manager of an anarchist defence fund. He lived until 1951.

◆

The public debate surrounding Riel in 1885 was in many ways similar to that in 1870 when he led the provisional government in Manitoba. Again, there was agitation in Ontario to have him hanged while public opinion in Quebec demanded that he be spared. In 1885 the federal government received petitions from Manitoba, the United States, and even England and France requesting mercy. However, Prime Minister Macdonald, who wanted him dead, believed at first that this tempest would subside. Macdonald was quoted as saying of Riel, "He shall hang though every dog in Quebec bark in his favour."

When the furor continued, Macdonald responded by appointing two physicians, neither of whom were experts in mental illness, to interview Riel and to report on the state of his sanity. One said that he was sane. The second said that Riel was normally sensible but that when it came to discussing political or religious subjects he was not. Lieutenant-Governor Edgar Dewdney sent a summary of the doctors' findings to Macdonald. In it, he simply chose to ignore the final portion of the second doctor's conclusion. Dewdney's telegram to Macdonald indicated that the doctors, except for minor semantic differences, agreed that Riel could discern right from wrong. It was this information that was provided when Macdonald's cabinet met to take a decision. There was internal disagreement, with Quebec ministers making dire predictions about the political consequences of hanging Riel. Sixteen of Macdonald's seventeen Quebec MPs also sent him a telegram pleading with him not to carry out the sentence, but to no avail. Riel was hanged in Regina on November 15, 1885.

A few days after the execution, a massive forty-thousand-person rally occurred in Montreal. One of the speakers was provincial politician Honoré Mercier. He used the execution to create the Parti National in Quebec, which swept to power in the election of 1886. Although that government fell after one term, Riel's execution remained part of a bitter narrative in the province. Wilfrid Laurier, the de facto leader of the federal Liberals in Quebec, also spoke to the Montreal rally. He departed from his usual cool reserve to say, "If I had been on the banks of the Saskatchewan, I, too, would have shouldered my musket." Laurier, though, soon became alarmed at what he considered Mercier's excesses in using Riel's execution to create a French-based nationalist party. He soon retreated to a more pragmatic stance.

There was a good deal of political calculation in everyone's position. Macdonald wanted to be rid of Riel and was determined that he should hang. He was able to convince his cabinet ministers from Quebec not to criticize him about it publicly. In Ontario the population, incited by newspapers, was calling loudly for an execution. Laurier, despite being a Quebec politician, also kept an eye out for reaction in Ontario and the rest of Canada. He and Liberal leader Edward Blake attacked Macdonald for ignoring the petitions of the Métis and causing them to revolt. But Laurier also said that he believed Riel was an egotistical madman. There was rife hypocrisy involved in Blake's criticism that Macdonald ignored the Métis petitions. It was Blake who, as the Liberal leader in Ontario, had personally offered a reward of $5,000 for the capture of Riel after the events in Red River.

The Catholic hierarchy was also in a delicate position. They had denounced Riel for his perceived religious heresies and for challenging their hegemony in the North-West. But they were now confronted by the popular uproar in Quebec. They were alarmed by the fervour of the nationalist movement being led by Mercier following the execution. They feared its liberal and potentially revolutionary zeal. So the hierarchy chose to support the Conservatives as they had in the past. They continued in their hostility toward Laurier and the Liberals, albeit less overtly than in earlier years. Macdonald and the Conservatives won the 1887 and 1891 federal elections with only somewhat reduced support in Quebec. But the Liberals were to supplant the Conservatives after 1896. One cannot say without reservation that the execution of Riel was the only factor in the rise of the Liberals, but it was certainly one of the important factors.

◆

Riel remained a galvanizing figure in Canadian history and popular culture for many years, and he remains a prism through which much of the nation sees itself. There are still those historians who believe that he was a sick man consumed by delusions of grandeur or at the least a hopelessly ineffective leader. They concede, though, that they have lost the battle of mythologies. Riel is now accepted as a Canadian hero, a father of Confederation in Manitoba, a Western populist, and a symbol of Indigenous resistance to European colonialism, not to mention a victim of its grasping and voracious ways.

Riel's characterization has changed with time. In the nineteenth century most French Canadians considered him to be a martyr and victim, while in English Canada he was demonized as a traitor in novels, plays, and poems. Then he mostly disappeared from view to be resuscitated in the years following the Second World War as a much more sympathetic, even heroic figure. It is that positive image of Riel that reigns among most artists, writers, academics, and even the political class today. There are books and plays written about him, schools and streets named after him, and even a major highway in Saskatchewan called the Louis Riel Trail.

There are ironies in all of this. Riel is popular among English Canadian writers and myth makers but less so in Quebec. There his devout Catholicism and mysticism have made him an unlikely hero for Quebec nationalists. There are also those, of both European and Indigenous extraction, who believe that the Métis warrior chief Gabriel Dumont is a more fitting icon than Riel for the aspirations of the Métis. Yet it is Riel's words, both in his plentiful written works and his oratory at the trial, that ensure his enduring legacy in our culture and our consciousness.

NELLIE MCCLUNG ON WOMEN AND THE VOTE

JANUARY 28, 1914

"Man was made for something higher
and holier than voting."

Nellie McClung was a ball of fire. She grew up in rural Manitoba, became a small town teacher, and later a successful writer, speaker, and unremitting activist for women's rights. In January 1914, Manitoba Premier Rodmond Roblin met in Winnipeg with McClung and a delegation of several hundred from the Political Equality League, which was seeking the vote for women. Roblin treated them condescendingly and flatly refused. The following evening McClung and others turned the encounter with the premier into a piece of burlesque theatre. McClung played the part of Roblin and made a mock speech to a fictitious group of men appearing before women legislators to request the right to vote.

◆

Nellie Mooney was born in 1873 on a farm in Grey County near Owen Sound, Ontario. She was the youngest of six children. Her father, John Mooney, had emigrated from Ireland in 1830 and eventually settled on a free, but rock-strewn fifty-acre farm. Nellie's mother was Letitia McCurdy, Scottish-born and twenty years younger than her husband. Eventually the family was in despair over trying to grow crops amid the rocks. In 1880 they moved west to settle on a homestead southeast of Brandon, Manitoba.

Most of what is known of the Mooney family life, or of McClung's personal life for that matter, is of her own description in the sixteen books she was to write: two volumes of autobiography, as well as novels, essays, and reminiscences. She describes her parents as solid, hard-working, and devoutly Christian; her mother was loving but strict, her father also devout but witty and light-hearted.

In Manitoba, the Mooneys took advantage of the government's homestead land grant and improved upon their farm through determination and hard work. McClung records in her autobiography that the family lived for a time at Red River and considered settling there, but her mother feared that eventually her children might intermarry with the Métis. She did not want that. Nellie quotes her as saying: "There are too many jet black eyes and high cheekbones here. I like them well enough in my neighbours' children but I would not like them in my grandchildren." McClung also records the strong sentiments in her homestead community near Brandon against Riel, the Métis, and First Nations people during and after the resistance at Batoche in 1885. According to her telling, she took Riel's side in these arguments, repeating the sympathetic comments that she had heard from a teacher in her one-room school. Her mother was not pleased. McClung was later in life to remain sympathetic toward Indigenous peoples but their cause was never to become an object of her activism.

There was no school to attend in her remote rural area until she was ten but once enrolled she loved it and soon learned to read. She described herself as a willful although not rebellious child who was marked by her parents' values, their fervent religious faith, and their disapproval of alcohol. She did chafe at the often bleak lives of farm women and escaped that fate by following her older sister in 1889 to study at Normal School in Winnipeg. She received her second class teaching certificate in 1890. She read voraciously while at school and was particularly smitten by the writing of Charles Dickens. She decided that she would become a writer and a tribune for the oppressed.

In August 1890 she began to teach in a small rural school south of Portage la Prairie and while there she met Annie McClung, the wife of the Methodist minister in nearby Manitou. She was a member of the Woman's

DENNIS GRUENDING

Christian Temperance Union (WCTU) and an advocate for women's issues. Nellie was later to write: "She had all the sweetness, charm, and beauty of the old-fashioned woman, and in addition to this had a fearless, and even radical, mind." This description was also one that defined Nellie. She was a reformer but her values were in many ways old fashioned; she was always conscious of decorum and loved to dress well. Photos of her, usually taken at a writing desk, invariably show her in well-tailored dresses. She also had a penchant for stylish, even rakish hats. Those same photos portray a woman with abundant curly hair, a wide forehead, and a strong chin. Her eyes are dark and her gaze direct.

In 1892 Nellie became a teacher in Manitou and lived with the McClung family. Their son Wesley was to become her husband in 1896. He was a pharmacist and they lived above the store. She found him to be compatible and supportive of her egalitarian ideas and emerging activism. Her teaching career ended, by convention, after their marriage, and while he tended the pharmacy, she threw herself into both motherhood and community activity. She joined the WCTU and became involved in its projects, which included advocating for women's right to vote and their property rights, as well as opposing the use of alcohol. The WCTU believed that liquor was a major cause of hardships faced by many women and children. McClung was devoutly Methodist throughout her life and in her mind feminism, activism, and social gospel Christianity co-existed seamlessly. When the United Church came into being in 1925 through an amalgamation of several Protestant churches, McClung remained involved in its many projects, including a struggle for women's ordination, which came about in 1936.

It was in Manitou where McClung became a professional writer. In 1902 her mother-in-law encouraged her to enter a short-story contest for *Collier's*, a prominent American magazine. McClung did not win but did later transform her story into the initial chapter of a novel called *Sowing Seeds in Danny*, published in 1908. The book eventually sold one hundred thousand copies and was the first in a trilogy built around a character named Pearl Watson, whose persona and experiences closely paralleled those of McClung. All of her writing, including her fiction, was unashamedly didactic, dealing primarily with the issues facing rural women and their families and advocating social and political remedies.

It was in Manitou, as well, that McClung was launched as a public speaker. The event was a WCTU convention for seventy-five delegates from throughout the province. McClung provided a welcoming address on behalf of the local chapter. "I remember the effect it had on me," she was to write in her memoirs. "I saw what could be done with words, for I had the vision of a new world as I talked." Her growing popularity as a writer combined with her zeal as an articulate reformer made her a speaker in demand not only in Manitoba but throughout Canada and even in the United States. She made two American tours to speak about female suffrage and prohibition. The first one lasted for two months and she spoke almost every day.

◆

In 1911 Wesley McClung was offered a position with an insurance company in Winnipeg and the family moved into the city. Nellie McClung already knew many of the reform-minded women and was welcomed into their midst. She writes fondly of weekly gatherings at the Canadian Women's Press Club and says they were about more than eating chicken sandwiches and olives. In 1911 the group hosted Emmeline Pankhurst, the British feminist and suffragette, an event that reinforced its determination to win the vote for women in Manitoba. Pankhurst led an all-women suffrage advocacy group that was met with hostility by the political establishment. Eventually she and others engaged in militant tactics, smashing windows, assaulting police officers, blowing up mailboxes, and even committing arson. Some of the women were put in prison where they engaged in hunger strikes and were force fed. McClung was determined but more pacific in her activism. In 1912 she and about a dozen other women in Winnipeg organized the Political Equality League (PEL), which became their preferred vehicle for advocating the vote. McClung also belonged to the Local Council of Women. She and a female friend convinced Premier Rodmond Roblin to accompany them on a visit to several of Winnipeg's sweatshop factories. Their deplorable conditions surprised the premier but did not move him to act.

McClung's concern for the working conditions of factory women did not, however, extend to sympathy for labour unions that would bargain collectively to improve those conditions. In her novel *Painted Fires,* McClung created the character of Anna Milander, a fictional Finnish immigrant waitress in Winnipeg. McClung used her character to paint an unflattering picture of organized labour. Milander has joined a union and McClung has her mouthing anti-capitalist slogans. She wrote, "Anna dreamed pleasantly of a golden age of which the street corner leaders told when there would be leisure and luxuries for the workers and confusion for the capitalists …" McClung had been somewhat involved with the local mission work of J. S. Woodsworth, but she was aghast at the 1919 Winnipeg General Strike in which he participated and was arrested. McClung did not appear to distinguish between revolutionary and democratic socialism of the kind advocated by Woodsworth and others.

She was socially well connected and recalls in her autobiography how one day she called "on impulse" and asked for a meeting with Premier Roblin. Remarkably, within a short time she was seated in his plush office, and she described to him the work being done by the PEL. She advised him that women in Manitoba were going to be granted the vote either by him or another premier. She suggested that he should do it and take the credit. According to her account, he was astonished by her impertinence and opposed to her proposal. But he did tell her to come back another time if she wished. She informed him that he had just missed his chance and that he would be hearing more from her. He asked if that was a threat. She replied that it was a prophecy.

McClung and members of the PEL received a warmer reception from the opposition leader T. C. Norris, who invited them to attend the provincial Liberal Party convention and to make their case for women's suffrage. The Liberals incorporated that demand and another for the prohibition of alcohol into their party platform for the next provincial election, which occurred in 1914. Roblin suspected, and was correct, that McClung and members of the PEL were supporting the Liberals.

According to descriptions in McClung's books, Roblin was a pompous dinosaur, but he was, in fact, a more complex and even impressive figure. He was born in Ontario twenty years prior to McClung and moved to Manitoba in 1877 at age twenty-four. He was involved in business and built a fortune in the grain trade. He became premier in 1890, a position he was to occupy for almost fifteen years, winning four elections. He was a strong provincial rights advocate and received a knighthood after successfully negotiating an extension of Manitoba's eastern border with Ontario in 1912. It was under Roblin's leadership that the province bought out the Bell Telephone Company and created a successful government telephone system. He tried and failed to create a publicly owned system of grain elevators, in response to farmers' demands.

The late Manitoba historian W. L. Morton described Roblin as an accomplished leader and a "pillar of strength." Morton added that Roblin was at the same time, "pompous in speech and manner" and possessed of a self-confidence that verged on arrogance. Those traits became more established as his tenure lengthened. Roblin was also a fierce partisan who fought the Manitoba Liberals and the Laurier government with equal vigour and by any means available. There were three notorious by-elections in 1912 to 1913 in which the Liberals and Conservatives accused each other of dirty tricks, including having dead men vote and offering bribes to the living. Roblin was the unchallenged leader of the Conservatives and set the tone for a political machine that was prepared to wrestle in the mud.

Roblin was opposed to women having the vote and equally unimpressed by the growing demand for prohibition. Those policies were embraced by a reform movement that included the PEL and the WCTU, as well as the leadership of the province's labour and farm movements. Early in 1914 the PEL devised a strategy that would at once embarrass the premier and give added life to their campaign. They would secure an audience with Roblin and members of the legislature, asking them to support a bill granting voting rights to women in Manitoba. McClung and the others presumed that their demands would be rejected. Roblin had already said publicly that the idea was one supported by "short-haired women and long-haired men." The delegation's visit and Roblin's response to it would be used as the plot for a mock parliament, a theatrical satire that would parody and lampoon the premier. In the play, a group of legislators, all of them women, would receive a delegation of men petitioning for the vote and other reforms. McClung, playing a thinly veiled fictitious premier, would respond with grandiose condescension.

◆

On January 27, 1914, the real life delegation met in the legislative chamber with all MLAs sitting as a committee of the whole. The group assembled went well beyond the PEL to include speakers from the Manitoba Grain Growers Association, the WCTU, the Winnipeg Trades and Labour Council, and the Icelandic Women's Suffrage Association. There is no official record of the meeting because the legislature did not have a Hansard service at the time. However, the event was covered by several newspapers, including the *Winnipeg Telegram*, a paper that supported the Conservatives, and the *Free Press*, which was Liberal in its sympathies. *The Telegram* reported that the delegation "numbered several hundred men and women ..." The rival *Free Press* reported that the legislature was packed for the event and that "standing room on the floor of the House and in the galleries was at a premium."

Five presenters sat at a table in the middle of the room and each one prior to speaking rose and bowed to the chairperson and to the members on both sides of the House. McClung spoke about the long struggle for women to get the vote and said that it was the next logical step to be taken. It was, she said, a question of the rights of women and of justice. She rejected the "stock argument" that a woman's place was in the home. The *Free Press* quoted her as saying: "Woman's place was in the home or out of it, wherever she was called as a mother or a sister to guard those she loved and to improve conditions for them." She ended with a plain-talking metaphor addressed to the premier. "This is the day of your opportunity. We are standing on the last ditch; you have the power to pull us over. Now it is your move."

The premier's remarks were reported on in detail. Here is the lead sentence from the story in the *Winnipeg Free Press*: "Straight from the shoulder, Premier Sir Rodmond Roblin yesterday told a delegation of women that he is absolutely opposed to woman suffrage." Roblin was at first complimentary to the delegation and specifically to McClung, but the session became tense and he did not have an easy time of it. "Some of the premier's remarks," the *Free Press* said, "elicited emphatic signs or dissent from the audience that crowded the floor and galleries of the council chamber. When he said, for instance, that the prevalence of divorce in the United States was due largely to the effect of the suffrage agitation, he called forth a storm of denial." That outburst by the crowd prompted Roblin to respond: "I did not dispute you when you were speaking. You will be good enough to listen to my reply." At another point he said, "Your 'Noes' do not have any effect upon me."

According to the *Free Press*, the crowd exhibited "decisive signs of incredulity" when Roblin said that during his many years in Manitoba politics he had "never unearthed the slightest trace of corruption." He responded testily: "When you say that things are corrupt, it is only the imaginations of a wicked and vile mind." The newspaper also reported that as the delegation was leaving, McClung took a parting shot at Roblin, telling him: "We'll get you yet." The first payback occurred on stage at the Walker Theatre on the following evening.

Winnipeg's most elegant theatre had been booked in advance. The props had been created and the actors chosen. McClung says in her autobiography that she had been away from Winnipeg on a speaking tour and found out only upon her return that her friends had cast her in the leading role. A member of the PEL had learned of a mock parliament being staged in Vancouver and the Winnipeg group decided to borrow the idea. Reform-minded women had staged several such events in various Canadian cities dating back to 1880. They were feminist theatrical parodies, collectively inspired and created, in which the roles of men and women were reversed. The mock parliament would be humorous and entertaining but had as its object the serious political objective of winning the vote for women.

McClung writes with relish in her autobiography about how during the PEL delegation's appearance at the legislature she had listened closely to

Roblin's remarks, observing both his diction and studying his mannerisms. She says, for example, that he placed his thumbs in the armholes of his coat, twittering his little finger and teetering on his heels when he was portraying a jocular mood. When rendering cold reason, he held his elbows close to his body with palms outspread. He was ingratiatingly friendly when he welcomed the delegation but later switched to the authoritative tone of a leader who would brook no opposition. When McClung returned home from the event, she wrote a speech that would mimic Roblin's, and she rehearsed it before her husband and her oldest son. The draft remains in her papers at the Provincial Archives of British Columbia.

MCCLUNG'S SPEECH

Gentlemen of the delegation, it gives me great pleasure to welcome you here today. We like delegations, and although this is the first time you have asked us for the vote, we hope it will not be the last. Come any time and ask for anything you like. We wish to congratulate you, too, on the quiet and ladylike way in which you have come into our presence; and we assure you that if the working men in England had fought for their franchise in such a pleasing and dignified way, the results would have been entirely different. If they had used these peaceful means and no other, they might still be enjoying the distinction and privilege of waiting on members of Parliament.

This is theatre. McClung is an accomplished public speaker and loves the podium. In her stage role she mimics pomposity. Just as Roblin had done, McClung welcomes the delegation expansively and congratulates them on their quiet ways, contrasting that to the way in which men have pursued the vote in England. Roblin, in his remarks to the PEL delegation on the previous day, referred on several occasions to suffragettes' disruptive tactics in that country. Thousands of British suffragettes sought the vote for women but Prime Minister Herbert Asquith responded with indifference, as did Premier Roblin in Manitoba. McClung's reference to "come any time and ask for anything you like" likely refers to Roblin's remarks to her when she had gone previously, on short notice, to talk to him one-on-one about women and the vote.

In her stage role, McClung uses satire and humour to parody the premier and the political status quo. She mimics Roblin in a theatrical setting that faithfully reproduces the previous day's legislative setting. This is a case of art consciously imitating real events and rhetoricians even have a name for the device, which is mimesis. The entire speech is built on an inverted irony, where there is a huge gap between what is said and what is actually meant.

But I cannot do what you ask me to do, for the facts are all against you. Manhood suffrage has not been a success in the unhappy countries where it has been tried. They either do not vote at all, or else they vote too much, and the best men shrink away from the polls as from a pestilence. So obnoxious has the very name of polls become, that when one man wishes to call another a particularly obnoxious epithet he calls him a "poll-cat." Now sire do you wish our beloved husbands, fathers, and brothers to be subjected to such insult as this? Good men would not use the ballot, and when a ballot is not used it spoils, and that leads to political corruption—I have never seen it but I have heard of it!

Manhood suffrage would plunge our fair province into a perfect debauchery of extravagance, a perfect nightmare of expense. Think of the increased size of the Voter's List—we have trouble enough with it now. Of course with the customary hot-headedness of reformers you never thought of that—oh no, just like a man you never thought of the expense ... Yet though I love them, I know their frailties. If once they are [left to] vote, they become addicted to it, and even if the polls are only open once every four years, I tell you, I know men, they are creatures of habit, and they'll hang around the polls all the rest of the time ...

If all men were as intelligent as you and your worthy tho misguided followers, I might be justified in considering your case, but they are not: seven-eighths of the police court offenders are men, and only one third of the church membership. Hadn't you better reform your own sex before you come here asking us to do anything for you?

Despite her fondness for the men of the delegation, Premier McClung says she cannot grant them the vote because "the facts are all against you"—a direct quote from Roblin's earlier remarks to the PEL delegation. McClung's reference to having "men shrink away from the polls" is another lift from Roblin. He told the delegation that in Colorado, which had introduced women's suffrage, "they shrink away from the polls as from a pestilence"—but he cited no source for his information. *The Winnipeg Free Press* reported that those remarks by Roblin had drawn a hearty disagreement from people in the galleries at the legislature. McClung also takes the "shrinking" reference in the other direction, saying that in places where men can vote they do so either too little or too much. McClung is referring to common practice in Manitoba's elections, where political parties arranged for some men to vote multiple times. McClung goes on to describe such individuals as "poll-cats," a descriptive metaphor that compares someone who plays dirty politics to an animal such as a weasel or a skunk. McClung, in her inverted role as premier, imitates Roblin in saying that political corruption does not exist in Manitoba. His claim had been met with laughter when he made it in the legislature and was likely the cause of mirth in the theatre performance as well. When McClung accuses the men appearing before her of being hot-headed and misguided she is echoing Roblin, who had patronizingly said to the delegation: "In your enthusiasm and interest no doubt you believe you are right."

Oh no, no, man was made for something higher and holier than voting. Men were made to support families and homes which are the bulwark of the nation. What is home without a father? What is home without a bank account? The man who pays the grocer rules the world. In this agricultural province, man's place is the farm. Shall I call men away from the useful plough and the necessary harrow to talk loud on street corners about things which do not concern them? Shall I cheat the farm by turning honest ploughmen into dishonest and scheming politicians? I tell you no, for I was born on the farm and I am not ashamed to say so—the farm, the farm, the dear, old farm—we'll never mortgage the farm.

In the United States of America, when men vote, there is one divorce for every marriage, for politics unsettle men, and that leads to unsettled bills, and broken furniture, and broken vows. When you ask me for the vote, you are asking me to break up peaceful and happy homes and wreck innocent lives, and I tell you again, frankly, I will not do it. I am an old-fashioned woman; I believe in the sanctity of marriage. Politics unsettles men, and enters every department of life, with its blighting influence. It even confuses our vital statistics. They tell me that where men vote, when the election is very close, men have been known to come back and vote years after they were dead. Now, do you think I am going to let the hallowed calm of our cemeteries be invaded by the raucous voice of politics?

Roblin's most determined argument against women's suffrage was that politics would distract them and so ruin the home. He said as well that women were too good and precious to be sullied by politics. McClung faithfully reproduces those arguments and again she inverts them in an ironical way: "Man was made for something higher and holier than voting." She adds, mischievously: "The man who pays the grocer rules the world." This is a reference to Roblin's telling the delegation that a woman has more influence around her dinner table than she would have in the marketplace. McClung repeats another of Roblin's arguments but with a gender twist—in the United States when men vote there is a divorce for every marriage. Roblin had made that claim to the PEL delegation, again without referring to a source for his information. When that created a negative reaction among his audience, he responded sharply: "I say so … You will be good enough to listen to my reply."

McClung echoes the premier further in an inverted way by saying that politics unsettles men and has a "blighting influence" upon them. She adds another jibe about dead men voting, something that she says invades the calm of cemeteries. She is referring to the practice, well known in Manitoba, of having living impersonators vote in the place of men who had died.

Men in politics have given us many unhappy examples—Nero, Herod, King John are not worthy heroes, and yet you want me to hold up these men before our young people; I wonder any man ever dare ask for the vote in the light of such examples as these.

There is one part of your address to me, which it would have been better for your cause, if you had left it unsaid. It certainly will not get you anything. You basely, falsely, impertinently accuse us of extravagance. With your little brain you cannot grasp what it means to run a government such as this. Brains like yours come only in boys' sizes. But you think you can dictate to me, a woman who was busy running government when you were sitting in your high chair, drumming on a tin plate with a spoon. You would set

DENNIS GRUENDING

your little judgement against me—you only succeed in making yourself ridiculous. This is a place where most women would lose their tempers, but I never do. A woman in my position cannot afford it, and I never do, never, except when I feel like it, and am pretty sure I can get away with it.

You, very indelicately, have alluded to the amount of money it took to elect one of our women in a constituency north of here. I admit that we did spend money freely on that election, but we had to, there were peculiar local conditions which had to be overcome. We are not wizards, we must take things as we find them, and in this constituency the roads were very wet and the people were very dry.

We have not been extravagant. Every dollar of public money, which we spend on the public good is first examined carefully on all sides by all of us, to see if we couldn't make better use of it ourselves. And we practice very practical political economy in every election. We always get the greatest number of votes for the least possible amount of money.

McClung's reference to Nero, Herod, King John being "unhappy examples" of men in politics goes beyond anything Roblin had said. Similarly, her description of the delegation before her as people with a "little brain" exceeds Roblin's comments. She exaggerates for effect. She is pointing a verbal dagger at the premier for political corruption and for his reputation as an egotist who exercised a tight control over his MLAs and the civil service. Her reference to the amount of money it took to elect someone likely refers to the provincial by-elections, which had become notorious for their corrupt nature. McClung's remark about "[getting] the greatest number of votes for the least possible amount of money" would have resonated with her audience. In reporting the event, the usually hostile *Winnipeg Telegram* described it as "the choicest of sarcasm."

I have built for this province magnificent public buildings, scrimping and saving every cent of the money and of the meagre salary I pay myself. Did I get gratitude for it? Ah no—but then I did not do it for gratitude, I did it for something quite different ...

You have seen fit, in your puerile wisdom, to criticize our platform—you have hinted that we are not progressive. I resent that very deeply. Our platform is better than progressive, it is elastic. Any plank can be added at any time. We will let no party outdo us in planks. The Rainy River Lumber Co have nothing on us when it comes to planks.

We are particularly proud of our temperance plank, which helped to float us to victory on that bright and suspicious day when we came into our own in this province. We had such respect for that plank that we immediately put it away carefully wrapped in cotton batting and preserved it in alcohol. We still have it and will use it again; it is in excellent condition, not a scratch on it. Some immature politicians do not know how to use a good platform—they think it is something to work on. That is all wrong—a platform is something to get in on and then set carefully away. All this we have done ...

You flatter me, sir, when you tell me that I dominate this government. I am too mild a woman to dominate anything. I never insist on my own way. I never need to. My way naturally becomes their way.

The members of this government are all women of strong personal opinions and private principles. I allow them to have as many as they like, provided of course that they keep their opinions, merely personal, and their principles private. Of course their natural delicacy would forbid them intruding their personal opinions on me, and they soon see that principles are out of place here. One set is all that is needed, and I always carry a set of my own, a splendid set, too, elastic, adjustable and reversible, and everything but washable.

I have never spoken a harsh word to any of my members—a look is usually sufficient. I have rarely had to use the axe—I am proud and happy in their undivided admiration. I know they respect my long political experience, and my superior educational advantage. I taught school in a highly favoured country neighbourhood for years. I know I am a factor in the affairs of this province. If it were not for this fatal modesty which on more than one occasion has almost blighted my career, I would say that I know I have written my name large across the province, so large indeed we had to move the boundaries to get it all in, and my most earnest wish for this bright land of promise is that I may long be spared to guide its destiny among the nations of the earth. I know there is no one but me who can guide the ship of state. I actually tremble when I think what might happen to these leaderless lambs. But I must not dwell on such an overwhelming calamity, but go forward in the strong hope that I may long be spared to be the proud standard-bearer of the grand old flag of this grand old party, which has gone down many times to disgrace but, thank God, never defeat.

McClung's reference to "magnificent public buildings" is prescient irony. By 1915 Roblin would be driven from office over a scandal involving kickbacks from construction companies building the provincial legislative building. Perhaps McClung has some inside information. She also has some fun using an extended metaphor to describe the Conservative platform and its "planks," which are "elastic" and can be changed at will. One of those malleable planks was Roblin's promise, later broken, on prohibition, an issue close to McClung's heart. She never forgave him for what she saw as his lack of honesty on prohibition. She was one of those who convinced the opposition Liberals to put prohibition into their platform.

McClung ends with an allusion to Roblin's reputation for tightly controlling his MLAs. As the female premier she is "flattered" by the accusation but says she never insists on getting her own way. "I never need to. My way naturally becomes their way." She refers to the province having its boundaries extended. That occurred under Roblin and he was knighted for it. In McClung's telling, the province's boundaries had to be enlarged to contain the premier's ego. Finally she engages in a pompous and ironic peroration, a kind of grand finale with fireworks. She hopes that she may long be spared to guide the ship of state and to provide grand leadership. She hopes to lead a Conservative Party that may be disgraced but never defeated. Again, McClung is prescient. Roblin was to win the election in 1914 but it would be his last hurrah before being replaced by the Liberals. McClung was to be more than just a spectator in that campaign.

THE IMPACT OF MCCLUNG'S SPEECH

The mock parliament at the eighteen-hundred-seat Walker Theatre attracted full houses for two nights and it was later repeated in Brandon. In Winnipeg, it was reported that on the first evening, two Liberal MLAs had abandoned a civic dinner and "secreted" themselves among the theatre goers. The audiences would have been aware of the PEL's appearance before Premier Roblin and members of the legislature on January 27 because it had been thoroughly reported in the local newspapers. The Walker Theatre performance was covered as well and the Conservative-leaning *Telegram* reported that it was "packed to the roof." The newspaper said that McClung's "choice bit of sarcasm" was amusing but somewhat overdone. McClung was later to say that she did not indulge in sarcasm, which she described as an ugly word, but rather in burlesque. She wrote: "We had one desire: to make the attitude of the government ridiculous and set the whole province laughing … "

The crucial twist comes in what one critic has called the "rhetoric of reversal." McClung plays the part of a premier at a time when a woman cannot be the premier; women cannot even vote. It is only men who vote and who make the political and economic decisions in society. But in the mock parliament it is the men who are told they cannot possibly be involved in politics because they are too precious for that; it would destroy their marriages; and it would ruin society to have them so involved in politics that they neglect their farms. When the same arguments frequently used against women are reversed to apply to men, the audience is entertained by the absurdity. Members of the PEL hoped that the audience, having seen the play, would never look at the issue in the same way again. McClung believed that the plays were an important factor in moving public sentiment toward supporting the enfranchisement of women. The performances were so popular that they raised enough money to pay for the entire campaign mounted by the PEL.

Roblin stood firm in his opposition but he was to face the electorate several months later in July 1914. McClung campaigned vigourously against him, shadowing him and speaking in almost every location he visited. She reportedly addressed one hundred meetings on behalf of the Liberals and was so effective she was burned in effigy by the Conservatives. Roblin was re-elected but the results were closer than he or anyone had expected—the Conservatives won twenty-eight seats, against twenty for the Liberals and one Independent. Early in 1915, however, Roblin's government was forced to resign after a report commissioned by the lieutenant-governor found Roblin's administration guilty of corruption in the awarding of contracts for new legislative buildings. T. C. Norris and the Liberals were called upon to form a new government.

There was another election in August 1915 and this time the Liberals won in a landslide. By this time, though, McClung had bidden a tearful farewell to Manitoba and moved to Edmonton. Her husband's insurance company had transferred him in the autumn of 1914 and there appears to have been no doubt that she would accompany him. Nellie McClung had become a fixture in Winnipeg and Manitoba, widely respected or reviled depending upon one's gender politics. The move to Edmonton was a wrenching one for her.

When the election was called in 1915, she caught the train back to Winnipeg and once again she stumped the province on behalf of the Liberals. On election night she was to return to her old haunt at the Walker Theatre, where the Liberals held their victory celebration. At age forty-two, she received wild cheers on what was likely the pinnacle of her career. She had played an important role in the demise of the Conservatives and the subsequent implementation of a reform agenda. She wrote in her autobiography that if she had continued to live in Manitoba she could have sought office for the Liberals with a good chance of winning election. In that event, she believed that she would have been in the cabinet, perhaps as minister of education.

The Norris government enacted legislation in 1916 providing the vote to women. Saskatchewan and Alberta enacted women's suffrage later the same year; British Columbia, Ontario, and the federal government did so in 1918. Several other provinces made their move in the 1920s. In Quebec, where the powerful Catholic hierarchy was opposed, women did not receive the vote until 1940.

◆

McClung did win election as a Liberal in 1921 but it was to the Alberta legislature. She found the discipline imposed by party politics constraining. Her husband was transferred to Calgary in 1923 so she commuted between the two cities for much of her term. She ran in Calgary in the 1926 election and was defeated. In 1927 she was among a group of five prominent Alberta women who petitioned the federal government to ask the Supreme Court of Canada if women were eligible to be appointed to the Senate. For years prime ministers had claimed that the British North America Act did not allow for that. The all-male Supreme Court subsequently ruled in

1928 that women were not "qualified persons" according to the definition of the BNA Act and thus could not sit in the Senate. The case then went to the Imperial Privy Council in Britain, which was the High Court of Appeal for the entire British empire. There in 1929 the council's Judicial Committee overturned the Canadian court's ruling. It took years, but in 1979, a governor general's award was created in honour of the "Famous Five." A statue of them was unveiled in Calgary in 1999 and a replica was placed on Parliament Hill in 2000. In 2009 the Senate voted to name the five posthumously as Canada's first "honorary senators."

After her political defeat in 1926, McClung resumed her career as a writer. She and her husband moved to Victoria in 1932 and she published four books between 1935 and 1945, including two volumes of autobiography. Charlotte Gray, a recent McClung biographer, says that her fiction—sentimental and didactic—came to have a dated feel to it but that her journalism remained vigorous. McClung always remained unapologetic about her moralizing.

McClung's spirited campaign for women's right to vote in Manitoba was the finest hour in her varied and distinguished career. She did not achieve that victory single-handedly but she was its most prominent advocate. Her participation in the delegation to appear before Roblin in 1914 was important but even more so was her performance in the mock parliament. It portrayed dramatically that the premier was out of touch with his province and his times. When the previously unimpeachable Roblin became a laughingstock, his political end began to beckon. The vote for women became at first a possibility and then a fact.

ARTHUR MEIGHEN
ON CONSCRIPTION

JUNE 21, 1917

"A choice between fidelity and desertion"

Arthur Meighen is an historical footnote among prime ministers. He occupied the office briefly from 1920 to 1921 and again in 1926, but on both occasions he was defeated and replaced by his political foe and nemesis Mackenzie King. But in his years as a Conservative member of Parliament, Meighen had a well-deserved reputation as a fierce and consummate debater. He used those skills in 1917 to introduce and speak to the contentious Military Service Act, which introduced conscription to Canada. Meighen's prominent and uncompromising role in that debate made him a polarizing public figure. He was someone who could both defend himself in debate and go relentlessly onto the attack.

◆

Arthur Meighen was born in 1874 near the hamlet of St. Mary's, near Stratford in southwestern Ontario. His paternal grandfather, Gordon Meighen, had emigrated from Londonderry in Northern Ireland in 1839 to settle on land in Upper Canada. When Gordon died, his son Joseph left school to run the farm. Arthur was the second of six children in the family of Joseph and mother Mary Jane and he showed more interest in books than in chores. His parents moved from their farm to the outskirts of town so that Arthur could more easily attend school, at which he excelled. His formation in a Presbyterian family placed a firm priority, as he said often later in life, upon industry and thrift.

He enrolled at the University of Toronto in 1892, a campus that he shared with his contemporary Mackenzie King. Meighen was no socialite but rather someone who focused on studies, read voraciously, and participated in the university's mock parliament. He graduated in 1896 and the following year earned his teaching qualifications at the Ontario Normal College. He was hired by a high school near Brantford in 1897, but within the year he had a dispute with the board chair and his career there was a brief one. In 1898 he moved to Manitoba. After teaching briefly in Winnipeg, he began to article at a law firm and in 1902 he relocated to Portage la Prairie, ninety kilometres to the west. There he met Isabelle Cox, a teacher in a nearby town, and they were married in 1904.

Meighen joined the Young Men's Conservative Club in 1904 and worked in the federal election held in that year. By 1908 he was the Conservative candidate in the Portage riding and, improbably, he wrestled the seat away from the Liberal incumbent. The Liberals under Wilfrid Laurier won the election so Meighen sat on the back benches of a Conservative opposition led by Robert Borden. The Laurier government was growing stale but found a new issue in 1911, campaigning for reciprocity with the United States. Borden and the Conservatives preferred to maintain tariffs and the National Policy first enunciated by Sir John A. Macdonald, albeit with some tweaks. They defeated Laurier in 1911 but Meighen did not at first go into the cabinet. He did impress Borden by manipulating the rules of the House of Commons in a way that allowed the Conservatives to shut down a debate in April 1913, ending a Liberal filibuster that was delaying passage of a Naval Aid Bill. Borden responded in the same year by appointing Meighen as solicitor general, a post which at that time was not a cabinet position.

Borden came to depend heavily upon Meighen, who became what biographer Roger Graham describes as "a versatile extra minister of everything that mattered much." In 1914 Meighen was given the sensitive task of dealing with a crisis created by the insolvency of the Canadian Northern Railway. Although he was a committed free enterpriser, Meighen arranged pragmatically for the government to guarantee the company's bonds in return for Ottawa's assuming a share of the common stock. Officers and shareholders of the rival Canadian Pacific Railway were offended and angry. Meighen also shepherded the ensuing bill through Parliament. In October 1915 Borden elevated him to become secretary of state.

By then Canada was at war and all had changed. The First World War, which began in August 1914, was prompted by a chain of events that began when a Serbian nationalist assassinated Austrian Archduke Franz Ferdinand and his wife, Sophie, in Sarajevo on June 28. Austria-Hungary invaded Serbia and soon alliances among Europe's major powers came into play with Serbia being supported by Great Britain, France, and Russia against Austria-Hungary and its German ally. It was a war among great powers, precipitated in large measure by Britain's competition in a budding arms race with Germany. As a British colony, Canada was automatically at war, as Borden announced in a sombre speech to the House of Commons on August 14, 1914.

Most Canadians believed the war in Europe would be a brief one and initially there was a rush of eager volunteers. The conflict, however, dragged on in trench warfare and sporadic large battles that claimed tens of thousands of lives. The Canadian government promised fifty thousand troops but that pledged number was added to several times. By January 1916 Borden was promising to send five hundred thousand men to fight in Europe. Initially he was confident that Canada could provide them through voluntary enlistment. Indeed, there was social pressure placed upon young men to "knit or fight." As late as December 1916, when Borden made a speaking tour to promote voluntary enlistment, he was saying publicly that conscription would not be necessary; but Canadians were not enlisting in large enough numbers to fulfill Borden's promise to Great Britain. At one point Meighen apparently wanted to enlist himself. Borden was opposed and told him that he was of more use in the government.

In February 1917 the prime minister attended meetings of the Imperial War Cabinet in England. While there he visited with Canadian troops, particularly those wounded and in hospital. He was shocked and moved and he returned to Canada in May committed to conscripting men for military service. He promptly convened his cabinet and told them of his plans. He introduced the bill on May 18 in the House of Commons, but most of the heavy lifting was left to Meighen who had by then been named to the powerful post of interior minister. It was he who drafted the conscription legislation and would steer it through the House. The government's plan to force military enlistment was only one part of a more comprehensive package.

Normally there would have been a federal election in Canada in 1915 but Borden sought and received Wilfrid Laurier's support to postpone it because of the war. At first the opposition Liberals offered their full support. With a debate on conscription looming, however, the Conservatives saw a way to split the Liberal opposition and to siphon support away from Laurier. Canadians of British extraction were generally in favour of sending young men off to fight. But that eagerness was not shared by many of Central European origin whose families had more recently immigrated to Canada. Nor was the enthusiasm shared in Quebec, where people had little allegiance to Britain. In any event, nationalist leader Henri Bourassa and others were already angry about the undermining of French language education throughout Canada. Liberal MPs were divided as were their constituents.

On May 25, a week after Borden announced his policy of conscription, he invited Laurier and the Liberals to enter into a coalition government, which would further delay a federal election. In making his offer, Borden insisted that any Liberals participating in a coalition would have to accept conscription as a fact of life. Laurier refused. He knew that Quebec would never agree and the province represented the bedrock of Liberal support. He was aware, though, that the Conservatives were approaching other members of his caucus in an attempt to splinter the Liberals. While Borden was contacting Liberal MPs and provincial Liberal leaders, it was Meighen who piloted the legislation that he had prepared through the House of Commons.

Various observers have described Meighen as one of the finest Canadian parliamentary orators ever. He was lucid, knowledgeable, and sharply analytical with a keen recall of facts. Usually he spoke without prepared texts and seldom used notes. Senator Grattan O'Leary once wrote that he had heard Franklin Delano Roosevelt, Winston Churchill, Arthur Balfour, and Lloyd George—and that Meighen was a better orator than any of them. In Canada, O'Leary said, only Laurier, D'Arcy McGee, and Joseph Howe dwelt on the same plain as Meighen. "In clearness, in logic, in cogent and relentless reasoning," O'Leary wrote, "he was without an equal. He could state his case, argue it, illustrate it and prove it with a persuasiveness that was irresistible."

Meighen's critics, though, claimed that he was too austere and lacking in both passion and humour to be a great orator. O'Leary denied that but it is interesting that he felt the need to mount the defence. Meighen was a plain speaker whose physical appearance exuded at once a combination of physical fragility and severity. As a young man he had a slim blade of a face with thin lips and clear, piercing eyes. He had a high forehead and receding hairline. Meighen was often caustic in debate and in his relentless partisanship he frequently conveyed contempt for his adversaries. He exuded a certain mean-spiritedness with an accompanying sense of cynicism. Those were attributes more suited to the cut and thrust of parliamentary debate than they were to wooing voters at large. He was, in the description of his biographer, "forensic" and dealt with his audiences much as he would a judge and jury. His speeches lacked the wit and vitality found in those of Nellie McClung, just as they lacked the elegant architecture of an address by Laurier, whose more decorative form of address was no longer in vogue by 1917.

Borden introduced the Military Service Act into the House of Commons on June 11. Laurier spoke at length on June 18. He said the Liberals had supported Canada's going to war and had for three years backed the government in its efforts. He reminded the Conservatives that Borden had promised not to introduce conscription but to recruit Canada's fighting force through voluntary enlistment. Borden, when he led off the debate, had argued that the new legislation did not change anything other than the administrative means to be employed in conscripting troops for deployment in Europe. He said that the existing Canadian Militia Act already provided for the government to raise troops for the defence of Canada. In contrast, Laurier argued that the Militia Act gave the government the authority to deploy troops within the country but not to send them to Europe. He also took issue with the prime minister's claim that the troops were needed for "the defence of Canada." They might be needed for the defence of Britain and France, Laurier said, but Canada was in no danger of being invaded by Germany.

Laurier acknowledged that Quebec had provided fewer volunteer soldiers than other provinces but said there were reasons for that. The French had been in Canada for a much longer time than many people who arrived from Britain and they had fewer ties to Europe; they had been disarmed after the conquest in 1659 and thus did not have an arms-bearing tradition. Laurier also criticized the federal government's recruiting efforts in Quebec, saying that they had chosen English-speakers to do the job. He warned that the conscription bill would cause a "deep cleavage," not so much among provinces as among classes of people. He pointed to opposition by many people in the "working classes" but did not mention in his speech the opposition of immigrants from Central Europe.

Finally, anticipating criticism of his refusal to lead the Liberals into a coalition government, Laurier pointed out that Borden had extended the invitation only after he had announced his plan to introduce conscription. The Liberal leader ended his speech by moving an amendment to the proposed Military Service Act. He called for the bill to be deferred until the question of conscription had been put to a national referendum. He would, he said, abide by the result once the people had spoken. Meighen, when he rose to speak in the debate on June 21, 1917, was at the height of his power and influence in the Borden government.

MEIGHEN'S SPEECH

No one could be present during this debate, or, if not present, could look out with intelligent mind on the manifestations of sentiment everywhere appearing, without being convinced that this discussion is of greater consequence than any that has ever before taken place in this Parliament. I say that not because the issue is in doubt. Substantial unanimity, though not entire unanimity, on this side of the House would perhaps carry the Bill. But the courage of certain hon. gentlemen on the other side of the Chamber—courage in an hour of trial—has placed the issue beyond all doubt at all. It is the enforcement of the Bill that we must keep in mind. It is not so much the enactment of law as obedience to law that counts. That is why this Bill should be thoroughly considered, and why the debate should be conducted in such a spirit, and with such a purpose, as will afford an example to the people of Canada. The right and honourable thing must be done. The right and honourable thing will be done. The right and honourable thing is embodied in this Bill. But the important duty of members of Parliament is to see that we make plain to every reasonable man to the four corners of this Dominion, that we pass this Bill, and enforce it, only because it is the right thing to do—that we do so, far from any spirit of vindictiveness, or for any unworthy or insufficient reason, but because, in this crisis of the nation, it is the only right thing to do.

Meighen is usually a plain talking and bare-knuckled debater but here he begins his speech using passive voice and he departs from the normal order of words for the sake of emphasis—"manifestations of sentiment everywhere appearing"—a rhetorical device known as anastrophe. He is assuming the role of statesman, signalling that the debate should be conducted on an elevated level. It should provide an example and an inspiration that will ensure public support. Despite talk of statesmanship, he does aim a stiletto at the heart of the Liberal caucus. He praises the courage of "certain honourable gentlemen" in the Opposition; those who had chosen to abandon Laurier and support the conscription bill. Meighen describes that as a courageous act that places the issue beyond all doubt. The Conservative strategy to divide the Liberals is working. Meighen uses repetition and parallelism, playing on the phrase "right and honourable thing" to describe the decision being made. Significantly, he appeals beyond the precinct of Parliament to "every reasonable man" in the Dominion. But he leaves out half of the population. Despite the best efforts of Nellie McClung and others, women in 1917 were not able to vote in federal elections. Meighen had never been a supporter of a universal franchise for women; nor, to be fair, was Wilfrid Laurier. Even as he spoke in the House, though, Meighen was quietly working on drafting legislation for the next election that would grant the vote to only a select group of women—those closely related to soldiers fighting in the war.

I regard the forwarding of troops to the front as a necessity, as an all-out essential, as something we cannot shirk. Does anybody dispute that? Whatever means are necessary to procure these men, they must be sent, and whatever action is necessary on our part to support our army at present in France, we must adopt. No one has seriously argued in this House—and I give every hon. Gentleman the credit of saying no one seriously believes—that we can dispatch 350,000 men overseas, commissioned by us to stand between our country and destruction, and leave them to be decimated and destroyed. The obligation of honour is upon us, it is the plainest obligation that was ever placed on a nation. The obligation of honour is fortified by the primary obligation of all people to protect the security of the state. There is no other way in which the honour or the security of the state can be preserved ...

Here Meighen shifts to the first person and becomes more direct and emphatic in his use of language. This is the major theme of his address: conscripting men and sending them to the front lines is "something we cannot shirk." It must be done and it will be done. Then he engages in a hypophora, a favourite technique of his, where he both poses a question and answers it. "Does anybody dispute that?" He amplifies the answer to his own question: "No one has seriously argued" and "no one seriously believes" that Canada can send men and then abandon them. He follows with a series of strong parallel constructions built around the phrase "obligation of honour" to assert the need for action to preserve the security of the state.

Who can contend, with justification, that the voluntary system has not been adequately tried in Canada, both as to vigour of effort and as to length of time? The member for St. John (Mr. Pugsley), if I understood correctly an interruption that he made yesterday, feels that the voluntary system is now doing enough. Well, for twelve months it has produced an average of 6,000 to 7,000 men a month, while the wastage in Canada and in England amounts to a very substantial portion of that figure. In the two months through which we have just passed, the voluntary system yielded us not one man for four of those who were casualties among our armies in France. Add casualties in France and wastage in England to wastage in Canada, and it is as plain as any rule of arithmetic that further reliance on the voluntary system will in time—perhaps in a very short time—so reduce our forces that we shall have no substantial representation in the war.

It has been suggested that everything has not been done which might have been done. Perhaps that is so, all I know is that we have done everything that we were able to devise, that the resources of the Administration were able to evolve, to make voluntary enlistment successful. Has there been, during the whole course of this debate, a suggestion of any practical step which might have been taken and which was not taken? I have not heard one ...

I know of no resource that was not adopted; the system became at last one which was a system of voluntary enlistment only in a very modified and attenuated sense. It became a system rather of conscription by cajolery—and not altogether too creditable to Canada. Consequently, speaking from the viewpoint, not only of the Government, but of the Dominion, there is no other way of getting men than by adopting this measure. The men must be had; we have them to send; and there is no other way of procuring them and sending them. The business of the country, therefore, is by this system to get the men and to send them overseas ...

Meighen now turns to answering criticisms that have been raised by Laurier and picked up by other Liberal MPs during debate. Again he begins by posing a question and answering it. Who can contend that the voluntary system of raising troops has not been tried? Responding to a speech by an MP named Pugsley, Meighen says that soldiers are not being recruited in sufficient numbers to replace the casualties and "wastage." This is an accepted, but rather odd word, not to describe casualties but rather those who leave the forces for one reason or another, either in Europe, or in training before they get to Europe. He warns that without conscription Canada's forces will become so much reduced "that we shall have no substantial representation in the war."

Meighen then pivots to criticize the voluntary enlistment effort as "conscription by cajolery." He does not say it but those eligible men in Canada who chose not to enlist were despised as shirkers. However, Meighen's argument here is logically weak because he is denouncing voluntary enlistment, something in which his government was hugely invested and had until now praised with gusto. Prime Minister Robert Borden had toured the country only a few months earlier telling people how well voluntary enlistment was performing. Now Meighen is criticizing the practice as "cajolery" and describing conscription as the only way forward.

We are told, however, that, although we have power as a Government and certainly power as a Parliament to declare that our troops in this war shall go overseas beyond Canada for the defence of Canada, we should not exercise that power. Why? The leader of the Opposition assures us that he is not afraid of an invasion of Canada. The hon. member for Bonaventure (Mr. Marcil) is also brave; he is not afraid of an invasion either. These hon. gentlemen in their predictions—because at best they are only prophecies—are either right or wrong. If they are wrong, and if there is danger of an invasion of Canada, then we had better get ready as soon as we can and fortify ourselves at the vital point in Europe, against that invasion. They will admit that themselves. If, on the contrary, they are justified in expecting that there will not be an invasion of this country—that we as Canada are not in danger—I ask why are we not in danger? Why are they so brave? Why do they rest so comfortably? It is because the defence of Canada is being fought over there in France. If the defence of Canada is not made secure by success in France, then Canada is in danger of an invasion. And if our defence is bound up with our success in France, then it is our bounden duty under the Militia Act to send out troops there for our defence. Let us come to grips on this question. If there is any weakness in that argument I would like to know what it is. One or the other is true: either we are in danger of invasion right now or later as a result of this war, or we are not in danger. If the first is true, then we should certainly send out troops to repel the invader, imminent or apprehended. If the second is true, then our defence is being fought out over there, and it is only by our success over there that we can possibly avoid invasion. It is because the right hon. gentleman (Sir Wilfrid Laurier) believes that the troops of the Empire and of France and Italy will succeed on the western front and the troops of Russia succeed on the eastern front that he sits comfortably in his seat and feels that this country is not in danger of invasion. That means they are fighting out there the defence of Canada. If that is the case, how can he decline the duty that he must surely feel upon his heart of sending the troops of Canada to sustain the defence of Canada overseas?

Laurier and others have argued that Canada had never before conscripted soldiers to fight abroad and that, in any event, a war in Europe does not equate with the defence of Canada. Meighen is having none of it. He engages in an argument that is logically constructed and that he presents as being irrefutable. Either Canada is in danger of invasion as a result of the war or it is not. If it is, then send men to defend her. If Canada is not in imminent danger, the men should be sent anyway because it is the soldiers of France and other nations who are defending Canada, as well as themselves, on the battlefields of Europe. Meighen is contemptuous of his political opponents. Laurier and others, he says with sarcasm, are "brave" and "rest comfortably" because they know that the armies of the European powers will defend them. How, asks Meighen, posing another rhetorical question, can Laurier "decline the duty" to send troops overseas in order to defend Canada? Logically, these are weak arguments on Meighen's part, despite his tautology. Canada is indeed enmeshed in a bloody war, but is in no danger of invasion.

I pass on from that and proceed to take up certain of the contentions that have been advanced in support of the amendment moved by the leader of the Opposition. It had been a matter of great interest, and indeed of curiosity, to observe the wonderful collection of opinions that are massed behind this referendum amendment. The referendum amendment is really not an amendment at all. At all events it is not a policy: it is the negation of policy. Why is it adopted? Merely as an expedient to avoid facing the issue, and to collect behind the Opposition leader all support he can get. What are the opinions behind the amendment? It is seconded by the honourable member for Edmonton (Mr. Oliver), who complains that we have already waited too long on this matter: that we should have taken this course and had a referendum started a year ago. It is moved by the leader of the Opposition, who complains that we have dashed this Bill upon them too suddenly and too soon. What is the ground of the leader of the Opposition? He argues that the Bill is going to bring about disunion in this country, and will be met with opposition, if not with resistance on the part of French Canada. His amendment is seconded by the hon. member for Edmonton who wants a bill that will take all of these 100,000 men out of French Canada alone.

MR. OLIVER: *I would like my hon. friend to keep closer to the facts than that. Hansard is my record.*

MR. MEIGHEN: *I would not have said so if it had not been in Hansard. The hon. gentleman's words are capable of that interpretation, and of no other interpretation. I know he did not use those words with the intention that the interpretation should be applied.*

MR. OLIVER: *Thank you …*

MR. MEIGHEN: *Here is an amendment moved by the leader of the Opposition because he himself is against conscription. It is seconded by the hon. member for Edmonton because he is in favour of conscription. And its first sponsor is the hon. member for Bonaventure (Mr. Marcil) who does not know whether he is in favour of conscription or against it. It will be clear to everyone that the purpose of this amendment is to evade rather than to face a very great issue at this time. It is to avoid rather than to enforce the performance of duty. It is a refuge of discord—a haven of the disunited. It is not a declaration of faith, it is a declaration of scepticism. We cannot win a war by referendums.*

Meighen turns to the core proposal made by Laurier, who says that conscription is such an important national question that it should be put to the people in a referendum. Laurier had also argued that a government in office for six years lacked a mandate to impose conscription by a simple vote in the House of Commons. Meighen is scornful in his response. The call for a referendum, he says, is a cover for Laurier's opposition to conscription. Laurier had never said that he was opposed, although that was probably true. His espousal of a referendum would buy him time and political space. He could continue to say that he was neither in favour of nor opposed to conscription and that it should be left to voters to decide. He hoped that his position would allow Liberals to bridge the divide between English and French Canada and also between competing sentiments within English Canada. Meighen hits back.

A referendum, he says, is not a policy but rather "the negation of a policy." He asks rhetorically, "Why is it adopted?" Once again he answers his own question: Laurier wants to avoid the issue and to gather all the support he can muster. Laurier, he says, argues that conscription will be opposed and resisted in Quebec. At the same time, Frank Oliver, an MP from Edmonton, is against the bill because too many men from his constituency in Alberta have enlisted while too few have enlisted from Quebec. Laurier, however, is describing reality because a riot had broken out in Quebec City on May 24, shortly after Borden announced that conscription would be implemented. As for Frank Oliver, he objects to Meighen's characterization of what he had said.

To parse the Liberal position, Meighen uses a rhetorical device called antithesis, in which contrasting phrases are deliberately used in consecutive phrases or sentences. The Liberals, he says, want to evade the issue, not face it; to avoid rather than to enforce the performance of duty; not a declaration of faith but rather of scepticism. He concludes: "We cannot win a war by referendums."

Do hon. gentlemen realize that the passing of this amendment will bring joy to friends of Germany in every part of the world? It will be welcomed at Potsdam. It would be supported, were he here, by the head of the German nation itself. It will be welcomed by every German newspaper on this and every other continent. It will be welcomed by every slacker all over Canada. That is the company the hon. gentlemen are in who support this referendum. The passing of this amendment would be a subject of rejoicing to every poolroom loafer, to every movie veteran, to every sporting fan, to all who have shrunk from duty. But it would be a subject of resentment, regret, and pain to the men who have nobly done their part to preserve the liberty, and uphold the honour, of Canada ...

Meighen then goes further and says that Laurier's proposal will comfort the enemy; it will bring joy to friends of Germany; it will be welcomed in Potsdam; it will be supported by the Kaiser, and reported in the German press. This is a heavy-handed rhetorical tactic equating questioning the government's prosecution of the war as providing comfort and solace to the enemy. The message is that any such questions are disloyal. This is a time-honoured "with us or against us" argument meant to silence disagreement. Laurier's call for a referendum, Meighen says, will be supported by the "poolroom loafer," the "movie veteran," and the "sporting fan," all of whom he says "have shrunk from duty." He contrasts them with the enlisted men who have "nobly" volunteered to fight. This has the overtone of military orations that have existed in rhetoric since antiquity. Meighen's attack on those who do not want to fight is at odds with a claim earlier in his speech that voluntary recruitment exposes those who choose not to enlist to "cajolery." He is the one who is now cajoling.

Let us rise to the level of our duty, let us not be afraid to lead. We have been execrated from end to end of Canada for failure of leadership and all the rest. Many of those men who have lagged behind but who ought to have gone to the front have lampooned the leader of this Government because of alleged failure of leadership. Newspaper after newspaper has thundered that out. Well, here is some leadership. Here and now is a chance to follow. Let us as a Parliament get in front; let those who lagged behind and cried for leadership walk up now, close the gap, and stand beside the Prime Minister. The people of Canada, we have oft been told, call out to the Parliament of Canada for strong and fearless leadership. Are we going to answer that call with our hands up in the air and cry out to the people: "For heaven's sake, lead us." Such is the amendment of the right hon. Leader of the Opposition.

It is all very well to deliberate upon something that is left for us to decide, but we have already decided on the carrying on of this war, and of carrying it on with all our might. If there ever was a time for a referendum—which I deny—it was in August 1914; it is not now. We have committed ourselves as a nation, we have signed the bond, it is for us now to discharge the obligation.

Meighen issues a clarion call for leadership but his entreaty has a bitter edge to it. The laggards and the newspapers have lampooned the prime minister for a lack of leadership. Those people now have their chance to support him. Meighen usually bases his arguments on logos or logic, but here he makes an ethical appeal (ethos) to elicit sympathy for Borden. In the face of Borden's true leadership, Meighen says, all Laurier has to offer is a referendum. If ever there were a time for a referendum, Meighen says—and he immediately denies that there was one—it would have been when Canada entered the war in 1914, but not now. Then he uses a tricolon, or list of three, which gains strength by its cumulative effect in his call for Canada to "discharge the obligation."

I want to say something else, and I do so with special earnestness. It may be that in the heat of discussion I do not avoid animosities perhaps as carefully as I should; but I say this to those hon. Gentlemen opposite whose position with regard to this bill is surrounded by embarrassments much heavier than those that surround us, I say to them that this Bill is not designed and it is not framed to be unjust to the province of Quebec or to any other section of this country … We of English-speaking Canada have the kindest feelings towards our French Canadian compatriots. We realize that there are certain considerations having to do with this subject of recruiting that apply to them that do not apply with the same force to us. I want to say to the members from Quebec that this Bill as drafted is not intended to, and will not, if I understand the Bill, work unfairly to that province …

Surely the prosecution of this war with the whole might of Canada is not a subject which is now left to us to decide. That question has been passed upon. Its prosecution is now a matter only of good faith: 300,000 living men and 20,000 dead are over there, the hostages of our good faith. All that is left to us now is a choice between fidelity and desertion, between courage and poltroonery, between honour and everlasting shame …

We are told this action will result in disunion. I see no reason why it should produce disunion. It is framed to avoid disunion. But let no man deceive himself. We do not avoid disunion by dropping back to where we were, any more than we avoid disunion by going ahead with this measure. I see no more peril in the one course than in the other … While we would do almost anything to avoid disunion, we cannot purchase union at the cost of national disgrace …

I appeal to hon. Gentlemen opposite, and to hon. gentlemen around me, for party divisions as we once had them are not just the same today, I appeal to all hon. Members to take the course which, in my belief, alone can command the respect of this House, of Canada, and of the world.

Although Meighen has said that he is confident the conscription bill will not create disunity, he is clearly sensitive to Laurier's claim. When Borden had on May 17 announced his intention to conscript, two of his three French Canadian cabinet ministers warned that it would kill the party for twenty-five years in Quebec. Later in May there were riots in Quebec City. In June, E. L. Patenaude, a French-Canadian minister, had resigned, warning that the conscription law "imperils national unity."

Meighen alludes, briefly, to his reputation as venomous debater. "It may be that in the heat of discussion I do not avoid animosities perhaps as carefully as I should," he says. This is a rare attempt at conciliation. He reassures the House that the conscription bill was not designed to punish Quebec and will not do so. He says that English-speaking Canadians are fond of their French-speaking compatriots. Following that brief nod, he returns to his prescribed lines. The war will be prosecuted come what may: "All that is left to us now is a choice between fidelity and desertion, between courage and poltroonery [cowardice], between honour and everlasting shame." These are fine lines and should have been his peroration but he decides to make one more comment about unity: he says it cannot be purchased with national disgrace. Then he ends with an attempt at broad and universal appeal. Members of Parliament should take the only decision that can command respect in the House, in the country, and in the world.

THE IMPACT OF MEIGHEN'S SPEECH

The conscription debate of June to July 1917 was epic and one of the most controversial in Canadian parliamentary history. Ninety-nine MPs, forty of them French Canadians, participated and the nation's attention was focused upon all of them. Borden spoke upon the introduction of the bill on June 11 but after that it was left mostly to Meighen to ferry it through the House. He spoke as planned on June 17 but rose again a month later on July 24 immediately after Laurier had made an impassioned speech on the bill's final reading. Laurier knew that the legislation was dividing his party and spoke wistfully of being "estranged from friends." He freed his MPs to vote their conscience, knowing that he could not compel many of them to vote with him in any case. He predicted that the country at large was facing a "cleavage" that could tear it apart. He ended by saying, as he had in an earlier speech, that he opposed the bill because it would sow "discord and disunion" and because it was coercive: "All my life I have fought coercion; all my life I have promoted union."

Meighen was immediately on his feet following Laurier's remarks to deliver an impromptu speech. "Nothing was farther from my mind," he said, "when I entered the House this afternoon than to speak upon their reading of this Bill." Laurier, in his speech, had criticized Meighen but in a respectful manner; now he receives a barrage in return. Meighen began by saying that Laurier's many friends had become "profoundly disappointed at the course of [Laurier's] public life in recent years" and that they would not be impressed with "his deliverance today." Turning to the issues at hand, he spoke of the "vigorous" and "red-blooded men" fighting on behalf of Canada in Europe. He contrasted them with the "persons of alien enemy origin" in Canada. It was from them, he said, that Laurier was drawing support. He spoke of a "backward and a forward portion of the population," adding: "If we can only produce union by walking at the speed of and abreast with the backward portion of the Canadian people, then I do not want union in Canada. I am ready to face disorder and dissension." Finally, he placed the responsibility for "disunion" upon Laurier who, he said, had been invited to participate in a union government but had refused. "If there is one man between the shores of this country who is responsible for the shadow of disunion I say it is the leader of the Opposition." Even Meighen's sympathetic biographer Roger Graham admitted that such an attack upon the aging Liberal leader, and his contrasting of the "red-blooded" and "forward" elements of the population against those who were "backward" would have been better left unsaid.

When the vote was taken on the Military Service Act, every French-speaking member of Parliament opposed it and almost all the English-speaking MPs were in support. The eight English-speaking provinces also endorsed Borden's move while Quebec opposed it. The act became law on August 29, 1917, and it made all male citizens aged twenty to forty-five subject to call-up for service through to the end of the war.

Meighen predicted in his speech that if MPs were to tell their constituents of the merits of the conscription bill there would be no discord or resistance. Once they had introduced conscription, Meighen and the

Conservatives were to find that it did divide the country. For the most part English Canada backed Borden and Meighen but a significant number of people did not. They included many trade unionists, farmers, non-British immigrants, and pacifists. Most French Canadians in Quebec, including almost every French-speaking member of Parliament, were opposed.

Borden and the Conservatives spent much of the summer of 1917 attempting to entice Liberals and political independents into a union government while preparing for an election. During this time, Meighen was preparing legislation that would tip the electoral scales in the government's favour whenever an election did occur. The Wartime Elections Act extended the right to vote to women but only those women closely related to Canadian soldiers. The same bill removed the right to vote from "aliens" who had been born in Germany or the Austro-Hungarian Empire if they had become naturalized Canadians after 1902. Many of those people were Liberal supporters. They remembered that it was Laurier's government that had welcomed them to settle in Canada. Meighen's bill also removed the vote entirely from Mennonites and Doukhobors, who were pacifists for religious reasons. In addition, anyone who identified as a conscientious objector was also to be denied the vote. Meighen had recommended this as a course of action to Borden as early as October 1916.

Several Liberals and independents decided to accept Borden's invitation to run as coalition candidates. On October 12 he announced the formation of a Union government whose cabinet contained twelve Conservatives, nine Liberals or Independents, and one person who described himself as a labour representative. Borden called an election for December 1917. The campaign became a nasty one-issue contest over conscription, featuring a bitter division reminiscent of the Riel controversy. The Wartime Elections Act also created a legal open season on "aliens" of Central European extraction and some of the language in the campaign was ugly. The Unionists led by Borden trounced the Liberals by a vote of 153 to 82 and triumphed in every province except Quebec and Prince Edward Island. In Quebec, the Liberals won sixty-two of sixty-five seats and the three won by Unionists came from English-speaking areas. Borden and Meighen had their way in 1917 but their actions destroyed Conservative prospects for decades in Quebec and also among some ethnic and immigrant groups.

When conscription was implemented in 1917, Borden and Meighen found that many men preferred to remain in Canada rather than going to fight in Europe. Once again there were riots in Quebec City. In rural Canada, farmers were so upset to learn that they (or their sons) might have to serve that five thousand of them marched on Ottawa in protest. Of the first 400,000 men summoned for military service 380,000 appealed, a reluctance to serve that went well beyond Quebec. Eventually 125,000 men were added to the Canadian Expeditionary Force but only 24,000 made it to France by the war's end in November 1918.

By 1920 Borden was burned out and he retired after having been largely absent from Ottawa for months. Meighen had been the workhorse of the government while his leader was away in Britain during the war and in France during the peace conference to follow. As solicitor-general, Meighen had acted in draconian fashion to put an end to the Winnipeg General Strike in 1919. He considered the strikers to be revolutionaries bent on destroying the constituted order and he had no sympathy for them. He approved the arrest of strike leaders and wanted them deported. Shortly after the strike ended, he crafted amendments to the Criminal Code known as Section 98. This legislation was used for many years to harass and spy upon communists, trade unionists, and anyone, including members of the clergy, who spoke or acted on progressive causes.

Despite his loyalty and the arduous work that he had performed, Meighen was neither Borden's nor the cabinet's choice as a successor. However, the Unionist caucus preferred him and he was eager to serve. He became the party leader in July 1920. Laurier had died in 1919 to be replaced by Mackenzie King. Meighen and King were to contest three elections, with King winning in 1921, Meighen in 1925, and King again in 1926. In that election Meighen also lost in his own seat and resigned as leader. He returned in 1927 to contest the leadership but lost to Richard Bedford Bennett, who appointed him to the Senate in 1932. He served there until 1941 when, briefly, he became Conservative leader once again after Bennett's departure. But Meighen lost in the by-election that was to return him to Parliament. He remained as leader, but without a seat, until 1942 when he resigned for a final time from public life. He maintained business interests in Toronto and took little part in public activities for the last fifteen years of his life. But he remained, in words used in the title of his book of collected speeches, "unrevised and unrepented."

AGNES MACPHAIL ON POLITICAL REFORM
FEBRUARY 28, 1928

"A very considerable number of people in the country believe what we believe. They believe that our present system of government is outworn ... "

Agnes Macphail made history when in 1921 she became the first woman elected to the House of Commons. She was treated well by some MPs but others, who believed that women had no place in politics, were nasty and condescending. Macphail was not easily silenced. She was quick, blunt, and sharply humorous. She was such a good orator that during summer recesses she performed as a professional speaker on a Chautauqua speech-making circuit in the United States. She was a passionate champion of full equality for women. She was deeply concerned about peace issues and a proponent of changes to the prison system, but she remained above all an advocate for democratic reform and a voice for the farm people who sent her to Ottawa in five federal elections.

◆

Agnes Macphail was born in a log house in 1890 in Grey County, Ontario, seventeen years after Nellie McClung was born in the same region. The two women were to become friendly although they met only infrequently. Macphail's great-grandparents had been landless Scots who abandoned the cruelties of their landlords in the mid-1800s to settle near Guelph in what was then known as Canada West. When her grandfather came of age, he trudged farther north in Ontario to take land of his own near the village of Ceylon, about forty kilometres from Owen Sound. Her mother and father were Dougald Macphail and Henrietta Campbell and she had two younger sisters. Agnes liked school and passed her high school entrance exam at age fourteen. Much to her disappointment, her parents decided that she must stay home to work on the farm. She was a headstrong young woman and lobbied furiously to continue her studies. Her parents relented and in 1906, at age sixteen, she moved to Owen Sound where she lived in a boarding house and attended the four-storey brick collegiate. She finished a four-year matriculation course in half that time. She was to recall in later years how she felt mocked and ostracized as a rural outsider whose plain wardrobe and manners failed the prevailing style test.

In 1908 she moved to Stratford to attend a new teachers college for two years and then she accepted the first of several rural positions, which she was to occupy over the next decade. It was a time of economic and political ferment in rural Canada. Farmers in Ontario and the West were becoming increasingly agitated over the National Policy created and implemented by John A. Macdonald and the Conservatives. It built a tariff wall that protected Canadian industrialists against imported goods. Farmers believed that as a result, they were paying too much for machinery and other products. They also looked longingly at a burgeoning US market and wanted tariff-free trade with the Americans. They believed that would provide access to a market that had largely been unavailable to them. At the same time it would allow for cheaper imports of machinery and other manufactured goods. Added to the trade irritants, farmers had to accept the prices on offer, not only when buying machinery and other inputs but also when selling to grain merchants, meat packers, and creameries. In Western Canada, particularly, there was an added frustration about the railways' ability to charge high freight rates because of the farmers' isolated and landlocked situation far from their suppliers and from markets.

Agrarian unrest in the United States had preceded that in Canada, where farmers watched what was happening south of the border with keen interest. The United Farmers of Alberta (UFA) was created in 1909 to promote political and educational interests. The United Farmers of Ontario (UFO) was organized in 1914 for much the same reason. In 1919, the UFO decided to get into provincial politics and won enough seats to form a coalition government with the support of members elected by the Independent Party. In 1921 the UFA swept to power in Alberta and in the same year the United Farmers of Manitoba won the election in that province.

The ground was also shaking at the federal level. In 1919 Thomas Crerar, minister of agriculture in the Unionist government led by Robert Borden, resigned following the delivery of a budget he believed did not pay enough attention to farm issues. The Progressive Party was founded in 1920 with Crerar as its leader. Many farmers and their organizations believed that both the Conservatives and Liberals had betrayed them; that these parties were self-serving, corrupt, and in the pockets of big business. The farm populists wanted to reform the political system and infuse it with a more direct democracy in which elected members would go to Parliament essentially as independents representing farmers. The Progressives believed in co-operation rather than competition in politics. They wanted individual MPs to be able to introduce legislation; and they wanted free votes in which parliamentarians could make decisions based on merit rather than party discipline. They called for public referenda on certain issues and for providing constituents with the power to propose legislation in citizens' initiatives. They also wanted electors to be able to recall their MPs if they were not happy with them. The farm activists were supported in much of what they sought by candidates from the labour movement, who also felt frozen out of the political process. In reply, politicians within the two old-line parties said the agrarian populists were naive. The only system that could succeed in a large and diverse country, they said, was representative democracy where citizens elected MPs to speak for them between elections.

All of this was of consuming interest to Agnes Macphail. Women were playing a far more prominent role in populist farm movements than elsewhere. By 1917 Macphail caught the attention of the editor of *Farmer's Sun*, the UFO newspaper, and he invited her to write for the publication. Soon she was in demand not only as a writer but increasingly as an exceptional orator on the rural circuit. As the 1921 federal election approached, she left her teaching job in the countryside near Toronto. She returned to Grey County ostensibly to tend to an ailing grandmother, but she had also conveniently relocated to an area that had sent three UFO members to the provincial parliament in 1919.

She was named as one among 150 delegates to the UFO-Independent Labour nominating meeting in September 1921, and hers was one of twenty-five names put forward as a candidate. Five ballots and many hours later she won the nomination. She had in previous months prudently avoided appearing too eager for the prize. But on the day following the nomination, when the riding executive came under pressure to have her withdraw in favour of a male candidate, she refused. Prime Minister Arthur Meighen called an election for December and Macphail waded through snowdrifts and made fifty-five speeches to defeat the incumbent Conservative. She was the only female among 235 MPs to be sent to Ottawa in the first election in which all Canadian women (with the exception of Indigenous women) were allowed to vote. It was also the first election in which women were able to run as candidates. Meighen and the ruling Conservatives were trounced. The Liberals won 118 seats, one short of a majority. The Progressives, competing in their first election, won fifty-eight seats. That number did not officially include Macphail, who ran under the banner of the UFO, which was loosely affiliated with the Progressives. Two other candidates won on behalf of the UFA and J. S. Woodsworth was elected along with two other labour candidates. This political earthquake cracked the solid facade of the two-party system that had reigned since Confederation. Canada has had third, fourth, and even fifth parties in the House of Commons in every election since 1921.

Macphail saw herself as representing farmers above all but her interests and passions were diverse. She was a champion of ordinary people who, she believed, were preyed upon by a system tilted toward wealth and privilege. She demanded full equality for women. She was less likely than other feminists, such as Nellie McClung, to focus on the role of women as natural caregivers and mothers of the nation whose participation in public life would provide a civilizing force on society. In her first brief speech in Parliament in March 1922, she opposed changes to the Elections Act because she said they were not based on gender equality. Amendments to the law would have granted voting rights to certain non-Canadian women only if they were married to men who were citizens. Macphail argued that the vote should be granted based simply upon whether or not the women themselves were citizens and not upon their marital status. "I think that what women really want today," she said, "is perfect equality with men, and therefore if the striking out of Section 29 of the Dominion Elections Act in its entirety does not confer upon women perfectly and entirely equal rights with men, then, I think it is not going far enough."

Macphail, along with other farm and labour MPs, worked for a decade to have Parliament modify divorce laws that were fraught with discrimination against women. For example, in some provinces men could divorce their wives on the grounds of adultery but a woman seeking to divorce her husband had to prove cruelty or desertion in addition to adultery. Further, a woman seeking a divorce had to file for it wherever her estranged husband lived because his address was considered to be their domicile, even if that location was far from where the couple had lived together as spouses. Most MPs in the old line parties were stubbornly opposed to reforms and some accused Macphail of seeking to undermine marriage and ruin the home. She countered that accusation during a debate in 1925:

> I believe the preservation of the home as an institution in the
> future lies almost entirely in the hands of the men. If they are
> willing to give to women economic freedom within that home; if
> they are willing to live by the standard that they wish the women
> to live by, the home will be preserved. If the preservation of
> the home means the enslavement of women, economically or
> morally, then we had better break it … When we have a single
> standard for men and women, both morally and economically,
> we shall have a home that is well worth preserving, and I think
> we can be quite sure it will be preserved …

Within a month of occupying her seat in the House of Commons, Macphail also spoke out in favour of coal miners in Cape Breton who were being told by the British Empire Steel Corporation that they must take a 35 per cent reduction in pay. She opposed capital punishment and demanded prison reforms that would allow inmates to work and to receive rehabilitation. She was a pacifist who opposed refurbishing the Peace Tower in Ottawa because she said it glorified war rather than supporting peace. She put forward a motion that would refuse money for training cadets. She proposed that the government create a new department to promote peace and disarmament. She was at times accused of being influenced by communism and even accused of treason when she criticized militarism and imperialism.

Her early days in the House of Commons were not easy. Macphail had never been to Ottawa and in January 1922, not long after being elected, she visited the capital for the first time. Naturally, she went to see the Parliament Buildings. There remains a photo of her standing before a stone archway wearing an old coat that is too large and a dowdy hat. That wardrobe camouflaged the appearance of a handsome person with thick dark hair pulled back from a high forehead. She had a straight and comely nose and hazel eyes that could twinkle when she smiled or turn hard when she was challenged. When she returned to Ottawa in March, Macphail found a rooming house in which to stay, but she was lonely and far from home. She later confided to a friend that she had been miserable in those early days and she lost twenty pounds.

Macphail was at first the object of constant scrutiny and much of the attention was not friendly. Her manner of dress and her physical appearance were grist for commentary by reporters, some of whom were other women. Her status as an unmarried woman was also the object of frequent comment. One headline asked: "Does Agnes know what love is?" Mackenzie King and R. B. Bennett, leader of the Conservatives after 1927, were both lifelong bachelors but similar questions were never asked about them. When Macphail criticized the government of Quebec for refusing the vote to women, Premier Louis-Alexandre Taschereau responded by offering to find her a husband. In the House, some MPs attempted to be chivalrous while others were condescending; often those sentiments coexisted. She had quickly to develop protective armour but she possessed a quick wit and sharp tongue. One day in debate a fellow MP asked: "Doesn't the honourable member wish she were a man?" Macphail replied: "No, doesn't the honourable member wish he were?"

Before long, however, she became acquainted with a group of other Progressive MPs, particularly those representing the UFA. She became fast friends with Muriel Kerr, an Ottawa teacher who was also president of the Business and Women's Professional Association. The two often invited friendly MPs to Kerr's home for evening visits that would sometimes end in their going dancing. Macphail's fashion sense was soon to emerge and later photos of her show someone who is always tastefully, although not elegantly, dressed. She did not manage her money well. For example, she believed that MPs were paid too much and in her first year she returned some of her salary to the government. She learned to her chagrin that she had to pay income tax on it in any event. She did not, in future years, repeat that gesture. She was also a generous friend who shared her bounty. As a result, she was often short of money.

Macphail was a riveting speaker. During summer recesses she was recruited to the Chautauqua lecture circuit in the United States. It was a travelling talk show intended to introduce people to new ideas and issues of public concern. As she toured and spoke throughout the US, Macphail's favoured topics were women in politics, currency reform, and Canadian-American relations. In the 1930s she shared a New York booking agent with British politician Winston Churchill.

The Progressives in 1921 had elected enough members to become the official Opposition, but many of those MPs did not believe in the party system so they refused. That handed the task back to Meighen and the Conservatives, who had won only forty-nine seats. The Progressives had no national organization and their MPs were in essence independents. Some, including former Unionist minister Thomas Crerar, wanted to make a deal with Mackenzie King and the Liberals who had not elected enough members to form a majority. Macphail was among those who robustly opposed any alliance with the Liberals and she was against the Progressives becoming a political party. She was prepared to support or oppose the government depending upon what legislation it brought forward.

Mackenzie King capitalized on disunity among the Progressives to remain in power for a full term until 1925. By that time Crerar had resigned as Progressive leader to be replaced by Robert Forke, another ex-Liberal. In 1926 Forke and other Manitoba-based Progressives decided to run for election as Liberal-Progressives. Once elected, they supported another King minority government that remained in power until 1930. Both Forke and Crerar became Liberal cabinet ministers. Macphail and nine other rural MPs from Alberta, Saskatchewan, and Ontario left the Progressive caucus. They began to co-operate with J. S. Woodsworth and other independent labour MPs in what they called the Ginger Group, or the "co-operating independents" as Woodsworth preferred to call them. Macphail participated but she continued to define herself as a Progressive and as a representative of the United Farmers of Ontario. The UFO, however, lost power provincially in 1923 and later decided to get out of politics and become an occupational organization once again.

Macphail believed that old line parties had undercut democracy in Canada and she preferred a form of government in which MPs would be responsive to their constituents and to their group—in her case the farm community. These concepts remained vague and undeveloped but Macphail continued as an earnest voice for rural constituents at a time of growing urbanization. It was on their behalf that she spoke on February 28, 1928, in response to the budget recently introduced by the Liberals. It was a caustically humourous speech that was frequently interrupted by both cheers and catcalls. She took direct aim at individuals in the Liberal and Conservative parties as well as those who had defected from the Progressives. She also talked about her ideas for a more direct and responsive democracy.

MACPHAIL'S SPEECH

We come again to a consideration of the budget brought down by the minister of finance (Mr. J. A. Robb). In the opinion of the members of the Liberal Party that budget is a good one and I am sure they support it. The Liberal-Progressive members, I am sure, do not think it is a good budget but they will support it. The Liberals from Saskatchewan, coming as they do from that part of this enlightened Dominion cannot like the budget and yet I am expecting to hear them say it is a good budget. The Conservatives think this is a good budget but they must declare it not to be so and having said that, they will not be

able to vote for it. I think it is a rich man's budget and I am in the splendid position of
saying that I do not like it and of voting in accordance with my views. So also are these
honourable members who sit around me ...

Macphail begins her speech with a heavy dose of irony at the expense of those MPs who are locked by party discipline into either supporting or opposing the budget. The Liberal-Progressives come in for special scorn as do the Liberals in the agricultural province of Saskatchewan, who she says "cannot like the budget" but will support it anyway. Macphail is staking out her turf in favour of a political system in which MPs vote in favour of what they approve and oppose what they do not. That, she says, is what she and the Ginger Group will do.

Agriculture is still the main business of the Canadian people. The nation's prosperity depends
on a bumper crop. It has been well said that the agricultural returns are the barometer of
national prosperity. The following words were used by Aristotle: "The first attention should
be paid to that which is in accordance with nature; for by nature agriculture is first; next come
all those things which are derived from the earth, such as mining and other arts of like kind."

Or as has been often said: "The well-being of the people is like a tree." Agriculture and
other primary industries are its roots, manufacturing and commerce its branches and its life;
if the root is injured, the leaves fall, the branches break away and the tree dies.

The roots of the tree of Canada's national life have been injured. We have, for a young
and rich country, a depleted and impoverished agricultural industry. In this young country
agriculture has not held its own people, nor its power and place of influence. I regret it, but
it is true. I do not think anyone in this house will care to deny that our educational, religious,
business and political policies have been framed, not with rural needs in mind but rather,
whether consciously or unconsciously, directly antagonistic to those needs. The result is clear
to anybody who cares to look around, namely, that our people are leaving the land in numbers
that would worry any government, even this one. It does not seem to go further than worry
with them, but still it worries them. This great mass of people is disappearing from the open
spaces into crowded places which we call cities in either Canada or the United States. To
my mind one of the saddest things is that the individual is lost in the great mass of human
beings and so this constant robbing of the open places does not enrich the cities to the extent
that it robs the country ...

As befits an agrarian populist, Macphail describes agriculture as the economic bedrock of the country. She then quotes Aristotle to make her point. Macphail was largely self-taught as were many rural leaders. She had taken teachers' training but did not follow any formal studies other than that. However, she read widely, and her speeches often contained quotes—some of them lengthy—from books and articles. She describes the well-being of people as resembling a tree. Agriculture is the root of the tree but it is being destroyed. Although it sounds like a biblical allusion, perhaps to Jeremiah or the Psalms, Macphail does not provide a direct reference. She would, however, have been familiar with the Bible because she had been raised as a Presbyterian. She became a Seventh Day Adventist when she lived with her aunt while attending teachers' college and later in life became a member of the United Church. She extends the tree image saying that the roots of Canada's national life have been injured. People are leaving the land and crowding into cities, and government policies have been "directly antagonistic" to the needs of the rural community.

Country life develops thoughtful, wholesome and genuine people, to a greater extent than any other life, and I think it is true to say that in the last analysis the conscience of the nation lies in the country. I think we can all bear testimony, if we care to, to the fact that in cities and towns the conventions of life veneer even the ways of our friends and it is in the country that we find the beauty of simplicity and sometimes the bluntness of unaffected candour. Country living makes for character and because of the need of character in all national undertakings, and because of the importance of agriculture in our national life, we see how disastrous the results must be if people continue to leave the land. Aside from economic consequences, it heralds the approach of the time when the country will no longer furnish that leadership in business and public life which has been so influential in shaping the course of events.

Macphail follows her elegy to a disappearing rural way of life with a statement that idealizes farm life as tranquil, uncomplicated, and virtuous. She is heavily invested in agrarianism, a political philosophy that sees rural society as superior to urban, and the independent farmer as superior to the urban worker. Various farm movements in Canada, including certainly the UFO, promoted this world view and Macphail believed it as well. Such comments would also have played well when inserted into letters to her constituents or quoted in hometown newspapers. For Macphail and other agrarians, sentiments such as these led to a demand for reform in which farmers and rural communities would receive what she liked to call a square deal.

The rural problem is a many-sided problem and I am not one of those who think that governments are so important that they altogether make the problem, or, to any great extent, solve it. I know there are many other forces which operate. It would take too long—and I never wanted to speak for forty minutes until I could not speak any longer— to go into all of the phases of this question, but I should like to mention one thing that I think has done much to aggravate our rural problem and that is our educational system. It is true that the whole educational trend is towards the city. Our educational system in Canada has acted simply as a "gangway" to life in urban areas. If I had the time I should like to quote some leading educational authorities, corroborative of this view, but I think I can ask hon. members to look around their own counties; if they do they will find it is true that more and more people are going to high school and that life in school and high school is utterly divorced from the life of people who live in the neighbourhood of the school and support them. The result is that too many people are rushed into city enterprises; we have an abundance of people hunting for white collar jobs and too few people who are willing to do the very much nobler and better work of nation-building in the open spaces. I am glad that I have not had too much of that kind of education to prevent me from thinking for myself, but we have an educational system that actually stuffs children with facts and creates in them a reverence for things as they are, and this is a great disaster to our children, because it hinders [them] in creating institutions to meet changed conditions ... "

Macphail moves on to describe the "many-sided" problem of rural neglect. She expresses frustration that she should be expected to do so in the forty minutes allotted to each speaker in the debate. That rule had been introduced into the House of Commons in 1927 much to the annoyance of some MPs who had previously an almost unlimited time in which to express themselves. Macphail had been a rural teacher and in her speeches she frequently uses the educational system as an illustration of how life in the country is undervalued. Schools become a "gangway" to life in the city. High schools in rural areas are "utterly divorced" from the people and places that support them. Students are prepared for white collar jobs in the city rather than the much nobler work of farming. To this Macphail adds another criticism—that the educational system as it exists "stuffs children with facts" and inculcates in them the status quo. By all accounts Macphail did not do that but rather was a teacher who encouraged independent thought among her students. She has to this point in her speech said little about the budget that she is supposed to discuss.

It would take much longer time than I have at my disposal to review the sufferings of the farmer in the political field. The farmers, because there are more of them and because they carry on the primary industry of the country, have suffered more than any other class from political policies framed by governments antagonistic to the farmer's economic needs. The full discussion of this question would take me into the economic realm of finance, transportation, and many other places into which I have not time to go, but I want to review, for the edification of this house and particularly of the Liberal party, a history of the political life in Canada as it related to the farmers just before and since 1896.

Prior to 1896 the farmers in Canada, to a very great extent, felt that the Liberal party did voice their aspirations and needs. That is, the Liberal party was the vehicle used by the farmers for the expression of their political needs. For the seventeen years prior to 1896 many able men, particularly Sir Richard Cartwright and Sir Wilfrid Laurier, impressed upon the people of Canada this fact. The farmers believed that the Liberal party was opposed to special privileges, and particularly special privilege as it is embodied in the national policy. Sir Richard Cartwright made some very able speeches opposing the protective tariff ...

I want to quote from a speech by Sir Wilfrid Laurier ... "We stand for freedom. I denounce the policy of protection as bondage—yea, bondage; and I refer to bondage in the same manner in which American slavery was bondage. Not in the same degree, perhaps, but in the same manner."

That was before 1896. Lovely speeches those! They went to the country, and the people, tired of privilege in high places sent the Liberals back with a majority. In 1897 the Liberals brought down their first budget, and I suppose that the low tariff people *of Canada never looked forward with as great a hope to any other budget. In speaking of the time following the bringing down of the budget and subsequently Mr. [Edward] Porritt has this to say at page 362: "The policy of the Laurier government with regard to protection has been characterised as a betrayal of Canadian Liberalism* ... "*

In 1911 the Laurier government was defeated, and from that time on they never did to any great extent regain the confidence of low tariff farmers in Canada. Some indeed were such good Liberals that they remained Liberals rather than farmers but for the most part the confidence of farmers in the low tariff principles of Liberalism was broken never to be mended again. This sank very deeply into the minds of farmers, and was really one of the causes of revolt which brought in the sixty-five Independents who came into this house in 1921. The farming people in the constituencies had voted for honest party men of their own class, men who spoke well in the constituencies, saying they would come to Ottawa and be true to the agricultural industry ...

Macphail now engages in a history lesson for the members going back to 1896 when Laurier and the Liberals defeated the governing Conservatives, the party of the National Policy. The Liberals claimed to champion farmers but did not pursue free trade in their fifteen years between 1896 and 1911. Macphail quotes a muckraking writer of the day as saying that under Laurier the party had betrayed Canadian Liberalism. This comment would have annoyed the Liberal members sitting across the aisle from her. They would argue that they campaigned on reciprocity with the US in the election of 1911 but the Conservatives enlisted big business to defeat them. However, Macphail's conclusion, one shared by the radical Progressive MPs, is that neither of the old line parties can be trusted.

Before I proceed further let me say something about our idea. We are here not to work as a party. In that awful session of 1926 we were accused every day of being Grits or Tories although as a matter of fact we were neither. We are not interested either in Liberals or Conservatives, except personally; as a party we are interested in neither. We want such amendments in the rules and usages of the House as will enable new groups to function; that is, we want to come closer to having representative government than we have had it before. We believe that questions should be debated on their merits, that private members should be free to vote on legislation on its merits; and more than that, that private members

should be able to introduce legislation and that this house should be free to vote on the
merits of such legislation. As it is now, legislation is all cornered by the government, and
only the legislation which the government approves of has any chance of getting through
this house. A very considerable number of people in the country believe what we believe.
They believe that our present system of government is outworn, that it possibly served
its day, but that day is over, and they want such amendments in the rules and usages of
parliament as will cause it more closely to resemble a representative institution ...

Macphail recalls how she and other radical Progressive MPs were pilloried for supporting or opposing Liberal and Conservative governments based simply upon the legislation they put forward. She argues that she and her colleagues have no personal interest in either party but just want good legislation and good government. She has concluded, along with other agrarians, that the "present system of government" in no longer adequate. Her ideal is for a more direct form of democracy rather than one where an MP, once elected, stands in as the representative on behalf of his or her electors for the life of a parliament. She believes that MPs should vigorously represent their constituents and also their group or class, rather than being docile members of parties. They should be free to vote on the merits of legislation rather than being "whipped" by their parties to vote as a block. In Macphail's universe any MP would be able to introduce legislation; indeed citizens could also take the initiative to propose legislation directly. Macphail and other agrarians also believe that cabinet positions in government should be awarded in proportion to the votes cast for various parties and that this would make for a more co-operative form of government.

Now I come for a moment or two to the budget. At last we have a "stable" government,
the government that the Prime Minister wanted. He made very entreating, very convincing
speeches to the country that he must have a majority in the House before he could bring
down legislation that was good for all the people, that he must not be hampered by
having to submit proposed legislation to the House and be humiliated possibly by having
it turned down. So he came back from the last election [in 1926] with a majority. He
was joined by our Liberal-Progressive friends, led by the Minister of Immigration (Mr.

Forke) who thought— and possibly still thinks—that the Prime Minister needed greater numbers to bring good government to Canada. I want to say here that my heart aches for the Minister of Immigration. He is an honest, but deluded man. So the Prime Minister comes back to the House with a majority, and now we are going to get legislation that is in the interests of all the people. We are going to get this thing that he has been desiring to give us since 1921. Last year, his first session, one could say that he had hardly begun, and the budget then brought down was not much; but we can overlook that. Now we come to the second year of his administration, and we get another budget. Well, if this budget is in the interests of the common people, then I certainly am not capable of representing their interests. We had the income tax reduced 10 per cent last session, and now there is another 10 per cent reduction, and we had the spectacle yesterday of the hon. member for North Battleford (Mr. McIntosh) getting up and entreating the rich men of the Dominion to make anonymous donations to wipe out the national debt. I do not understand why there should be all this modest anonymity ... The budget plays with the tariff just as a boy plays with marbles to see how many he can catch when he throws them in the air. There is no real reduction in the tariff. No one knows that better than the Minister of Finance. If there is any reduction at all it is on things bought by people who could very well afford to pay higher prices ...

Finally, Macphail talks about the budget but her remarks are limited because hers is mostly a political speech justifying her ideal form of government. She is sarcastic in describing Mackenzie King's plea in the 1926 election campaign for a "stable government." She also takes a swipe at Robert Forke, the former Progressive MP who is now King's minister of immigration. Macphail describes him as "an honest, but deluded man." The budget claims to reduce tariffs, Macphail says, but it just plays with them "as a boy plays with marbles." She uses the "marbles" simile here but it is worth noting that she does not often employ figures of speech. Her rhetoric is simple, unadorned, and declarative. We might ascribe that to the rural constituency from which she has emerged; but there was also a more widespread movement in North America in the early years of the century to replace the more decorative rhetoric of someone such as a Wilfrid Laurier with the brusque and plain-spoken language of a Teddy Roosevelt, to take an American example. Macphail would have been familiar with American rhetoric from her experience on the Chautauqua circuit. She is a plain speaker who is always colloquial. For the most part her remarks are off the cuff although there is evidence, in later years at least, that they were more carefully prepared. The budget, Macphail claims, reduces income taxes so much that one Liberal in the House has seriously proposed that rich people should be asked to donate anonymously toward reducing the national debt. She is contemptuous of that: Why, she asks, all this modest anonymity?

Now, a very great deal of criticism is directed to myself and others any time we try to point out that economic groups do function under parties, and that the only thing for us to do is to come out as an economic unit and find a place in this house, striving to have the rules and usages amended in order that our people may be given real representation ... and we say therefore that the only thing for us to do is to come out as an economic group—a class group, if you like, for I am not afraid of the word—and seek representation in the House of Commons—a genuine representation of the needs of our industry. Politics is a business, and agriculture being the basic industry in Canada, the most important single industry in the country, has a perfect right to find for itself honest and above-board representation in this House. I should not like to say that only functional or occupational groups should come to the House, but I do think that the two parties are simply that. I would not say that others should not come, but I do say that we live in an age of functional organization: and since political life is only a reflection of economic life it is only reasonable that these new class, or economic, or occupational groups in the country should seek re-election in the House of Commons and should not find it necessary—certainly I do not—to apologise for their place here.

When we have electoral reform, when the Canadian people grasp the idea more clearly, particularly when they know that the old parties are simply systems under which class groups operate we shall see an increase in groups. The day will come when members of our group, the members of the Labour group will increase, and when other groups not now named will appear and find representation in the chamber. When that happens the new groups will be too strong for either of the old parties to command a majority and carry on the government of the country in the old way. Modifications will have to be made and a new method found. It does seem to me exceedingly reasonable that the House of Commons and not the Prime Minister should decide when there should be dissolution.

Why should power be put into the hands of one man to determine when there will be dissolution of parliament and when the people of the country shall be called upon to bear the expenses of a general election? I know that some people have the idea that those of us who say these things are cranks. We are not. I am not saying, of course, that I am not, but I certainly say emphatically that the Canadian people are thinking new thoughts and that to them it does not seem at all reasonable that things should be as they are. Our institutions, whether educational or political, will change to meet the needs of changing times. That is only natural ...

I should hate to bear upon my shoulders the responsibility which rests today upon the shoulders of the Liberal-Progressive group in this house. They have done much to discourage progressive thought in Canada: they have, to my mind, a great deal to answer for. Indeed, I should not care to be the Liberal party: I should not care to bear the responsibility—I am not sure whether it is parliamentary—of false friendship such as they have shown towards the new groups in this house, from 1921 to this day. But speaking personally, I say it is better for them to realize that we are not people who will one day be Liberals: we have no such ambition. We represent agriculture. We are not Conservatives; we are agricultural representatives, and the sooner this house knows that, the sooner they quit wondering whether we are Tories or Liberals, the better it will be for all concerned.

Macphail, in her peroration, predicts that her hoped-for day of direct democracy will soon arrive. Rather than ending on this prophetic note, she cannot resist one final slap at the Liberal-Progressives, who opposed the party system but are now in the Liberal fold. Here her remarks almost resemble a sermon—she would "hate to bear" the responsibility for deception that rests upon them. She is equally scathing about the Liberals for having engaged in "false friendship"—a description that Macphail acknowledges flirts with being language the Speaker of the House might deem offensive and ask to have withdrawn. She ends by defending her position and that of other independents with self-deprecating humour. Her group, she says, is accused of being cranks. She may be one, she says impishly, but her colleagues are not. She ends with a defiant statement of support for her small, dissenting group of MPs: "We represent agriculture ... "

THE IMPACT OF MACPHAIL'S SPEECH

Agnes Macphail was a dominant parliamentary orator and her speech on the budget was filled with passion and barbs. The *Ottawa Journal* described it as "caustic criticism" and said that "she faced a well-filled House which laughed and cheered as shaft after shaft went home." The Liberals were annoyed and took the unusual step in the following days of having two of their MPs respond to Macphail in negative and personal terms. The milder of the two was Charles Dunning, the minister of railways. As a farm leader in Saskatchewan, he had rallied support for the Liberals. Later he ran for a provincial seat and became a cabinet minister. In 1925 he was a candidate and won in the federal election. Macphail in her speech had made a sarcastic reference to Saskatchewan Liberals and now Dunning responds directly. "I would like to say a few words with reference to group government, which was advocated so forcibly, so wittily and so cleverly yesterday by my hon friend from Southeast Grey ... We always enjoy her witticisms even at our own expense ... "

Dunning adds that while Macphail promotes "group government" in Canada as a progressive measure, it is, in fact a reactionary one. He cites Italy and Spain as examples of the "group system" producing dictatorships. He would have been referring in Spain to the pre-Franco dictatorship of General Primo de Rivera who took power in a bloodless coup in 1923. In Italy, Dunning was describing the rise of Benito Mussolini, who became prime minister in 1922 but established a dictatorship in 1925. There was great political and economic turmoil in Europe following the First World War. One of the solutions posed was corporatism, in which society would be organized around major interest groups, such as agricultural, business, and even the church. Autocrats and eventually fascists such as Mussolini used the corporatist philosophy as an excuse to eradicate representative democracy, which was weak in many European countries, and replace it with a fascist, strong-man rule.

It is unfair, however, to equate those examples to what Macphail and her colleagues are proposing. She is a populist democrat who argues that one group—big business—already has an undue influence on the political process through its access to the two old-line parties. She believes that the co-operative government she is proposing is more, and not less, democratic than parliamentary democracy as practised by the Liberals and Conservatives. Dunning's response is that Canada already has co-operative government and he expresses his resentment about the "abuse" that he and others receive from Macphail and members of the Ginger Group.

Ontario MP Mitch Hepburn makes an even more personal attack on Macphail. Hepburn is a political brawler who began his public life with the UFO before switching to the Liberals and getting elected federally in 1926. He says that Macphail advocates "occupational group government" but in so doing she does not represent the views of her constituents. He says that people in the Grey constituency vote for her because, as a female MP, she is a "novelty." He implies that she cannot truly represent women because she is not married: "The fact remains that they are still selling wedding rings, so I take it that the honourable member neither represents the sentiments of her riding nor the sentiments of women in this country." He then accuses Macphail of holding "extreme views" that would be harmful to Canada if she were in a position to put them into effect. Hepburn was to be re-elected in 1930 but chose in that same year to become leader of the provincial Liberals in Ontario and he later served as premier from 1934 to 1942.

Macphail's cherished ideas about democratic reform and co-operative government did not prevail. She continued to run for election as a radical Progressive and as a representative of the UFO even when that organization had ceased to exist as a political force. She began to co-operate with Woodsworth and the Ginger Group as early as 1924. In 1932, members of the group, along with academics from the League for Social Reconstruction, created the Co-operative Commonwealth Foundation (CCF) at a founding convention in Calgary. Macphail was not there but she approved. However, it was not until 1938 that she began to sit as a member of the CCF caucus. Although she was involved in the creation of a new party, she reserved her right to dissent from decisions taken by its caucus.

Macphail was the first female MP and an orator of renown. But she was, above all, a leading participant in a populist agrarian revolt that took a political turn. She and others disrupted the two-party system in Canada and created a tradition of multi-party parliaments. If Canada is better off with such a system than with a two-party arrangement such as that in the United States, then Agnes Macphail—a progressive in politics and an iconoclast in life—is one of the people to be thanked.

RICHARD BEDFORD BENNETT ON A NEW DEAL

JANUARY 2, 1935

"I am for reform. And, in my mind, reform means government intervention. It means government control and regulation. It means the end of laissez-faire."

R. B. Bennett was a large and a gruff man who favoured top hats and wore three-piece suits with watch fobs stretched across his ample paunch. A lawyer who had made a fortune in business, he was the caricature of a fat cat but he saw himself as a reformer. It was his misfortune to come to power in 1930 during the Great Depression and he was unable to tame it. He appointed his brother-in-law W. D. Herridge as Canada's ambassador to Washington in 1931 where Franklin Delano Roosevelt introduced his New Deal to reinvigorate the American economy. Roosevelt used the emerging medium of radio for fireside chats to win the battle for minds and hearts, speaking directly to the American people about what he was doing and why. Herridge sent long memos to Bennett urging him to do something similar. Bennett was reluctant but finally he decided to roll the dice. On January 2, 1935, he delivered the first of five radio addresses to the nation.

◆

Richard Bedford Bennett was born on July 3, 1870, in Hopewell Hill on the New Brunswick side of the Bay of Fundy and was the eldest of four children. His grandfather created a shipbuilding yard nearby to which Bennett's father, Henry, was apprenticed, later becoming a partner in the family firm. Henry had married Henrietta Stiles, a committed Methodist, a stern woman, and a teetotaler who emphasized austerity, hard work, and diligence. Henry was easier going, rather fond of drink, and ultimately not a success in business. He was forced to become a general merchant, blacksmith, and farmer and he did not prosper. Richard Bennett, called Dick by his family, never forgot the shame of those humble beginnings and he was determined to become rich. He took to heart his mother's advice about hard work and sobriety as well as her ambitions for him.

Tall, slim, and freckled, Bennett at age sixteen attended Normal School in Fredericton and became a teacher. In his spare time he worked at a law office and by 1890 he had saved enough money to attend law school at Dalhousie University in Halifax. He was a hard-working student who spent much of his time in the library and showed a keen interest in debating. Upon his graduation in 1893 he articled in a law office in Chatham, New Brunswick. The dean of law at Dalhousie recommended him to Senator James Lougheed, who had a lucrative law practice in Calgary. Bennett was hesitant to relocate to a raw western city that at the time was smaller than Chatham. However, he did decide to go west in 1897 at age twenty-six. When he got off the train in Calgary it was -40°F with a brisk wind and blowing snow. Bennett was a loner in a frontier town where he lived in a suite at the posh Palliser Hotel. He neither smoked nor drank and he read from Scripture every day. Even as a young man, he dressed more formally than his peers and reputedly was the first man in Calgary to wear a top hat. He possessed a restless energy and worked long hours. The Lougheed-Bennett practice grew rapidly, representing the Canadian Pacific Railway and a bevy of corporations, including those in the emerging oil industry. Bennett was an active investor in that industry as well as in companies involved in grain, meat-packing, cement, and hydro-electricity.

By the time he was elected as a Conservative to the House of Commons in 1911 Bennett was wealthy. He was generous with his money in a benevolent way—providing for his parents and siblings, and giving away 10 per cent of his income to students, widows, and a host of charities. He was also egotistical, judgmental, had an explosive temper, and was unforgiving of any slight, real or imagined. He expected a cabinet seat in Robert Borden's government and was bitterly disappointed when he did not receive one. Borden did appoint him in 1915 as director general of the National Service Board, whose task it was to determine the number of prospective military recruits in Canada. Bennett had actually attempted to enlist in 1915 but was turned down for medical reasons that have never been made public.

He chose not to run for election in 1917 and was angry when Borden did not keep what Bennett believed was a promise to appoint him to the Senate. He sent the prime minister a twenty-page letter of complaint but received no reply. Once out of politics, he threw himself into business and became deeply involved with the E. B. Eddy Company of Hull, Quebec. This connection arose as a result of his long friendship with Eddy's widow, Jennie Grahl Hunter Eddy, who Bennett had known since his youth in New Brunswick. When she died in 1921 she left her shares to him and to her younger brother. When the brother died in 1926, he willed the remaining shares to Bennett as well.

In 1920 Borden resigned as Conservative leader. The caucus chose Arthur Meighen as his successor and he invited Bennett back into politics. Bennett was narrowly defeated in the 1921 election, which Meighen lost to Mackenzie King and the Liberals. Bennett then engaged in a messy parting of ways with Senator Lougheed and set up his own law practice. Soon he was representing a prime roster of corporate clients. Most of his income, though, was derived from his investments and numerous corporate directorships. In 1925 Meighen lured Bennett back into politics once again and offered him the justice portfolio should the Conservatives win the election. This time Bennett won in Calgary with a comfortable majority, and across Canada the Conservatives took 116 seats to the Liberals' ninety-nine. However, King stubbornly clung to power in a coalition until his government fell. Meighen succeeded him briefly but there was another election in 1926. The Conservatives lost to King, Meighen resigned, and in 1927 Bennett, who was by then fifty-seven years old, succeeded him. Bennett proved to be an effective opposition leader who rebuilt the party's electoral machinery and, in the July 1930 election, the Conservatives won convincingly. In addition to his prime ministerial duties, Bennett took on the portfolios of finance and external affairs. He found it difficult to delegate responsibility. There was a joke about that if Bennett was seen talking to himself as he walked the streets of Ottawa, he was actually holding a cabinet meeting. He was a formidable figure in the House of Commons who spoke in such a rapid fire way that he became known as "Bonfire Bennett."

◆

King was prime minister when the US stock market crashed in October 1929—an event triggered by the failure of risky and unregulated investments. The Great Depression was to last for a decade and it spilled over into every country. The Canadian economy, heavily dependent upon the export of raw materials, was hit hard when those markets evaporated. Between 1929 and 1933 Canada's gross domestic product fell by 42 per cent and fully one-third of the labour force was out of work. The depression was accompanied by an extended and punishing drought in Western Canada where wheat prices fell by 90 per cent within two years. Across the country, bread lines, soup kitchens, and homelessness became the order of the day. People were desperate and frightened and began to question the very foundations of the economic system.

The prevailing economic wisdom was that the market was a law unto itself and that there should be no interference with it. In the United States, for example, President Hoover did not believe it was the government's responsibility to create jobs or provide economic relief to beleaguered citizens. In Canada, Mackenzie King was of much the same opinion. He insisted that the problem was short term and that looking after those without jobs or homes was the responsibility of local governments. By the spring of 1930, Bennett's opposition Conservatives were demanding action. King made clear his lack of empathy when he said that he might be prepared to discuss the matter with Western provinces led by "progressive" premiers. Then he added: "But, I would not give a single cent to any Tory government."

DENNIS GRUENDING

King came to regret those words. During the 1930 election campaign Bennett attacked him incessantly and promised action if elected. He won and six weeks later called a special session of Parliament to deal with unemployment. His government provided twenty million dollars for relief, equivalent to four per cent of the federal budget, a significant amount. Bennett's major thrust, though, was to raise tariffs on manufactured goods in the belief that Canadian industries would prosper behind the protective wall and create jobs for the unemployed. That provided no solace to farmers and others who relied on foreign markets to sell products such as wheat and timber. Bennett also attempted to negotiate preferential tariffs with Commonwealth countries, particularly Great Britain, but with little success.

The depression did not melt away as both industrialists and Bennett had predicted. By 1932 his government was creating relief camps in remote areas to warehouse young men without work. The economic crisis spawned unrest and agitation. Two new political movements, the Co-operative Commonwealth Federation (CCF) and Social Credit, arose in Western Canada. The CCF in particular demanded that government play a much larger role in the economy. Bennett churlishly denounced his critics and promised to crush them under "the iron heel of capitalism." He turned police loose on protestors at the slightest provocation and he insulted people forced onto relief. Their forebearers, he said, "did not ask governments to be a wet nurse to every derelict."

South of the border, Franklin Delano Roosevelt took a different approach. When he won the Democratic Party nomination at a convention in Chicago in July 1932, Roosevelt boldly promised "a new deal for the American people." It would provide economic recovery to industry and agriculture, relief to the unemployed, and reform of the financial system. Newspaper headlines and radio reports picked up on the "new deal" phrase and it soon became a permanent fixture in the American lexicon. Roosevelt was inaugurated as president on March 4, 1933, and in that speech he delivered his famous remark that "the only thing we have to fear is fear itself." However, there was soon a wave of bank failures. Roosevelt closed them all for four days and within a week Congress passed emergency legislation providing for federal deposit insurance. When the banks reopened, Roosevelt went on radio to deliver the first of his fireside chats. He spoke directly to an estimated sixty million Americans, using a medium that was quickly becoming commonplace. People gathered around trunk-sized radio sets in their living rooms, all listening to the same speech. Roosevelt talked about the banking crisis and described what he was doing to solve it. He assured Americans that everything was under control. He asked for calm, and it worked. The nation's banks were reopened and within a few days it became obvious that deposits were greater than withdrawals.

While Roosevelt's radio speeches appeared informal and effortless, they were finely crafted and rigorously edited. He employed a group of writers and advisors who came to be known as his "brains trust." They worked closely with him, meeting in a cabinet room adjacent to the Oval Office and at times even sleeping over at the White House. Roosevelt's speeches went through as many as a dozen drafts, with each being provided to the president for his perusal and comment. By the time they were completed he was intimately familiar with each word. Roosevelt told his writers that he wanted to speak to Americans in language they would understand. Samuel Rosenman, one of those writers, was to say: "[Roosevelt] looked for words that he would use in an informal conversation with one or two of his friends." The president's overriding intention was to reassure Americans and he warned his writers to avoid dramatic oratory. The fireside chats are credited with maintaining Roosevelt's popularity through perilous times and allowing him to pursue his New Deal agenda.

◆

Bennett's brother-in-law William Duncan Herridge was watching all of this closely. Bennett had appointed him as Canada's ambassador to Washington. Herridge was a handsome patent lawyer from Ottawa who had been decorated for bravery in the First World War. He knew Mackenzie King since childhood because his family had a neighbouring cottage at Harrington Lake in the Gatineau Hills near Ottawa. Herridge was close to King and a supporter but he later turned on the prime minister. He was upset over what he considered to be King's shoddy treatment of Governor General Lord Byng, who was one of Herridge's friends. Herridge had been married to the daughter of a wealthy Ottawa industrialist but his wife died in 1925. At some point prior to the 1930 election Herridge had lunch with Bennett and his vivacious younger sister Mildred. She was so close a confidante that she lived with the bachelor prime minister in his suite at the Chateau Laurier Hotel. She possessed the social and diplomatic graces that he lacked. It was she who protected him as much as was possible from social gaffes. She described herself at one point as the "bumper on his car." Bennett was impressed with Herridge at their lunch. When the election contest began in May 1930 Herridge was among a small entourage, which included Mildred, to accompany Bennett on his campaign rail car. Herridge gave policy advice and wrote speeches, providing some of Bennett's most memorable lines during that campaign. Mildred was obviously impressed because they became secretly engaged and were married in April 1931. Bennett appointed Herridge to Washington later in the same year.

Herridge was a cultivated individual and charming, as was Mildred, and they were popular on the diplomatic circuit in Washington. He was on friendly terms with members of Roosevelt's New Deal advisors. Dean Acheson, who was Roosevelt's undersecretary of the treasury and later served under President Harry Truman, was a friend. He described Herridge as "one of the ablest diplomats this country has received." Herridge used his privileged access to arrange for Bennett to have a private lunch with Roosevelt in April 1933 when the prime minister visited Washington. When, in May of that year, Roosevelt used one of his fireside chats to report on the New Deal, Herridge would have listened to it in minute detail.

Herridge was soon sending numerous and lengthy memos to his brother-in-law. In August 1933 he told Bennett that Canada should push for construction of a St. Lawrence Waterway as a major make-work project. "In the language of one of the phrase-makers of the NRA [National Recovery Administration]," Herridge wrote, "we simply prime the engine." That described Roosevelt's decision to use government spending on public works to reinvigorate the economy. In January 1934 Herridge proposed a "Bennett Recovery Programme." He wrote again in April. He said that he was not impressed by the New Deal's accomplishments, which he believed were oversold. But he was captivated by Roosevelt's masterful promotion of it on radio. Herridge wanted Bennett to follow Roosevelt's lead. In June 1934 he wrote to say, "The old fashioned Toryism is dead." His message in July was that "government is now in business ... to stay."

Eventually Bennett decided to accept Herridge's proposition, although he was to remain uneasy about it. He was at least open to convincing for several reasons. He was immensely frustrated about his inability to tame the depression. By 1933 he had become the butt of jokes. For example, cars towed by horses because owners could not afford gasoline were called Bennett buggies. He considered himself a reformer but believed he had gone as far as he dared in spending to combat the depression. As an election year approached in 1935 he faced a dire political situation. The Conservatives lost provincial elections in Ontario and Saskatchewan. The federal party also lost four of five by-elections. In addition, there was the resignation of Harry Stevens, a popular Conservative minister and one of the few progressives in cabinet. He had been roundly condemned by his cabinet colleagues for his speeches criticizing big business and they wanted him to apologize. He refused and sent a bitter letter of resignation to Bennett. The prime minister responded in kind, talking about "rodent[s]" escaping the government ship. Both men released their letters to the press. Bennett's heated antagonism to Stevens was seen by many people through the lens of a cartoon capitalist shutting down a champion of ordinary Canadians.

◆

Herridge was home for the summer in 1934 and retreated to his cottage at Harrington Lake to work on the new deal speeches. Bennett's private secretary Roderick Finlayson, a lawyer from Winnipeg who had worked with the prime minister since 1931, accompanied Herridge. According to Finlayson, he met Bennett in 1929 when the Conservative leader spoke at a partisan event in Winnipeg. Finlayson, who admits that he had too much to drink, disagreed vocally with Bennett's version of Canada's relationship to the British Empire. Bennett approached him following the event and told him that he had spoken well. Bennett won the election in 1930 and the next year he had his personal secretary call Finlayson to offer him a job. One of Finlayson's tasks as Bennett's advisor was to write speeches. But he claims that the inspiration for the new deal speeches came entirely from Herridge.

When Herridge returned from Washington that summer, Finlayson met him at the Ottawa train station and they immediately went to work at the cottage. Herridge was a good cook so they enjoyed meals after each day's work, accompanied, according to Finlayson, by a plentiful supply of imported Scotch whisky. When at summer's end Herridge returned to Washington, he left Finlayson with a bulky memorandum that contained an outline of the proposed speeches. They mirrored Herridge's language in his spate of memos to Bennett over the previous year. Herridge asked Finlayson to "sell" the speeches to the prime minister. Finlayson was uneasy with some of the content and would only promise to hand them over to Bennett without comment.

Bennett had been in Geneva during September and much of October of 1934 at meetings of the League of Nations. Upon his return, Finlayson provided him with the material. Bennett seized on the word "reform," mentioned often in the speeches. He reached for a nearby copy of Hansard and showed Finlayson his first speech in the House of Commons. Bennett said that it demonstrated his pedigree as a reformer. When Herridge next returned to Ottawa, the three men met. Bennett asked for an opinion on the speeches and Finlayson said that they were too general in nature. Herridge disagreed. He believed that the magic of the new deal was in the concept and warned against providing too much information about policies and programs. For him, this was to be largely an exercise in public relations. Roosevelt's speeches had sparked a recovery in national confidence and Herridge hoped that Bennett could do the same.

Herridge's strategy was for Bennett to secure radio time (he did so, paying out of his own pocket) and deliver a series of five evening radio addresses early in January 1935. The plan was that Bennett would then move quickly to call an election. The prime minister set the stage for the radio addresses by speaking in five cities during December. Herridge spoke on an economic reform theme to a Canadian Club luncheon in Ottawa at mid-month. Late in December, Bennett's office issued a news release saying that he would make a series of radio broadcasts in January over a network of forty stations. Finlayson arranged with the press gallery to release the text of the first speech in order to get maximum coverage in the morning newspapers. On the evening of January 2, Bennett stood in front of a microphone at Ottawa's CRCO Radio. The station had been part of a network owned by the Canadian National Railway but which in 1933 was taken over by the new Canadian Radio Broadcasting Commission.

Bennett made history as the first prime minister to speak directly via radio to a pan-Canadian audience. His use of Herridge and Finlayson to craft the radio speeches was also new. For the most part, prime ministers who came before Bennett, including Macdonald, Laurier, and Meighen, prepared their own speeches and delivered them extemporaneously. Radio is a medium that suggests natural speech but ironically the presence of studio microphones and the need to talk to time make it more likely that remarks will be scripted—as they were for R. B. Bennett on January 2, 1935.

BENNETT'S SPEECH

The time has come when I must speak to you with the utmost frankness about our national affairs, for your understanding of them is essential to your welfare. This is a critical hour in the history of our country. Momentous questions await your decision. Our future course must now be charted. There is one course, I believe with all my heart, which will lead us to security. It is for you to decide whether we will take it. I am confident that your decision will be the right one, when, with care and diligence, you have studied the facts. Then you will support the action which your judgement decrees to be imperative; you will strive for its success, for its success will determine the future of Canada.

Bennett begins in a dramatic fashion and addresses his radio listeners in the first person. This is a style of speaking that differs from parliamentary debates. On radio, Bennett's sentences are brief and simple in construction, as is appropriate for the medium. He indicates that he will appeal to his listeners with facts and logical argument. However, he also uses ethos in this speech, speaking from the heart in an attempt to win sympathy from his listeners. This is a gamble because he has become a most unpopular figure during the long years of the depression.

In the last five years, great changes have taken place in the world. The old order is gone. It will not return. We are living amidst conditions which are new and strange to us. Your prosperity demands [changes] in the old system, so that, in these new conditions, that old system may adequately serve you. The right time to bring about these changes has come. Further progress without them is improbable. To understand what changes and corrections should be made, you must first understand the facts of the present situation. To do that, you should have clearly in mind what has taken place in the past five years; the ways in which we have made progress, the ways in which we have not. To do that— to decide wisely—you must be in a position to judge those acts of government which have palliated your hardships, which have preserved intact our industrial and financial structure, and which have prepared the way for the reforms which must now take place.

Canadians are not those from whom unpleasant facts should be concealed. The people of this country were born optimists, but they were born realists as well. They demand the truth, however disturbing it may be. And the truth IS disturbing. The world is in tragic circumstances. The signs of recovery are few and doubtful. The signs of trouble are many, and they do not lessen. The world is searching pathetically for safety and prosperity. It will find them only when each nation, resolute to effect its own regeneration, will come to a meeting place with all the others, in the spirit which declares that even the most powerful among them has no real economic independence of the rest. That time has not yet come. Meanwhile, dangers abound.

Bennett tells his audience that he will explain the changes that have occurred in the world, but he does not immediately provide any details. Rather, he shifts to a dark statement about the old order being gone. Then, after providing brief praise to Canadians as being both optimists and realists, he continues with alarming descriptors about "tragic circumstances." This is in contrast to Roosevelt's approach. During a time of despair and uncertainty, Roosevelt wanted, through his calm and confident tone and demeanour, to convince Americans that all would be well. Bennett, on the other hand, engages in almost apocalyptic talk and his remarks are anything but reassuring. The difference may be that Bennett is preparing for an election while Roosevelt had won his and was selling his program. Still one must question the tactics of Bennett and Herridge. They want to establish Bennett as the country's saviour from disaster; but he has been in power during five years of the depression so it is difficult to cast him as the one who can conquer it. Further, no good speech writer would use the phrase "palliated your hardships." Bennett is referring to actions of his government that may have made the depression less severe but did not remove its causes—hence the need for real reform; he could well have used a simpler term.

This discussion of our national affairs will take time. It must be thorough. All phases of the situation will be dealt with, for it is vital that you be put in complete possession of the facts. To accomplish this, I have decided upon a series of half-hour broadcast talks. I ask you to give me your earnest and patient attention. I wish with all my heart that I had nothing but good news for you.

When one has been head of the government of this country for more than four years and has done his level best, and has worked with all his might to bring you security, it is with inexpressible regret that he speaks as I must now speak to you. But the facts, grave as they are, do not cast me down. Nor will they you. I am deeply anxious, but I can never doubt this country's coming triumph if you will range yourselves on the side of progress and reform. For then we will fight on, you and I, and we will win.

Bennett appeals to a combination of ethos and pathos. He wants his listeners to be on the side of "progress and reform," which he has yet to define in any way. But he also extends a plea for sympathy: he has done his best, he has worked hard, he is "deeply anxious," but he believes that the battle can be won. Then he begins an apologia for his government's record. He has a problem, though, because in the 1930 election campaign he criticized Mackenzie King roundly, and with justification, for doing little to combat the emerging depression.

First of all, I shall have a few words to say about conditions as they were in 1930, and as they have been since that time. Then I shall tell you what the policy of the government has been during that unhappy period. I shall discuss the nature of the measures taken by the government. You will realize that they were the only ones which the circumstances permitted. You will say, I think, that they were the only ones which were wise. I shall then show you that the time has come for a radical change in the policy of the Government. You will, I know, agree upon its necessity and approve its timeliness. I shall exactly explain what this policy is and develop my plans for its execution. After you are fully acquainted with what has taken place and with the conditions of today, I am confident that this policy will receive your enthusiastic support. Without your support, I am unable to carry it out. Therefore, when you have had an opportunity to thoroughly examine the whole condition of affairs, I will ask you for a decision. You will not be hurried. You will have ample time to test this programme of reform and to decide upon its value. I will then invite your considered opinion as to whether reform is in fact necessary, and as to whether my programme of reform is wise. If you say yes, then I will not rest until I have put it into operation. But if you say no—if you are satisfied with conditions as they now are, if you think that there is not need for reform, if you feel that the government is not required to do anything more—then I am not willing to continue in this office. For if you believe that things should be left as they are, you and I hold contrary and irreconcilable views. I am for reform.

And, in my mind, reform means government intervention. It means government control and regulation. It means the end of laissez-faire. Reform heralds certain recovery. There can be no permanent recovery without reform. Reform or no reform! I raise that issue squarely. I nail the flag of progress to the masthead. I summon the power of the state to its support.

In the 1930 election Bennett had rashly promised to end the depression or "perish in the attempt"—but he had failed. Now he must defend the measures taken by his government. He wanted to do more, he says, but conditions would not allow it. Consider that Roosevelt was elected during the same depression. He had acted boldly in 1933 and his brains trust had helped him to expertly publicize that activity. Bennett, however, had dithered and lived in denial. Now, he says, it is time for a radical change in government policy. He sets up a straw man argument for his listeners. If they are satisfied and see no need for reform then he will resign. He promises "the end of laissez-faire" and he equates reform with government intervention in the economy. His language here is almost a verbatim lift from the memos that Herridge had sent from Washington in 1933 and '34: Herridge had written: "The policy of laissez-faire must be abandoned."

Who will oppose our plan of progress? It will be interesting and instructive to see. It seems to me that the party which supports laissez-faire, which demands that Government does not interfere with business, which says that the state has no such part to play in these critical times—it seems to me that that party may have a change of heart when it sees how the rest of us feel about the matter, and may decide to come along with you and me. Well, if it will denounce its hereditary chieftain, which is reaction, abandon its creed of inaction, and pledge its allegiance to action, to progress, to reform—it will be welcome if it is really sincere. For I am working, and working grimly, to one end only: to get results. And so, honest support from every quarter from men and women of good will, of every party, race and creed, I hope for and heartily invite.

There must be unity of purpose. There can be no success without it. I earnestly entreat you, be in no doubt upon that point. I am not. If I cannot have your whole-hearted support, it is wrong for me to assume the terrible responsibility of leadership in these times. I am willing to go on, if you make it possible for me still to serve you. But if there is anyone better able to do so, I shall gladly make way for him. And it is your duty to yourselves to support him, and not me. Your country's future is at stake. This is no time to indulge your personal prejudices or fancies. Carefully and calmly, look well into the situation. Then pick the man and the policy best fitted to deal with it. And resolutely back that man and that policy. The nation should range itself behind them. In war you fought as one. Fight now again as one. For the task ahead demands your war-time resolution and your war-time unity.

Bennett is attempting to lay a trap for the Liberals, as he had discussed with Herridge. The radio speeches are part of a calculation to build support for his proposed reforms and to lure Mackenzie King into opposing them and thus defending the status quo. Bennett asks a rhetorical question about who might oppose his reforms. Of course, he is talking about Mackenzie King. Then he returns to his earlier threat to step aside, saying that he will resign if there is someone better equipped to lead. These are odd statements. There had earlier been speculation, some of it fuelled by Bennett himself, that he would not lead the party into the 1935 election. But in October he had decided to stay on, in large part because he did not want to be succeeded by his nemesis Harry Stevens. Bennett's remarks in the radio speech then can be understood only as an empty and rhetorical threat.

In the beginning of its term of office, the policy of the government was determined by the critical nature of the times. The economic system had broken down. Dismay and uncertainty prevailed. We were storm-tossed in turbulent seas. Swift and decisive measures were needed to avert shipwreck. The emergency demanded emergency action. It was no time for changes or reforms in the economic system. The only sensible thing was to get behind the system and make the best of it, until the fury of the storm had abated. This your government did. We gave unswerving support to finance. We stood behind industry. We aided agriculture in all the ways we might. You know what we did. It was singularly effective. Look at conditions in your country during the worst period of the depression, and compare them with conditions in other countries. I think you will agree that our relatively fortunate state is the surest proof that your government faithfully supported our people in their splendid struggle against the depression.

This government was not long in office before demands for reform were made upon it. Such demands were natural. But, in your interest, they could not then be heeded. The ship was pounding in mountainous seas. That was not the time to try to recondition it. We had first to save the ship and guide it into less troubled waters. I do not think that even my most irrational opponent will cavil at the sanity of that course ...

You will see that a false step might have led us to disaster. I ask you to pass judgement upon these points. I ask you to say whether the government's emergency measures were sound. When you have done so, you will then be required to determine whether the government's new policy of reform is also right and whether we have chosen the proper time to introduce it.

Now, you will understand that by recovery measures I mean measures which work no change in the economic system. They are emergency measures designed to support the system during the depression, but do not interfere with its operation, and do not, of course, contemplate any modification or correction in it. Recovery measures of the proper kind minimize the dangers and ameliorate the hardships incident to the depression. They also stimulate the movement toward recovery. This kind of assistance is sometimes known as "priming the pump."

Reform measures, on the other hand, are measures designed to effect a change in the existing system. They are measures to be taken when it has been decided that the existing system is faulty in some major or minor respect, and that this fault must be cured before the system can satisfactorily function again. These reforms may be, as you can imagine, of very many different types and of varying significance; but, whatever their importance or character, they are all refutations of the old idea that government should leave business alone. This old doctrine is known to some people as the doctrine of laissez-faire, and it originated at a time when business as we now understand it, was very young and, presumably, very innocent.

Measures of reform should normally, of course, be initiated and carried out, not in times of depression, but in times of comparative prosperity. That is obvious. Indeed, I suppose that ideal and timely measures of reform might avert a depression by removing the causes of it. But we never have worked ideally, and probably we never will. So if, through lack of reform, depression follows, the next best thing is to introduce reform as soon as the conditions of the depression will permit. I did not have a chance to effect reforms before the days of the depression. I will be perfectly candid and tell you that, in those days, I doubt whether anyone fully realized the need of reform. How much I wish that in this country or in the world there had been a man with vision to see the abyss upon which we were rushing and with power of action to arrest the movement. I say, I did not have a chance before the depression. This is my first opportunity. I am determined to take it. In fact, I have seized upon it already, as will soon be disclosed to you …

Here Bennett returns to his apologia and he employs a rare extended metaphor about turbulent seas and avoiding shipwreck to explain his government's lack of action. He defends that inaction by saying he had to delay until the fury of the storm had abated. Demands for action were natural, he says, but he could not heed them until he had righted the ship of state. Now the time is right for bolder action, for true reform rather than emergency measures.

Nowhere in this first speech does Bennett describe what those reform measures might be. This was to be primarily a public relations but not a policy exercise. But after the first speech, Finlayson argued that Bennett should provide more detail. In the second and subsequent addresses Bennett did talk about unemployment, agriculture, the Bank of Canada and financial reform; but in the first thirty-minute speech he stuck only to generalities that were not convincing. In his fifth and final address, Bennett trained his guns on the Liberals. If his listeners wanted the status quo, he said, they should support the Liberals; if they wanted change, he was their man.

Bennett and Herridge would have been wise to have more closely imitated Roosevelt not only in tone and diction but also in his views about overexposure. The president resisted when some of his advisors wanted him to go on radio more frequently. One of them described Roosevelt's "dread" that if he spoke too frequently his talks would lose their effectiveness. Bennett did not often speak on radio but his choice to do so for five nights within ten days was unwise. His "brains trust" was decidedly modest as compared to Roosevelt's and he was not as skilled a communicator. As one commentator put it, the broadcasts were not so much reassuring fireside chats as they were evangelical sermons from the mount.

THE IMPACT OF BENNETT'S SPEECH

Bennett's new deal speeches had an immediate, if brief, impact upon the fortunes and morale of the Conservatives. The party claimed that his final address on January 12 had an audience of eight million Canadians. That hardly seems possible since the country had a population of only eleven million at the time, including children, and not everyone had a radio. The addresses did, however, create a stir. Stephen Leacock, the noted McGill University economist and an active Conservative, wrote that the speeches had "quickened the spirit of the country." CCF Member of Parliament Angus MacInnis suggested mischievously that Bennett cross the floor and join the democratic socialists.

The addresses caught Bennett's cabinet and caucus completely off guard because he had not bothered to consult them. Once the shock had subsided, at least some of the party's stalwarts were hopeful and guardedly optimistic. Former leader Robert Borden said that the speeches had "animated" the Conservatives and provided them with new hope. Minister of Railways Robert Manion approved and, from the West, perennial candidate John Diefenbaker said the speeches had been received with enthusiasm. On the other hand, Arthur Meighen, who Bennett had appointed to the Senate, was not impressed and in a private conversation the two men exchanged sharp words. Charles Cahan, a cabinet minister from Montreal, was so upset that he planned to resign. He was close to business interests in what was then Canada's primary financial centre. They urged him to stay and oppose Bennett's proposals from within cabinet.

The reaction from the press was mixed but mainly negative. The *Montreal Gazette*, long considered a mouthpiece for business and the Conservative Party, attacked Bennett even before he had made the last of his speeches. On January 7, the *Gazette* accused him of trying to copy Roosevelt in his national recovery plans and quoted *The Wall Street Journal* as saying that those plans were failing. On January 10, a *Gazette* editorial accused Bennett of "acute pessimism" at a time when business leaders were predicting that "happy days" were just around the corner.

The *Winnipeg Free Press* was a staunchly Liberal newspaper whose editor John Dafoe had been a confidant of Laurier's and to a lesser extent of King's. Dafoe now engaged in a campaign to undercut Bennett and used his staff to assist. In a January 4 memo that began "Dear chief," Grant Dexter, the Ottawa correspondent for the *Free Press* reported to Dafoe on some Parliamentary Press Gallery gossip. Dexter said that people believed Bennett had "made rather a mess" of his first speech. He had rushed through it, "stumbled and fumbled," and was "not his usual oratorical self." Dexter also described "trouble in cabinet" with at least four ministers opposed to what they had heard in the speeches. Dexter believed that Bennett's and Herridge's plan was to accept any challenge from opposition leader Mackenzie King as a pretext to call a snap election. Here Dexter had information most useful to the Liberals. It was provided, perhaps inadvertently, by Grattan O'Leary who wrote for the *Ottawa Journal* and was sympathetic to the Conservatives. Dexter said that on the afternoon of the first broadcast, Bennett had called O'Leary into his office. Bennett showed him a draft of the first two speeches and asked for his opinion. O'Leary said that the speech lacked detail. Bennett replied that his main goal was to arouse public interest. Bennett then confided to O'Leary that he could not be more specific in his speeches about measures to be taken because the follow-up legislation had not yet been drafted.

Dexter reported to Dafoe again on January 7, saying that opinion in the Conservative caucus was "gradually crystallizing" against Bennett's policy announcements and the "two interlopers"—Herridge and Finlayson. Later in January, Chester Bloom, the *Free Press* correspondent in Washington wrote to Dafoe to say that Herridge was the major author of the speeches. Bloom promised to undertake a comparison of Bennett's remarks with those of Roosevelt. He also confided that Herridge was close to the "New Deal crowd" in Washington and cultivated them. It is clear from their correspondence that neither Dafoe nor his correspondents approved of Roosevelt's New Deal.

Mackenzie King raged against Bennett's speeches in his diary. They were, he wrote, an exercise in "nauseating self-sufficiency and egoism" and they filled him with "indignation too great for utterance." Yet he claimed that Bennett had "plagiarized" his ideas from King's book *Industry and Humanity*, published in 1918. That begs a question. King had been prime minister for years and could well have put his own ideas into practice—but he had not done so.

Bennett's aide Roderick Finlayson had been given the task of drafting the Speech from the Throne, which would open the parliamentary session and tout Bennett's new deal. In a memoir Finlayson recounts how at a meeting of their "troika," Bennett and Herridge had an argument about the speech. As a result Bennett banished Herridge from the office and he returned to Washington. Bennett and Finlayson completed the speech, which was a toned-down synopsis of the radio addresses. The governor general delivered it in Parliament on January 17, 1935.

King, despite his private fuming, made a key strategic decision that may have been informed by intelligence provided by Dafoe and other Liberals, not to mention Grattan O'Leary. Rather than challenging Bennett's new deal and opposing it, King urged him to introduce the legislation immediately so that it could be debated in the House of Commons. Bennett, of course, was not ready. He did introduce several bills, including those on a minimum wage, maximum hours of work, and a weekly day of rest. These would ratify the International Labour Organization treaties to which Canada had consented.

Then in February Bennett became ill with fainting spells. He was overworked, overweight, and under great stress, much of it self-induced because he failed to delegate work and responsibility. He spent four weeks in bed in his Chateau Laurier suite. The Conservatives were left in an embarrassing lurch because he had kept the contents of the proposed reform bills to himself. The Liberals made legislative life even more difficult by offering little or no opposition and calling on the Conservatives to keep their promises regarding numerous pieces of new deal legislation. The cabinet bickered over the legislation, watering much of it down; and from his sick bed even Bennett appeared to be retreating from his zealous radio broadcasts.

He was well enough to travel to England to celebrate the King's jubilee in May. Given his poor health, there had been some jockeying in cabinet in anticipation of his retirement. He wanted at all costs to prevent Harry Stevens from succeeding him and in June he informed his MPs that he would lead the party into the election. Stevens was banished from caucus and went on to create the Reconstruction Party, which threatened to drain votes away from the Conservatives in the election. When that election occurred on October 14, it became clear that people were tired of Bennett and the Conservatives. The Liberals won 173 seats to just thirty-nine for the Conservatives, a stunning loss of ninety-five seats compared to 1930. New parties also appeared on the scene. Social Credit won seventeen seats and the CCF won seven. Stevens also won a lone seat for his Reconstruction Party. The Conservatives were not to taste power again until John Diefenbaker won with a minority government twenty-two years later.

There is an enduring debate among historians about whether Bennett was a sincere reformer or just a poseur using his radio addresses in a desperate attempt to win re-election. What is beyond debate, however, is that those addresses represent a watershed moment. In them a prime minister signalled that the days of laissez-faire capitalism, in which only the market ruled, were over. The government, Bennett insisted, did have a larger role to play in the economy and in providing security for its citizens.

The new deal broadcasts helped to make that philosophy respectable and did so in a medium heard by millions of people. Mackenzie King, prodded by the CCF and the expectations of Canadians following the Second World War, introduced much of what Bennett had promised but never delivered. Bennett's message—death bed conversion or not—was one that has informed governments to this day.

TOMMY DOUGLAS
ON MEDICARE

OCTOBER 13, 1961

*"It is not a new principle ... when we're talking about
medical care we're talking about our sense of values."*

*Tommy Douglas was one of Canada's great political orators. He was involved in
theatre and debating while studying for the church ministry at Brandon College.
Douglas further honed his speaking skills as a Baptist preacher in Weyburn,
Saskatchewan, during the Great Depression, which led him to look to politics for
solutions to widespread poverty. He won election to the House of Commons in 1935
but in 1944 he returned to Saskatchewan and led the Co-operative Commonwealth
Federation (CCF) to electoral victory. He promised that his government would provide
for publicly financed health care when the province could afford it. That came about in
1961, when the legislation was introduced and Douglas spoke to what would become
the first such plan in North America. That set the stage for a tense standoff with the
CCF and its supporters on one side, and the political opposition along with doctors and
health insurance companies on the other.*

◆

Thomas Clement (Tommy) Douglas was born on October 20, 1904, in
Falkirk, Scotland. His parents, Annie Clement and Thomas Douglas, also
had two younger daughters and theirs was a family where grandparents
played an important role. Thomas was a skilled tradesman who volunteered

to fight in the Boer War. A few years after his return, the family left a deteriorating economy in Scotland and immigrated to Winnipeg. Thomas found work there in a foundry. However, that life was disrupted when he enlisted to serve in a Scottish ambulance unit during the First World War. His young family returned to Glasgow to live in cramped quarters with Annie's parents. Tommy Douglas soon withdrew from school to work in a cork factory to help support his mother and siblings. When the war ended, the family returned to Winnipeg where they lived in a multi-ethnic neighbourhood and Thomas again found skilled work.

The younger Douglas, age fourteen, and a friend watched from a rooftop in June 1919 when police on horseback charged the crowd during the Winnipeg General Strike. A worker was killed in the melee. One of the strike supporters was Reverend James Shaver Woodsworth, the Methodist minister at All People's Mission, which provided services to Winnipeg's immigrant slum dwellers. Douglas frequented the mission, participating in youth events and using the gym and library. Woodsworth had become a leading proponent of the Protestant social gospel, which attempted to apply Christian principles to social conditions. That led him to a passion for social reform and eventually into politics.

Douglas was a precocious young man although his formal education was limited. He left school and found work as an apprentice in a printer's shop where he spent five years and earned his papers as a journeyman. He was an avid reader, became involved in amateur theatre, and was a Scout leader. He also took up boxing and in 1922 he won the flyweight championship for Manitoba, a title he defended successfully the following year. By then, and perhaps incongruously, he decided to enrol in Brandon College to study full-time for the ministry. He completed his high school matriculation at the college and then entered its Faculty of Arts. It was at Brandon that his intellectual formation began in earnest. His studies and life experience led him to believe, as Woodsworth did, that Christianity should be more concerned with improving conditions in this world than with an afterlife. Douglas did well in his courses, competing for the academic gold medal in three of his four years. He became a champion debater, participated in drama, and took classes in elocution. In his final year he served as president of the student body. He paid for his education by preaching at Sunday services and delivering monologues and poetry recitations at church suppers and service club meetings. He was especially fond of Scottish poet Robert Burns and memorized much of his work. While filling in as a preacher in nearby Carberry, he met a young farm woman named Irma Dempsey who was to become his wife.

Following his ordination in 1930, Douglas and Irma moved to Weyburn, Saskatchewan, where he became the minister of Calvary Baptist Church. The depression had begun and in Saskatchewan it was accompanied by a prolonged drought and dust bowl. Under Douglas the church became a drop-in centre for the poor and unemployed. He became involved in a new Independent Labour group that was building ties with an increasingly politicized farm movement. Douglas became a farmer-labour candidate in the 1934 provincial election. He was defeated but the new party elected five members to the legislature. At the national level, farm and labour groups met in Calgary in 1932 to create the Co-operative Commonwealth Federation (CCF). The party's 1933 convention in Regina stated boldly in its manifesto that it would not rest until capitalism in Canada had been replaced by a full program of socialized planning. The new party also made it clear that it was committed to non-violence and democratic means.

Douglas missed the 1932 convention in Calgary because he was completing long-distance studies for a master's degree in sociology from McMaster University in Hamilton. During those studies he had unfortunately become enamoured with eugenics, a belief that through social engineering, societies could improve the human population. Policies advocated by eugenicists included prohibiting marriage in some cases and the forced sterilization of people deemed unfit to be parents. That list often included those with mental or physical disabilities, convicted criminals, and members of minority groups. Eugenics had been developed as a theory in England and had both an academic and a popular following across the political spectrum in Europe, the United States, and Canada in the early 1900s. Nellie McClung was a prominent advocate and supported the passage of eugenics legislation in Alberta in 1928. Judge Emilie Murphy, a member with McClung of the "famous five" women involved in the

Person's Case, was an even more outspoken advocate of eugenics and forced sterilization.

Douglas, in his thesis based on fieldwork in Saskatchewan, proposed that couples seeking to marry should have to be certified as mentally and morally fit. Those deemed to be subnormal would be sent to state farms or camps, while those judged to be mentally defective or incurably diseased would be sterilized. Douglas changed his mind about all of this well before he became Saskatchewan's premier. His government stayed away from such policies even while they were being pursued in some other jurisdictions, including Alberta.

In 1935 Douglas became the federal CCF candidate in Weyburn. His defeat in the provincial contest in 1934 had taught him some lessons about public speaking. Rather than overloading his audiences with information, he became adept at explaining complex issues in ways that were simple and entertaining. He made people laugh while attempting to win them over. He won in 1935, albeit narrowly, along with six other CCF members, including M. J. Coldwell from Saskatchewan and J. S. Woodsworth from Winnipeg. Douglas soon gained a reputation as a witty and tenacious parliamentary debater. He also became a favourite on the CCF convention and speakers' circuit.

Although he had pastoral training and was a good listener, he loved to speak and enjoyed the limelight. People who worked with him over the years recalled that he was a demanding taskmaster. He was at his most peevish when event organizers failed to provide an audience for him. He was not a political theoretician but rather an effective popularizer of socialist ideas. He did that, in part, by creating parables about the economic and political system. One of these was a story in which a city slicker visits a farm and helps with the chores by turning the handle on a cream separator. Douglas used the cream separator as a metaphor for a system in which the owners of capital feasted on cream while those providing the labour had to settle for skim milk.

Douglas was re-elected in Weyburn in 1940 but CCF activists in Saskatchewan urged him to return and lead the strife-ridden provincial party. He became party president in 1941 and leader in the following year. Oddly, he remained an MP until 1944 even while he was leading the provincial party. When the governing Liberals called an election for June of 1944, Douglas and the CCF were ready. Under his leadership the party had overcome its divisions, improved its organization, and developed a thorough but easy to explain nine-point program.

During the campaign Douglas maintained a frenetic pace, usually speaking at three public meetings per day and at family picnics on Sundays. He was an engaging platform performer. He was approaching forty years of age in 1944 but possessed a lively and boyish demeanour. A diminutive man, he had an actor's poise and a prize fighter's physical grace. He dressed in smart and well-cut suits; his wavy but receding hair was carefully groomed; and the light glinted off of his rimless steel glasses. He combined humour, sarcasm, irony, anecdote, and self-deprecation in ways that allowed him to both inform and amuse his audiences. He was sparing in his use of figurative language and kept his sentences short and snappy. He enunciated carefully and even cultivated a slight stutter, which gave the impression that he casting about for just the right words to describe his proposals or his opponents.

Author L. D. Lovick lists a range of physical gestures and postures that Douglas would use to underscore his verbal arguments: the pointed finger; the arms widespread or folded; the hands slowly clapping as the point is hammered home; the fingers folded as the points are enumerated; arms folded as he ponders the gravity of an issue; and hands in the pockets as he tells a story. Douglas was adept at handling hecklers and the one-liners he sent their way could be cutting and sarcastic; but he gave full and patient attention to audience members who would surround the stage to talk to him following a speech.

He also loved radio and used it to good effect during the 1944 campaign. He was familiar with Roosevelt's fireside chats. Douglas cultivated a persona on radio that portrayed him as reasonable and sympathetic rather than his more dramatic approach in public meetings. R. B. Bennett may have pioneered the use of radio by a Canadian politician but it was Douglas who perfected the art. He was to continue using radio regularly during his entire seventeen years as premier.

In 1944 Douglas and the CCF won handily over the shopworn Liberals and after winning power the new government initiated an ambitious reform agenda. That demanded a more sophisticated capacity for research and planning than had been the case with previous governments. Douglas was able to attract talented civil servants and planners from across the country, as well as from Great Britain and the United States. His government's desire for innovation, however, was combined with an orthodox approach to expenditures and deficits. Saskatchewan slowly paid off the public debt left by the previous Liberal administration and Douglas never once ran a budget deficit.

It was in health care, though, where he would leave his most indelible mark. He had always believed that people should not be denied medical care based on their ability to pay for it. Agitation for publicly financed medical and hospital insurance had occurred considerably earlier than 1944. During the depression in Saskatchewan, many patients were poverty stricken and doctors found it difficult or impossible to collect for their services. The Saskatchewan Medical Association endorsed public health insurance in 1933. The Canadian Medical Association (CMA) supported the idea in principle in 1934. Following the Second World War, the Liberal government of Mackenzie King, prodded by the CCF and the public, considered introducing Medicare. The proposal foundered when the governments of Ontario and Quebec objected to federal intrusion into their jurisdiction for providing health care services.

That stalemate prompted the Douglas government to go it alone in creating Canada's first publicly financed hospital insurance plan in 1947. Ten years later, John Diefenbaker and a newly elected Conservative government in Ottawa put in place a similar program by providing each province with grants to cover half of its costs in hospital spending. That freed up money that Saskatchewan had been spending on its public hospital insurance program. Douglas decided to use the extra cash to create Medicare, which added a publicly financed plan to pay for patient visits to the doctor. He announced in 1959 that the government was considering such a plan. By then the doctors' earlier endorsement had gone the way of affluence. Doctor-controlled private plans were doing a thriving business. The CMA reversed its earlier position in favour of public insurance, saying now that a public plan would be tantamount to the "civil conscription" of doctors. The CCF campaigned on Medicare in the 1960 provincial election. It was a bitter event in which the CMA dedicated more money to anti-Medicare publicity than any of the political parties spent on the entire campaign. The CCF won by a seat count of thirty-seven to seventeen over the Liberals and captured 41 per cent of the popular vote.

Douglas had a robust political adversary in Liberal leader Ross Thatcher, a gruffly intelligent ranch owner who also owned a hardware store in Moose Jaw. Thatcher had been a former CCF member of Parliament. He was elected in 1945 but bolted from the party ten years later to become one of its most trenchant critics. He became leader of the provincial Liberals in 1959 and was determined to defeat those whom he excoriated as socialists who were ruining Saskatchewan. He led the party into the 1960 provincial election and focused on economic issues. On health care, Thatcher would say only that he was in favour of some form of medical insurance but he would not further define his position.

The 1960 provincial election was only a prelude for an even bigger battle to come. Douglas believed the election victory gave him the mandate he needed. He had established an advisory committee in April 1960, which included doctor representatives. But the College of Physicians and Surgeons said that it was "flatly opposed" to a publicly financed program unless it were limited to subsidizing people to belong to private plans. The committee appeared paralyzed by the demands of a small but influential group that had drawn a line in the sand. Finally, Douglas asked for an interim report, which was provided in September 1961. A majority of the committee's members supported a public plan while representatives of the medical profession and the chamber of commerce were opposed. The government prepared a bill and called a special session of the legislature for October 1961 to introduce the legislation.

◆

There was a backdrop to the drama unfolding in the provincial legislature. The CCF had played an important role in federal politics since its inception in 1933 but had failed to come even close to power. The party was almost wiped out in the electoral sweep accomplished by John Diefenbaker and the Conservatives in 1958. Some leaders of the federal CCF and the labour movement dreamed of building a social democratic party modelled upon the Labour Party in Great Britain. Those plans were forming in 1959 to 1960 just as Douglas was planning to introduce Medicare in Saskatchewan. With his rhetorical gifts and his sterling record as a premier, he had long been one of the CCF's greatest public assets. The new party would need a popular and effective leader and Douglas came under increasing pressure to run. Eventually he agreed to enter the race. On August 4, 1961, he was elected as the first leader of the New Democratic Party (NDP), which succeeded the CCF. Although he was on his way out as premier, Douglas was still in that office on October 11 when the Throne Speech in the Saskatchewan legislature provided details about the Medical Care Insurance Act. When Ross Thatcher spoke in reply to the Throne Speech, he was cutting in his remarks. He said that Medicare was not needed in Saskatchewan and that Douglas had no idea what the plan would cost. The speech that Douglas made in response to Thatcher was his last in the legislature. On one level it was a simple address; but it made expert use of the rhetorical style that he had perfected over the years.

DOUGLAS'S SPEECH

Mr. Speaker, this session of the legislature was called together as hon. members know, to deal with ... the Saskatchewan Medical Care Insurance Act, which has just been given first reading by this legislature. I think it is significant, that in his address yesterday, the Leader of the Opposition said nothing about the basic principles of medical care. His only references to a medical care program were those which were designed to throw cold water on the idea. First he said, "Why don't we wait for a national plan." Well, Mr. Speaker, I am sure there were a lot of people in Saskatchewan who heard that and who said to themselves, "How long are we supposed to wait?" … To say that we should wait for a national plan, is to ask the people of Saskatchewan to drag along and wait, as they have waited for thirty or forty years, for the federal government to act and knowing full well that they are not likely to act unless some province leads the way.

The other thing the Leader of the Opposition said about the medical care program was, "What's the hurry?" He said the government is just hurrying this plan through for the publicity effect in the federal election. Yet, I remember at the last regular session of the legislature, that at least two or three members opposite asked the government when we were going to get on with the medical care plan. They pointed out that the government had promised it in the election of 1960. They wanted to know what we were waiting for—how long was the medical advisory committee going to take to get a report down—what was holding us up? Mr. Speaker, this is surely a disorganized army. The rank and file are saying forward, and the leader is saying retreat. They had better make up their minds. Does the Liberal party believe we should have a medical care plan? Do they believe we should have it now? Do they want to postpone it? They can't be "forwards-backwards" all the time. They've got to take a stand. I think the people of the province have a right to know where they stand on this question. When the House votes on this matter they'll have a chance to see, and their constituents will have a chance to see what they think about a medical care plan.

Douglas is an orator adept at winning over his audiences through a combination of self-deprecating humour and didacticism. That approach does not lend itself to his audience in the Legislative Assembly, a bear pit where he is speaking to a controversial piece of legislation introducing Medicare. The members of his party support him although some are no doubt anxious about the political outcome of what they are doing. Douglas uses his speech to buoy their spirits and firm their resolve. On the other side of the aisle, Liberal leader Ross Thatcher has been scathingly critical of the CCF and its plan. The wider audience for Douglas, of course, is the entire provincial population. He launches quickly into a spirited rebuttal of Thatcher's speech. He chooses to create a mini-drama, complete with fictitious Saskatchewan people and dialogue, about the timing of introducing Medicare. He then describes the inconsistency of the Opposition's hurry-up-and-wait arguments. He paraphrases some Liberal MLAs who want the government to move more quickly while Thatcher criticizes Douglas for moving too quickly. This is reminiscent of how Meighen flayed Liberals over their conflicting criticisms over conscription in 1917. Douglas is trying to discredit the Liberals and to force their hand because they refuse to say what kind of health plan they would prefer. He is putting pressure on them to take a position.

There was one statement made by the Leader of the Opposition about medical care which astonished me. He said, "There's not a shred of evidence to show that any person in the province has been unable to get medical attention." Surely if ever a comment indicated that an individual was out of touch with people, it is that remark. It is like Marie Antoinette at the time of the French Revolution when the people were crying for bread, saying, "Why don't they eat cake?" To say that there is no evidence to show that any person in the province has been unable to get medical attention, is to fly in the face of all the facts.

The Canadian Sickness Report, 1951, conducted by the government of Canada shows clearly that the lower income groups in the period under study had more illness and more days of disability than did the higher income groups. It shows, conversely, that the volume of medical care received by the low income groups is much less than that received by higher income groups.

The low income groups because of poor diet, poor housing conditions and harder working conditions have more illness and have more disability. Yet the records show that they are the people who get the least medical care ...

Now I readily grant that no doctor has turned patients away. No doctor could do so without violating his Hippocratic oath. But what happens? First of all, patients are reluctant to go to the doctor if they know they can't pay. People fail to seek medical counsel and medical advice when they should get it and they oftentimes leave it until the situation is serious and even dangerous. The second fact is that many people who do go to doctors incur bills and debts which cripple them for years to come and this does not just apply to poor people. There are thousands of people in Saskatchewan and across Canada living on reasonably comfortable incomes who are able to make the payments on their houses and their cars and on their television set and who can get by providing two things, firstly—they don't lose their jobs and secondly, that the bread-winner doesn't get seriously ill. For such people, doctor bills amounting to large sums of money can put that family in a serious financial predicament for years to come.

Douglas feigns astonishment over another Thatcher claim, accurately quoted, that anyone in Saskatchewan who needs medical attention can get it. Douglas says that shows how out of touch Thatcher is with reality. The premier uses an allusion to French Queen Marie Antoinette about having hungry peasants eat cake. This is a rhetorical device known as sententia, where a well-known saying is used to sum up facts or details that have been presented. Douglas, in his rebuttal to Thatcher, refers to a federal report about who makes most use of the health care system. It is not the poor, Douglas says, because they are reluctant to go a doctor if they cannot pay. He hastens, however, to include those who are reasonably comfortable as well. Their lives can change quickly if they become ill and must pay medical bills. Douglas does not want to appeal only to the poor because he needs the support of many other people for Medicare as well. He uses colloquial metaphors to describe Thatcher's positions. First Thatcher "[threw] cold water" on the idea of publicly financed health care and now his claim about everyone having access to care "[flies] in the face of all facts."

The Leader of the Opposition yesterday spent a good deal of time talking about the terrible costs which this would place upon the taxpayers of the province. I thought some of his sentences were gems. He said, "The Liberals believe in a medical care plan if it can be done without hardship to the taxpayer." Now, which taxpayer is he worried about—the ones that are going to be paying less under this plan than they pay now, or the ones that are going to be paying more? Which is he worried about? He goes on and says, "Many people wonder if we can afford $20,000,000 at a time like this for a medical care plan." Many people wonder! Is he one of them? Are the members opposite among those who wonder if we can afford $20,000,000 for a medical care plan? Let them say so ...

I want to point out, Mr. Speaker, that the cost of a medical care plan is not a new cost to the people of Saskatchewan. The people of this province now are spending $18 million to $20 million a year for medical care. This is not a new cost. It is a different distribution of the cost—that is all. This money had to be paid before. Doctors of this province had to be paid. Everything has had to be paid for—their staff, X-ray technicians, lab technicians, these things all had to be paid for. But they have been paid for by those who were unfortunate enough to be ill. We are now saying they should be *paid for by spreading the cost over all the people. We propose that the family tax, which we admit is a regressive tax since there is a flat rate on every family and therefore bears no relationship to ability to pay, should be kept as small as possible. We propose that the balance of the cost—probably two-thirds of the cost—ought to be raised by factors which have a measure of ability to pay.*

Maybe this is why the Liberal press have been so vehement in their attacks on this plan. It may be that some of them begin to suspect that they are going to have to pay a part of the medical bill of some other people who are not able to pay their own.

Yesterday the Leader of the Opposition sneered at the idea of "I am my brother's keeper." He said, "There isn't much cream in Saskatchewan." I want to suggest that the Leader-Post *and the* Star-Phoenix, *the Sifton interests and the Leader of the Opposition have fattened quite a bit during the term of the CCF government in office, and it will certainly not hurt them at all to make some contribution towards the medical care for those less fortunate than themselves …*

Douglas uses mild sarcasm to rebut Thatcher's claim that Medicare would be too big a burden on Saskatchewan taxpayers. Turning to details, Douglas says that Saskatchewan people spend millions on medical care in any event. But now that amount will be paid through a tax-financed public program rather than by having individuals take out their wallets each time they go to the doctor. Douglas and Thatcher hold a classic difference of opinion regarding health care that exists in Canada to this day. Douglas believes it is a public good and Thatcher that it is a commodity provided in the marketplace. Douglas then shifts his attack to what he describes as the "Liberal press" in the province. In doing so he is attempting to settle scores both old and new. The daily newspapers in Saskatoon and Regina were owned by the Sifton family from Ontario and have long been opponents of the CCF. More recently they have been severe critics of the government's proposal for Medicare. Douglas personalizes the criticism by suggesting that the Sifton press may be so "vehement" in its opposition because owners and editors do not want to contribute toward Medicare for people less fortunate than they.

Then he begins to build his moral argument. Her says that on the previous day Thatcher "sneered" at the premier's mention of someone being his or her "brother's keeper." Douglas was fond of using such biblical allusions. We cannot know from the written record whether Thatcher actually sneered but he did accuse Douglas of trotting out allegories about "the jungle society, the elephant and the chicken, our brother's keeper, and so on." Thatcher also referred to Douglas using his cream separator parable. Thatcher said that under the CCF there was very little cream to siphon off and what there was went to friends of the government. This was a personal attack on Douglas implying that he doles out patronage or perhaps that he is corrupt, and Douglas does not appreciate it. He responds with a personal jibe of his own, saying that those who have "fattened" during the CCF government's term were the Sifton newspaper owners and Thatcher himself. That was a rather undignified personal dig because Thatcher was a rotund individual. Douglas is using an established although informal practice in political debate in which the tone one uses in reply matches that of the question or statement that has been made by one's adversary.

It seems to me to be begging the question to be talking about whether or not the people of this province, or the people of Canada can afford a plan to spread the cost of sickness over the entire population. This is not a new principle. This has existed in nearly all the countries of western Europe—many of them for a quarter of a century. It has been in Great Britain since 1948; it has been in New Zealand since 1935; it has been in Australia. The little state of Israel that only came into existence in 1948 has today the most comprehensive health insurance plan in the world. It has more doctors, and nurses and dentists per thousand of its population than any other industrialized country or any country for which we can get statistics.

It is not a new principle. To me it seems to be sheer nonsense to suggest that medical care is something which ought to be measured just in dollars. When we're talking about medical care we're talking about our sense of values. Do we think human life is important? Do we think that the best medical care which is available is something to which people are entitled, by virtue of belonging to a civilized community? I looked up the figures and I found that in 1959, the people of Canada spent $1,555 million, or eight per cent of their personal expenditures on alcohol and tobacco. I would be the last person to argue that people do not have the right, if they want to, to spend part of their income for either

alcohol or tobacco or entertainment, or anything else. But in the same period of time, the
people of Canada spent $944 million for medical and dental care, or four and one-half
per cent of their income expenses. In other words, in the year 1959 we spent almost twice
as much on luxuries such as tobacco and alcohol as we spent on providing ourselves and
our families with the medical and dental care which they require.

If we can afford large sums of money for other things such as horse-racing, and
many other things, and we do—I'm not arguing against them—then I say we ought to
have sufficient sense of values to say that health is more important than these things, and
if we can find money for relatively non-essential things, we can find the money to give to
our people good health …

Douglas wants to show that there is nothing scary about Medicare. Some
critics say that it is communistic, an accusation that he cannot allow to
pass. He points to a number of countries, including Great Britain, all of
whom have such plans. Public health care is not new. Then he returns to
his moral argument. Health care is about more than dollars; it is about a
sense of values. He extends his argument to a moralistic one by setting
out a contrast that is quite in keeping with his formation in the Protestant
social gospel movement. It contains a Puritan disapproval of drinking
alcohol, smoking, and gambling. Douglas says that people spend more
money on those pursuits than they do on health and dental care. Twice
he throws in qualifiers about not being opposed to that, but he is at the
least encouraging his audience to pass judgment on the value of booze,
cigarettes and horse racing versus medical care.

I believe that the people of this province want health security. I think hospital insurance
proves that. In spite of all the criticism we had when hospital insurance was set up,
and in spite of the protest of the Liberal party that we should allow it to be handled
by the municipalities, the fact is that today no one in this province in their right mind
would suggest abolishing hospital insurance. On the contrary, our pioneering in hospital
insurance proved so successful that today our example has been followed in every province
in this Dominion.

I believe that the great bulk of the people of this province support the idea of the
medical care plan. I believe they will indicate they are willing to pay for it, providing the

cost is spread equitably on the basis of ability to pay. The only ones who are likely to oppose it are those who fear that they will have to help those less fortunate than themselves.

You will note from the Speech from the Throne it says this medical care plan is to be a province-wide plan, with universal coverage. This was an important decision for the Advisory Planning Committee on Medical Care to make. They had before them briefs from which advocated a partial medical care plan. In very brief terms the recommendation was that the great bulk of the people who were self-supporting would ensure themselves by joining the private plan of their choice, and that the remainder should have an extra premium paid on their behalf to the private plan, providing they could show that they were in need. Private plans ordinarily do not take people who have congenital illnesses. But if these people are in need and if an extra premium is paid on their behalf by the government, they would get medical care from private plans.

Those people generally who, because of low incomes, were not able to pay the private plan premium would also be covered by the private plans if they could show they were in need and if the government would pay their premium ...

There are two basic weaknesses in the proposals which were put forward by those who wanted a limited coverage for medical care. The first is that private plans bear no relationship to ability to pay. I want to make it abundantly clear, Mr. Speaker, that the private plans such as Medical Services Incorporated and Group Medical Services have rendered a marvelous service to the people of Saskatchewan. In the absence of a government plan I have advised people throughout the years, if they can possibly afford it, to join these private plans. They have been well operated, and I hope that much of their experience and their facilities and staff may be made available to those who will be managing the government-sponsored medical care plan. But a private medical care plan can only raise money in one way, and that is by putting a flat premium on every family irrespective of whether the family's income is $20,000 a year or $10,000. They have no way of graduating premiums on the basis of ability to pay. Only the government can levy taxes on the basis of ability to pay. Only the government is in a position to say that those who have less will pay less, and those who have more will pay more. This is why, in my opinion, and in the opinion, apparently, of the majority of the committee, the idea of partial coverage was dropped.

The other weakness in the proposal of a partial medical care program is that a great many groups in the province would only get coverage if they could prove need. This means imposing a means test; this means probing into people's affairs, and this is a pretty *serious thing to do. I want to say that the time is surely past when people should have to depend on proving need in order to get services that should be the inalienable right of every citizen of a good society. It is all very well for some people to say that there is no stigma or humiliation connected with having to prove need. This is always said by people who know that they are in no danger of having to prove need. I am very glad that the committee recommended and the government decided that there will be no such stigma and that there will be no means test. Every person in the province who is self-supporting and able to pay a relatively small per capita tax, will be eligible for care and those who are not self-supporting will be covered by other programs …*

Douglas begins in a more dispassionate way to describe the plan that the government is putting forward. There had been criticism when in 1947 the government introduced publicly financed hospital care, but it worked so well that no one would suggest turning back the clock. Every other province in Canada has followed Saskatchewan's example on hospital insurance. Similarly, Douglas says that the "great bulk" of people support Medicare. He does not say so here but he believes that his party's victory in the hard-fought 1960 election is all the proof he needs.

Douglas dissects the proposal that Saskatchewan should rely on private, doctor-proposed plans. Those who can afford it would pay their own way. The government would subsidize the poor by paying on their behalf into the private plans, but only after a means test. Surely, Douglas says, the time is past when people have to prove need in order to receive a service that should be their right as a citizen. He does, however, favour a modest contribution by individuals and families toward the cost of medical care.

I believe that if this medical care insurance program is successful, and I think it will be, it will prove to be the forerunner of a national medical care insurance plan. It will become the nucleus around which Canada will ultimately build a comprehensive health insurance program which will cover all health services—not just hospital and medical care—but eventually dental care, optometric care, drugs and all the other health services which people require. I believe such a plan operated by the federal and provincial governments jointly will ultimately come in Canada. But I don't think it will come unless we lead the way. I want to say that when the history of our time is written, it may well be recorded that in October, 1961, the Saskatchewan legislature and the Saskatchewan people pioneered in this field and took a first step towards ultimately establishing a system of medical care insurance for all the people of Canada ...

May I just close by saying that this is the last Throne Speech debate in which I shall participate. I have had the high privilege of attending seventeen regular sessions of this legislature, and three fall sessions, making a total of twenty sessions in all. I would like to say that to me these have been most enjoyable and satisfying years. I would like to think that much good has been accomplished. I would be foolish if I were to say that in all these seventeen years no mistakes have ever been made, or that my judgement or the judgement of my colleagues has always been right. Any human being who would make such a statement would either be foolish or dishonest. But I do believe that in these seventeen years, we have done some things to make this a better province for the ordinary man and woman to live in; that there are more of the amenities of life; that there is a greater measure of security and a greater measure of equality of treatment; that there is greater freedom from discrimination; and that our people have, working together, moved forward. No government, of course can take all the credit for this. A government may give leadership, but in a democracy, unless there are people—thousands of them—who are prepared to work together for the mutual good of their community and their province and their neighbour, no government can accomplish very much.

If, when the history of our period is written, it can be said that we have taken some forward steps in the past seventeen years, then the major credit must go to the people of Saskatchewan ... there [are] no finer people in all the Dominion of Canada. Here are the people, who out of their hardships and out of their suffering, have learned to work together for their mutual advantage. They were the first people to set up union hospitals on this continent; the first people to set up municipal doctor plans; and the first people to establish an Anti-Tuberculosis League. They are people who have learned that they must help each other. They learned it in the hard days when neighbours had to co-operate with one another, or face the possibility of starvation, or freezing to death. Fortunately, the traditions of our forefathers had stayed with them. Ours is a great province of self-help and mutual co-operation ... I want to thank the people of this province who have made it possible to serve them, and I hope the record will show that I served them not too badly.

Douglas begins his peroration with a bold prediction that if Medicare is introduced in Saskatchewan it will become the "forerunner" of a national plan. His province will once again have led the way. Finally, he says his goodbyes as Saskatchewan's premier. His seventeen years in the job have been enjoyable and he believes that "much good" has been accomplished. He speaks poetically about Saskatchewan's people—of the suffering and hardship they have endured and how that taught them that they must co-operate to help one another. He ends the speech with understatement—what the students of rhetoric call meiosis—saying that he hopes he served the people of the province "not too badly." Douglas is not in the habit of asking for sympathy, nor of trumpeting his achievements, but here he is arguably engaging in ethos, an attempt to paint himself in a way that will have his wider audience look favourably upon him and lend support to his project, in this case publicly financed medical care.

THE IMPACT OF DOUGLAS'S SPEECH

Douglas was ultimately right in his prediction that if Saskatchewan led the way on Medicare it would one day be adopted throughout Canada, but in 1962 there was an epic battle in his own province. As the clock ticked down to the implementation of Medicare on July 1, the province's doctors warned that they would go on strike. They made good on their threat, leaving people with only emergency care. While the offices were shuttered, Keep Our Doctors committees began to hold rallies throughout the province. They insisted that Medicare was a totalitarian step on the road to communism and there were even calls for violence to prevent it if need be. Police began to watch the homes of cabinet ministers. The government had its own supporters in the CCF, in the farm, labour, and co-operative movements, at the university and among some churches. Those supporters began to organize consumer-based community clinics that attracted sympathetic doctors from Great Britain in an airlift organized by the Saskatchewan government. Eventually, Stephen Taylor, a member of the British House of Lords, was invited to the province to act as a mediator and after a bitter twenty-three days the strike was settled.

The desire for publicly financed health care arose during the hardships associated with frontier settlement in Saskatchewan and elsewhere in

Canada. The need became even more apparent during the depression when a growing number of people could not afford either hospital or doctors' care. In the 1940s Canadians worried that the pre-war depression might return and they demanded improved government safety nets. Douglas and the CCF came to power in 1944 promising action even though Saskatchewan was one of Canada's poorest provinces. It took three years for hospital insurance and almost twenty years for Medicare, but Douglas kept the promise.

As he did so, one of his old political rivals was watching from the sidelines. Emmett Hall was a Saskatoon lawyer, a long-time Conservative, and a former law school classmate of John Diefenbaker, who became prime minister in 1957. Diefenbaker promptly appointed Hall to become a judge in Saskatchewan and later named him to the Supreme Court of Canada. In January 1961 Diefenbaker also appointed Hall to lead a Royal Commission into health care. The prime minister acted at the urging of the Canadian Medical Association, which was casting a wary eye on the CCF promise to implement Medicare in Saskatchewan. The doctors wanted to head off any chance that what they considered a contagion would spread to the rest of Canada.

Hall brought his legal training and judicial bearing to the work. He assembled the evidence and closely questioned hundreds of witnesses who appeared before him in public hearings. He was struck by the obvious gaps in the health care system, the inequitable access to services, and the generally poor health of many Canadians. Studies prepared for his commission reported that thirty per cent of people had no form of medical insurance coverage in 1961. Hall came to the conclusion that it was preferable to have a publicly financed, single-payer health plan than to have governments subsidize the premiums of millions of Canadians with private insurers, as the Canadian Medical Association was requesting. When he published his report in 1964, Hall stunned the country by proposing a Medicare plan similar to the one in Saskatchewan.

The Liberal government of Lester Pearson, after some indecision, passed enabling legislation in 1966 and by 1972 Medicare was a reality throughout Canada. Douglas and Hall had been political rivals in

Saskatchewan, one a social democrat and the other a Conservative. But along with Pearson they embodied a political consensus around publicly financed health care. Douglas was to write to Hall in 1971: "I think we can both take some satisfaction out of knowing that we have helped push back a little the shadows of fear and anxiety from the lives of so many people."

Medicare has served Canadians well. It is available to everyone and removes the barriers that would otherwise prevent millions of people from being insured against treatment for illness. The quality of that care remains arguably among the best in the world. Despite its critics, publicly financed health care is far cheaper and more cost efficient than the bafflingly complex system in the United States. Canadians have not forgotten Douglas. In a national contest conducted by the CBC in 2004, almost eighteen years after his death, he was chosen in an online vote to be the Greatest Canadian. His passion to make life better for ordinary people, his vision, his sense of humour, and his gifted oratory won him an enduring place in Canadian hearts and minds.

LESTER PEARSON ON A NEW FLAG

JUNE 15, 1964

"This flag, if it is adopted by parliament, will stand for one Canada; united, strong, independent and equal to her tasks."

Lester Pearson lived a charmed life. He was born at the end of the Victorian era, survived enlistment in the First World War, and joined Canada's embryonic foreign service where he became a respected diplomat. Later he was recruited by the Liberals and became Canada's minister of external affairs under Louis St. Laurent. It was Pearson who devised a way out of the Suez crisis in 1956 and he was awarded the Nobel Peace Prize for his efforts. After the Liberals' narrow defeat at the hands of John Diefenbaker in 1957, Pearson became party leader early in 1958, just in time to preside over his party's near obliteration in the second election held in two years. Pearson and Diefenbaker were fated to be political adversaries through three minority governments. When Pearson won in 1963, one of his promises was to provide Canada with a distinctive new flag. But it was no simple matter. Diefenbaker accused him of sowing disunity and dug in his heels, setting the stage for a long and bitter parliamentary debate in 1964.

◆

Lester Bowles Pearson was born in 1897, the year of Queen Victoria's golden jubilee, and he was the second of three sons. His birth occurred in Newton Brook, then a community near Toronto and now within the confines of the city. His forebearers on either side had arrived from Ulster in the 1820s and 1840s respectively. In Canada they embraced Methodism, a faith that was English in its origin. Lester's grandfather and his father, Edwin, were Methodist ministers, as was one of his mother's cousins. His mother, Annie Sarah Bowles Pearson, was well educated and artistic. Edwin moved the family often as he accepted charges from various churches in southern Ontario. He was a popular minister, easygoing and athletic. He avoided controversies around the social gospel, which was so important in the lives of others, including Nellie McClung and Tommy Douglas.

There was an aura of old Ontario Anglo solidity about the family and Pearson was later to write in his memoirs about how pleasant and secure his childhood had been. The family was not wealthy but the Pearsons were reasonably well connected. Edwin Pearson received an honorary doctorate from the University of Toronto and Sarah Pearson's cousin was chancellor of Victoria University, a Methodist college. The family was living in Hamilton when Pearson graduated from high school in 1913 and enrolled at Victoria to study modern history. He was a good student who had also inherited his father's love of sports. He excelled at baseball, hockey, and lacrosse as a youth and at the university played on the rugby and basketball teams.

The First World War was soon to interrupt Pearson's studies and his life, as it did for his brothers and hundreds of thousands of other young Canadians. In April 1915, on his eighteenth birthday, he enlisted with a hospital unit and entered the Canadian Army Medical Corps. After basic training in Britain, he was posted, not to the killing fields of Europe but rather to Salonika in Macedonia, off the southern fringe of the Austro-Hungarian Empire. He longed to be closer to the real action and had his father intervene with General Sam Hughes, the Canadian minister of militia and defence, about a transfer that occurred in March 1917. Pearson supported the conscription legislation introduced by the Union government and steered through the House of Commons by Arthur Meighen. Pearson wanted to be a pilot and joined the Royal Flying Corps for training, but while in London he was struck by a bus during a blackout. John English, one of his biographers, says that the accident did not disable

Pearson physically but that he broke down emotionally while recuperating in hospital. A medical board sent him home to Canada in April 1918 and once there he received his discharge.

The war ended soon after and Pearson resumed his studies and graduated in 1919 with a specialization in modern history. He began to apprentice with a law firm in Toronto but he left within a week. Then he worked in Hamilton at the Canadian subsidiary of a business owned by his uncle. Soon he transferred with the company to Chicago. Business was not a good fit either and Pearson decided that he wanted to study at Oxford University. He was able to do so when Vincent Massey, later to become the first Canadian-born governor general, arranged for him to receive a scholarship in 1921. Pearson thoroughly enjoyed his two years at Oxford. In addition to his classes, he threw himself into the sports program, starring at rugby, lacrosse, and hockey. It was at Oxford that he met many of the British, American, and Canadian men with whom he was to work over many years in diplomacy and politics.

In 1923 he returned, at age twenty-six, to teach history at the University of Toronto. His education and life experience provided him with a maturity that was accompanied by a cheerful and almost jocular persona. He enjoyed teaching but was not particularly interested in academic publishing. A book that he contemplated did not materialize. As always he found a healthy outlet in sports, coaching as well as playing, and at one point the university proposed to move him into a leading position in the athletics department. It was his fourth-year history tutorial where he met Maryon Moody, a student from Winnipeg. The attraction was immediate and mutual and they were secretly engaged within a month. Such liaisons between a professor and student would be forbidden, or at least frowned upon, in universities today. They were married in 1925 when he was twenty-eight years of age and she twenty-three. They were to have two children.

In 1926 Pearson followed one of his history department colleagues in sitting for the foreign service exam and he joined the Department of External Affairs in 1928. Under the cautious direction of Mackenzie King, who kept that portfolio for himself, Canada was emerging from its long dependent status as a colony within the British Empire. Pearson was in the right place at the right time, seemingly diffident, but owning an "artfully concealed ambition." He was intelligent and good looking; he was pleasant and always polite; and he took to wearing a trademark bowtie. He was considered a good colleague and he knew people everywhere. He liked to describe himself as "Mike," a nickname given to him by an army drill master who thought that Lester was not a good name for a soldier. Colleagues were later to say, however, that no one really knew the man behind the pleasant smile. He was a professional extrovert whose public personality masked a much more private and impersonal individual, which was an advantage for a diplomat.

Pearson held increasingly important foreign affairs assignments. He was posted to London in 1935 where he found himself closely observing the British attempting to mollify Hitler. He was frustrated by Mackenzie King's caution and his reticence to see Hitler as a threat. When war was declared in 1939, Pearson remained in London while Maryon and the children returned to Ottawa. He returned to Canada in 1941 and was posted to Washington as a senior diplomat in 1942, not long after the Japanese attack on Pearl Harbor. Pearson was trusted by politicians and diplomats in the Roosevelt administration and popular with journalists. In 1945 he was named as Canada's ambassador to the United States and following the war he was a member of the Canadian delegation when the UN Charter was drafted in 1945.

Pearson was instrumental in forging Canada's position as a modest but significant player in affairs beyond its borders. His family, particularly his father, held British imperialist loyalties and Pearson was an anglophile who loved Oxford and most things British; but he was also a realist. He understood that the locus of world military and economic power had shifted away from Britain and toward the United States. Canada's evolution from colony to independent nation demanded a foreign policy that was at once astute and nimble.

Mackenzie King was by the mid-1940s contemplating retirement after a long career. King admired Pearson and spoke to him directly about entering politics. Pearson was interested although he did not want to appear too eager.

In order to smooth such a transition, he was brought back to Ottawa as the under-secretary (today we would say deputy minister) of the department under Louis St. Laurent. King resigned in 1948 and Pearson was appointed as external affairs minister even before his successful win in a by-election in 1949. As the minister, he distinguished himself during the dangerously volatile Suez crisis in 1956. Egypt's president Gamal Nasser nationalized the canal that was contained within his country, and in turn Britain, France, and Israel launched a military attack. Pearson and Canada did not support the imperial powers and he was deeply involved at the United Nations in crafting a solution acceptable to all parties. It involved the creation and deployment of a peacekeeping force in the region. In October 1957 he was awarded the Nobel Peace Prize for his diplomatic work. By then a spent and tired Liberal government had been defeated by John Diefenbaker and the Conservatives, who formed a minority government. St. Laurent resigned as leader soon after and Pearson succeeded him in January 1958. Diefenbaker called a snap election within two weeks and campaigned vigorously. The Conservatives won the largest parliamentary majority in Canadian history.

Diefenbaker and Pearson were fated to be locked in parliamentary combat for ten years and their initial wariness and mistrust developed into a bitter antagonism. There is much that was similar in their backgrounds but many contrasts as well. Both were born in southern Ontario in the 1890s into English-speaking Protestant families with a deep affection for Britain and its empire. Both remained unilingual throughout their lives and careers. Diefenbaker's family migrated to the North-West Territories in 1903, settling in what was to become the province of Saskatchewan. His father taught in a series of fledgling rural schools and tried his hand at homesteading before the family moved into Saskatoon in 1910. When Diefenbaker registered for studies at the University of Saskatchewan in 1912, the campus was just being built. He went into law with an early eye to politics. Meanwhile, the Pearson family lived a more genteel existence in a series of church manses. Pearson attended prestigious universities in Toronto and Oxford.

Both young men enlisted in the First World War and both had inglorious careers. Diefenbaker was sent to England in 1915 but he was sent home two years later without having gone to the front. His story, which he told often, was that he was working in a trench when someone inadvertently dropped a pickaxe onto his back causing him to hemorrhage badly and even to cough up blood. However, after painstaking research in military records, biographer Dennis Smith concludes that Diefenbaker suffered from fear and anxiety to such an extent that he was deemed unfit for service and sent home. Pearson was also ferried home more for psychological than physical reasons. The difference between the two men, Smith concludes, is that Pearson eventually was more truthful than Diefenbaker about his war experience.

Diefenbaker made his reputation as a flamboyant defence lawyer in small-town Saskatchewan. He ran for office in five civic, provincial, and federal elections but victory eluded him for fifteen years. He was almost ready to give up when he won a seat in the federal election of 1940. Within two years, he ran for the federal Conservative leadership and lost. He ran and lost again in 1948. He succeeded on his third try in 1956. By then Pearson had been the minister of external affairs for eight years. Diefenbaker was a product of the prairies and the Great Depression. He was very much a parliamentarian—a gladiator in the House of Commons and an awe-inspiring campaigner in elections. Pearson, a late arrival to political office, had moved in the world of diplomacy where tact, a discreet search for common ground, and a view to the long term were prized skills. Pearson lacked Diefenbaker's deep experience in politics; Diefenbaker lacked Pearson's international experience and his profound understanding of Canada's place in the new order that emerged during and after the Second World War.

Diefenbaker also bore the scars of a perennial candidate who had lost numerous elections and leadership contests. He had long harboured an almost messianic view of his own destiny, and his overwhelming victory in the 1958 election reinforced his belief that he had a mystical bond with voters. Despite his strengths as an opposition politician and campaigner, he had little by way of administrative skill and was distrustful of his ministers and advisors. By 1962 his massive parliamentary majority had shrunk and his government was reduced to minority status in the election of that year. That administration was short-lived and in 1963 it was Pearson and the Liberals who emerged victorious with a minority government. He depended upon support from either the NDP led by Tommy Douglas, the Social Credit from Western Canada, or Réal Caouette's Ralliement des créditistes from Quebec. On the day following the election, Pearson turned sixty-six.

During the 1963 campaign, the Liberals had promised "sixty days of decision" if they were elected. But what occurred in the description of one journalist was "sixty days of derision." The challenges of governing were many and Pearson often appeared to be weak and vacillating. In Quebec, the provincial government of Daniel Lesage wanted more power. Pearson was able to negotiate on these demands but he had also to contend with the rise of violent tactics by the Front de libération du Québec, a separatist paramilitary group founded in the early 1960s. Pearson responded to unrest in Quebec by appointing the Royal Commission on Bilingualism and Biculturalism. Diefenbaker, still smarting from his losses, was able to use obstructionist tactics to bring Parliament to a near standstill and the government was in retreat if not in chaos.

Pearson decided in early 1964 that it was time to introduce a distinctive new Canadian flag. He argued that almost one hundred years after Confederation the country still did not have an official flag. The Red Ensign that had been adapted for use had never officially been approved by Parliament for that purpose. The ensign displayed Great Britain's flag—the red, white, and blue Union Jack—as well as a Canadian coat of arms, all on a background of red. The Conservatives could argue with some justification that the ensign had evolved as the de facto flag and that many Canadians were attached to it. The question of Canada's having a distinctive flag had arisen in 1925 and again in 1945 when Mackenzie King was prime minister. In each case he allowed the matter to slide, probably because he feared it would become a divisive issue. However, the Pearson Liberals had promised in their 1962 and 1963 election platforms to produce a distinctive Canadian flag within two years of being elected.

Pearson had a mix of reasons for promoting a new flag. They included both principle and partisan considerations. His conviction was that Quebec nationalism and increasingly virulent separatism were threats to Canadian unity. He believed a distinctive flag that did not contain British symbols, as did the Red Ensign, would be welcomed in Quebec. The new flag would also be a symbol to other Canadians that the era of the British Empire was over and that Canada was exhibiting its maturity and independence. Pearson's immediate partisan consideration was that his government had proven to be confused and inept. His followers were disheartened. He and they needed both a focus and a political win. Pearson also believed that he could use the issue to undercut Diefenbaker's party leadership.

Shortly after the Liberal victory in April 1963, a backbencher named John Matheson wrote Pearson a twelve-page letter outlining his ideas about a flag. Matheson had been wounded and decorated for his service in the Second World War and was someone with an interest in flags and heraldry. He was also Pearson's parliamentary secretary. Matheson convened a small panel of experts and they produced some preliminary sketches featuring the maple leaf. From among the options provided, Pearson liked a design featuring three conjoined maple leaves on a white background with blue vertical borders to represent a Canadian sea-to-sea motif.

Pearson informed his cabinet in early 1964—and it seems he asked little counsel in doing so—that he wanted to have Parliament approve a new flag. He had already been preparing the way. On May 1, he spoke to the Canadian Legion branch in Espanola, Ontario, a small town in his riding of Algoma East. He talked about the importance of symbols in fostering national unity and made some subtle references to the maple leaf being one such symbol. On May 10, he spoke at a Freedom Festival in Toronto and again he mentioned a new flag. He had earlier, with proposed designs from Matheson in hand, arranged for the post office to create a new stamp that mimicked his favoured design. That stamp was released on May 14. On the same day, Pearson invited eight Parliamentary Press Gallery reporters to his home for what was intended to be a private and informal briefing. Two of the journalists decided to report on the gathering anyway. Members of Parliament were among the last to hear about the flag that they would soon be asked to approve.

Pearson and Matheson had also decided that he would make his first dramatic pitch during a speech that he was scheduled to give to the twentieth dominion convention of the Royal Canadian Legion in Winnipeg on May 17. Pearson knew that Legion members would not be a friendly audience. The organization had been using its monthly publication to attack any notion of a new flag and to insist that the Red Ensign continue to be used. Pearson wrote his own speech. He was a member of the Legion and Matheson convinced him that he should wear his war medals on that evening. When Pearson took the stage, he was almost blinded by a bank of television lights. He spoke to the audience of nineteen hundred as a fellow war veteran and Legion member. He told them that his advisors had warned him against talking about the flag. "That advice, of course, was well meant," he said. "It was also impossible to accept." He said he was aware of their position but that he wanted to be "square and honest" about it. He said that the flag question was contained within the larger issue of national unity. "We are all, or should be, Canadians, and unhyphenated, with pride in our nation and its citizenship, pride in the symbols of that citizenship. The flag is one such symbol."

He was interrupted by jeers and catcalls. Somebody shouted out that he should "drop dead." The Legion president stepped in to call his members to order, but he had also told the convention earlier that he believed there should be a national referendum to settle the flag question. Pearson waved him off, remarking: "As Harry Truman used to say, 'If you can't stand the heat keep out of the kitchen.'" Someone in the crowd shouted out, "You are selling Canada to the pea-soupers." Pearson remained unfazed and oddly enough he was given a standing ovation when he had finished. That may have indicated that the rude call-outs had been the work of a few overly lubricated rowdies, or that even if they disagreed with Pearson, the Legion members admired his courage.

Diefenbaker was waiting in the House of Commons early on the following week: "I would like to ask the prime minister, now that he has returned to Ottawa from the fields of prophecy, whether he would tell the House why the announcement as to the alternate designs he had in mind was not made in the House?" Diefenbaker also asked Pearson about his cozy meeting with journalists at his residence to show them variations of a flag design. He asked if Pearson had already chosen a design or whether he would submit options to his cabinet. Pearson indeed had deliberately ignored Parliament, preferring a public relations strategy that included a post office stamp, several speeches, and the evening with select journalists. Diefenbaker was angry about that and in his questioning on May 19 he introduced several themes in what was to become a passionate and bruising debate on the flag. He said that Pearson was creating disunity in the country. Pearson replied that his purpose was to bring about greater unity. The Conservatives asked Pearson whether he would hold a national plebiscite on the flag. He said no and that Parliament should make a decision. He was asked repeatedly if he would allow a free vote of MPs on the matter of which flag was to be chosen. At first he said he would and then he changed his mind, only to change it again later.

On May 26, cabinet approved Pearson's favoured flag design. Two days later the government introduced a resolution into the House of Commons to establish a new flag but to continue using the Union Jack on certain occasions related to Commonwealth functions. The debate on the flag began in earnest on June 15, 1964.

If Pearson had a motive for pushing ahead, Diefenbaker had his own reasons for making this the political fight of his life. One of those was principle. Although his ancestors were of Germanic and Scottish origin, he was an anglophile. For him the Red Ensign was a symbol of Canada's association with the empire. He had been on record since 1926 in opposing any suggestion that the Red Ensign should be abandoned. But Diefenbaker was also dealing with his own political survival. He won a minority government in 1957 and then a massive victory in an election held the following year. He should have been unchallenged in his success and prominence, but he bungled and underachieved. By 1964 he was seen by a growing number of his caucus and party members as a liability. In February there was an attempt to unseat him at the annual party convention in Ottawa. He held on stubbornly but the growing divisions worried him to the point of distraction. He needed an issue to gather his party around him. The enemy to be rallied against was Lester Pearson, someone whose international reputation and renown Diefenbaker envied but whose parliamentary skills he held in low esteem.

Diefenbaker believed that he could bring down Pearson's minority government on the flag issue. His strategy was to engage in a parliamentary filibuster and tactics of obstruction that would test Pearson's nerve and resolution. If the government did not fall, Diefenbaker planned at minimum to provoke Pearson into using closure, a tactic that would place a strict time limit on the debate. Diefenbaker hoped that would infuriate voters. It had worked for the Conservatives in 1956 during a debate on a trans-Canada pipeline. The Liberals responded to a filibuster by introducing closure and the Conservatives accused the government of being dictatorial. The bill passed but the debate discredited the Liberals in the eyes of voters and contributed to their defeat in the 1957 election. Diefenbaker thought it could work again in 1964.

When the flag debate began on June 15, Diefenbaker was soon to turn sixty-nine years of age and Pearson was sixty-seven. Diefenbaker looked his age and gave the appearance of someone more attuned to the past than the present. Pearson's days as a dashing young diplomat were long behind him as well, and his lithe and athletic physique had given way to a somewhat rotund softness. Unlike Diefenbaker, Pearson had never been a riveting orator. He was graceful and charming on relaxed occasions but his pitch rose unpleasantly in large public settings. He had a discernible lisp and as he spoke his head bobbed and weaved and his fingers poked awkwardly at the air. On June 15, 1964, it was these two men who took to the parliamentary stage in a debate that would not end until six months later.

PEARSON'S SPEECH

Mr. Speaker, I would remind the House that this is the 750th anniversary of the signing of the Magna Carta, and ... today is another anniversary, a little closer to home in both time and space. One hundred years ago today, on June 15, there was a dramatic moment in Canadian history when, in parliament, Sir John A. Macdonald and George Brown, two strong and even bitter political opponents, agreed to meet and try to end their long antagonism for the purpose of creating a Canadian confederation which one day would stretch from sea to sea. I hope that this resolution which is now being discussed one hundred years later will, when action is taken on it, result in a united effort, above party and above personalities, to strengthen and ensure the survival of the confederation which Macdonald and Brown, putting patriotism above all else 100 years ago, did so much to create ...

Pearson begins by invoking British constitutional history and the Magna Carta as well as the day when political enemies Macdonald and Brown set aside their animosity, temporarily at least, to co-operate on the project of nation building. Pearson is attempting to place the flag debate within an honourable political tradition and at the same time he is challenging Diefenbaker to be a statesman. Diefenbaker had wrapped himself in the Red Ensign and castigated Pearson for being insensitive to tradition and to Canada's English and its French heritage. As the debate begins, the Conservatives immediately interrupt Pearson to raise procedural objections and to call for a referendum. The NDP argues that the motion put forward by the Liberals is really two motions: one to introduce a new Canadian flag and a second to continue using the Union Jack for certain limited purposes and occasions. The Speaker agrees that the motion should be divided and it is. Pearson begins again but is once more interrupted by Diefenbaker. Pearson plods on.

Mr. Speaker, if I may continue, as I said a moment ago, this is a serious, a solemn and historic occasion and I venture to hope, as I also mentioned a moment ago, that the debate will be worthy of the occasion. This is the first time in our history that parliamentary action has ever been requested by a Canadian government to decide on a national flag.

MR. DIEFENBAKER: *In that regard, would the prime minister allow a question? Is it not a fact that the order in council of 1949 said that the red ensign shall continue to be the flag until parliament otherwise renders a decision?*

MR. PEARSON: *If my right honourable friend will conceal his impatience he will find that I am dealing with this as we go along ... Back in January 1960, following a broadcast I made, I issued a statement ... and I proposed in that statement on January 27, 1960, the submission by government to parliament of a measure which, if accepted by the representatives of people in parliament would, I hoped, settle the problem of a national flag by agreement on a distinctive design which, unlike the red ensign—a flag never given formal sanction by parliament—could not be confused with certain United Kingdom or colonial flags and which was easily identifiable as Canadian. This was the position I took at that time and it is the position I have taken consistently since that time ...*

At our party rally in 1961 which laid down the policy to be followed by our party, the statement of policy included these words: 'A Liberal government will establish a distinctive Canadian flag within two years of taking office.'

We are carrying out that policy laid down at the party rally. It was in the election platform of 1962 and, in 1963, the undertaking was repeated in exactly the same words … Our party's commitment to ask for a parliamentary decision on the flag extends over many years. The present resolution, therefore, should come as no surprise. We are not proceeding without due notice, nor are we ramming anything down parliament's throat as has been suggested …

Diefenbaker has accused Pearson of trying to foist his own preferred flag design on the Canadian public—he has referred to it elsewhere as "Pearson's pennant." The prime minister, however, is determined to show that he is being faithful to what has been Liberal party policy for several years and through two elections. In his manner of speaking, Pearson tends to use many qualifiers and does so here. This is likely a carryover from the world of diplomacy but it makes for tortuous oratory. Then he turns to the demand by the Conservatives that the flag question be decided at a federal-provincial conference or through a national referendum.

In dealing with this important resolution before us and the procedure that might be followed to bring it into effect, if it meets the wishes of parliament, there has been some criticism to the effect that the resolution should not be submitted to parliament at this time but that there should be a referendum or a plebiscite before action by government or parliament; or that it should be submitted—and this has been another proposal—to a federal-provincial conference for agreement and a decision.

As to the latter, surely this would not be the most effective or the right procedure to follow. Those provinces which have separate flags chose them without reference to the federal government or federal parliament, and they were, of course, right in doing so. The choice was within their own responsibility. Similarly, the choice of national flag is the responsibility of the federal government …

As for a referendum or plebiscite, I have received a great many representations on this emphasizing the desirability of following this course in a matter of such deep and wide national importance … There are strong arguments, I submit, against a referendum or a plebiscite. In the first place, I believe it is essentially out of keeping with our system of parliamentary democracy and responsible government. The very fact that we have had only two plebiscites in the entire history of this country and, so far as I am aware, none at all in the entire history of the United Kingdom indicates that it is not a part of our parliamentary system of government. The essence of our parliamentary system is that the people elect members of parliament on the basis of broad positions of policy and program and they expect the members of parliament to assume the responsibility of making decisions in the national interest based on those positions ...

Votes in a special referendum on a special subject would be by constituencies, and any cleavage on racial or geographical lines would be highlighted over the six or seven month period of the referendum and subsequent action. That seems to be a great disadvantage in the adoption of this constitutional procedure ...

Pearson argues that referenda have been used only rarely in Canadian parliamentary tradition and never in Britain. In Canada, he says people elect MPs to make decisions and expect them to do so. This is a contemporary version of the response provided by the Liberals to Agnes Macphail and other populist democrats in the 1920s when they called for direct democracy, including a more widespread use of referenda. The Liberals responded to that demand by arguing on behalf of representative democracy, much as Pearson is doing here. He also fears that a referendum on a flag would divide the country. Canada had referenda on prohibition in 1898 and on conscription in 1942. Both produced divisive campaigns, and the referendum on conscription also divided Canada bitterly along French and English lines. Interestingly, during the conscription debate in 1917, it was Liberal leader Wilfrid Laurier who called for a referendum. Arthur Meighen refused, using arguments similar to those that Pearson is now employing against Diefenbaker.

I believe that the time has come for the government, in our tradition of responsible government, to take action by submitting this resolution to parliament for decision. Parliament will then take the responsibility and parliament will decide. If the government resolution is defeated, then on a matter of such major importance the government has obviously lost the confidence of parliament. If an amendment is submitted, as I presume

there might be, substituting the red ensign for the maple leaf design, and if it were passed,
then that flag, by action of the parliament of Canada, would become the flag of Canada.

But if parliament accepts the resolution as it is now, then the flag in the resolution,
accepted by parliament, will be submitted to the Queen for a royal proclamation, as is the
proper procedure, and it becomes Canada's flag by true parliamentary mandate. It will
not be the flag of a person or a party; it will be the flag of the people of Canada by the
decision of their representatives in parliament ...

I believe that a national flag of the kind I have described in this resolution, that will
be exclusively Canadian, will bring us closer together; give us a greater feeling of national
identity and unity. Today especially, as [Governor General] Mr. Massey has reminded
us, we need faith and confidence in ourselves as Canadians, with pride in Canada,
devotion to our country. I believe that the adoption of this resolution will help to produce
that result. If I did not deeply and sincerely so believe, I would not be introducing it into
this House of Commons.

Pearson says that the proper democratic procedures are being followed
and the time has come for Parliament to make a decision about a flag.
Then he rolls the dice saying that if he is defeated on the flag his minority
government will resign. That would plunge the country into a third
election in three years. Pearson had initially said this would be a free vote
for MPs but now he appears to have changed his mind. His vacillation will
undermine the confidence that his colleagues have in him while sending a
signal to Diefenbaker that the Conservative tactics are rattling the prime
minister. Pearson also offers another indirect rebuttal of Diefenbaker's
claim about "Pearson's pennant." He says the flag will belong to no
person or party but will bring all Canadians closer together. Pearson is not
often personal in his remarks in Parliament but here says that he believes
sincerely in introducing the flag motion; if he did not believe in it he would
not be doing it. This is ethos, an appeal to his audience on behalf of his
own integrity.

In taking this position, I know there are others who are as patriotic and as Canadian as I
am or can ever hope to be, who disagree honestly and deeply. I respect that kind of honest
disagreement. I know also that a flag issue is bound to raise strong and deep and genuine

emotions. All national symbols have a deep meaning and create strong sentiments. This is why they are so important in national growth; in nourishing loyalty and patriotism among those who make up our nation. It is inevitable, therefore, that there will be strong emotional reactions when there is any suggestion that old symbols should be dropped, or adapted to new conditions and new needs.

Whatever our strength of feeling may be, however, on one side or the other I am sure we can discuss this matter in this House with respect for each other's views and in a way, as I said this afternoon, which will be worthy of the historic importance of this occasion. We have a responsibility to history in this debate and I am sure we all wish to be worthy of that responsibility, on whatever side of the House we sit. And when a decision is reached, whatever that decision may be, we will all, I know, abide by it and do what we can to secure its universal acceptance in this country ...

Pearson appeals to those who disagree with him, whether in the House of Commons, the Canadian Legion, or elsewhere. He asks them to respect opposing views in a polarizing debate. This is a reasonable and statesmanlike posture but it is also an attempt to isolate Diefenbaker and the most caustic and determined critics among the Conservatives. Pearson provides a brief lecture in civics and civility aimed not only at Conservative MPs but also at the media and the public, who Pearson believes are more open to persuasion. He recognizes that flags and other national symbols contain a potent meaning. He would have understood this well from his experience as a soldier, diplomat, and politician. In fact, he was humiliated when, during the Suez Crisis in 1956, the Egyptians objected to the presence of Canadian ground troops under the UN auspices because their badges and uniforms were too similar to those of the British.

It is argued, and I can appreciate the strength of the argument, that the flag of this resolution ignores our past. In my view, it does not. No one would deny, of course, that we have a responsibility to the past. But we have also a greater responsibility to the present and to the future ...

The red ensign has served Canada honourably and well since it was designated for such service by order in council; but those who are in favour of retaining it and making it permanent and official by parliamentary action must surely realize that basically—this is certainly no disrespect to the red ensign—it is the flag of the British merchant marine and that it is similar except for a different coat of arms, to the flags of certain British colonies.

Diefenbaker's opposition to the proposed new flag is based on his claim that Pearson is turning his back on the Red Ensign that Canada had been using for decades. Many of Pearson's opponents accuse him of disrespect toward Great Britain. He is also accused by some of discarding a British symbol to pander to Quebec and thus dividing the country.

I have done some research on this and I have no doubt other hon. members have too. It is true, and this has a bearing on the distinctiveness of the red ensign and its identification with Canada, that apart from Canada and its merchant vessels more than a dozen merchant navies, British companies and other countries, British colonies, use the British red ensign as a base for their flags. Indeed, half of these are British colonies. The majority of these flags based on the red ensign have a badge or coat of arms ... which, at no great distance, may be easily confused with the Canadian shield, or vice-versa ...

In an effort to clear up subsequent uncertainty as to what was the Canadian flag, even for government buildings, the colonial secretary in London stated in 1912 that the Union Jack was the national flag of Canada. And so it remained for many years; all through World War I, when the Union Jack was the flag of the Canadian forces under which Canadians served and under which many Canadians died. The red ensign, though many of my correspondents do not seem to appreciate this, was not in use during World War I in any way, shape or form for the Canadian forces.

It was not until January 26, 1924, that an order in council was passed authorizing the red ensign to be flown for limited use over all government buildings abroad, and that became essential because we were building up a diplomatic service and for obvious reasons we had to have some flag to fly over Canadian embassies that was not the Union Jack.

And so the situation remained until towards the end of World War II when in 1944, by order in council, the red ensign was authorized to be flown by our forces overseas. Then on September 5, 1945, was passed that order in council to which reference has already been made more than once, decreeing that, until such time as action is taken by parliament for the formal adoption of a national flag, the red ensign may be flown wherever place or occasion may make it desirable to fly a distinctive Canadian flag. That is the authority given in 1945, not by parliament but by order in council, by which the red ensign has been flying as a Canadian flag.

Pearson must meet and deflate Diefenbaker's most cogent argument—that the Red Ensign is steeped in tradition; that Canadians see it as their flag; and that it should continue to serve that purpose. Pearson, therefore, engages in a brief history lesson. He claims to have researched the topic. Actually he had delegated that task to MP John Matheson. He had advised Pearson that because Canada had no flag of its own, the Red Ensign was first authorized in 1892 for use on Canadian ships by the British admiralty. The Canadian and British governments later permitted its use for other purposes as well. Pearson claims that the Red Ensign was not—as some say—used in any way during the First World War by the Canadian forces. He is later to be challenged on this assertion by Conservative MPs who had served at the front, something which they pointedly remind Pearson he had not done.

Pearson also says that the Red Ensign had been authorized for use by orders-in-council, which are directives from the cabinet, but that it had never been formally accepted as Canada's flag by a vote in Parliament. While true, this is a fine point that would likely be of little interest or concern to most Canadians. The Conservatives can, and do, argue that Canadians have come to accept the Red Ensign as their flag even though it has not received full parliamentary approval. Pearson wants to "invent" a tradition by creating a new Canadian flag. Diefenbaker is attached to the Red Ensign on the basis of respecting an existing tradition, albeit one of quite recent invention.

In my view, the time has come for a further and final change. If, as I believe to be the case, Canada needs a national flag and if the red ensign is not the most appropriate design for this purpose, what should that design be? In my view, it should be based on three red maple leaves because that is our formal and emblematic link with our Canadian past. The record shows this conclusively. The maple leaf itself has been accepted as a Canadian symbol since long before confederation. It is deep in our history and in our traditions. Contemporary records all through the nineteenth century are full of references to it … In war it has become the emblem of the men in uniform; their official and their unofficial emblem. The words "maple leaf," in fact, are synonymous with Canada in uniform. Those words mean a great deal, as the maple leaf badge does, for all veterans of the two world wars. The official badges of the three armed services all include maple leaves, and have for a hundred years … Indeed, the three joined maple leaves have for us a historic and heraldic significance which, in my view, make them preferable on a flag, to a single maple leaf which has not the same significance and has not, in fact, any formal emblematic authority; but this does not necessarily exclude it from consideration …

Pearson had commissioned Matheson to advise him on a new flag; Matheson, in turn, had seized on the importance of the maple leaf as a Canadian symbol and pointed to its use in the military and elsewhere. Pearson recommended this design to Parliament. Diefenbaker is incensed for a variety of reasons but particularly because he believes that Pearson is forcing his own favoured design on members of Parliament and the country.

This resolution does indeed mark a break with the past, as every accepted stage in the evolution of men and nations must mark a break with the past. But this break does not dishonour or repudiate the past, or the flag symbols of that past under which many of us have served and lived … I have seen the Union Jack carried doggedly and heroically in combat; I have seen it flying defiantly over the fires caused by the bombing of London; I know something of the decency, the goodness and the fortitude of the British people. All this is part of our tradition, too, a proud part; it will not be betrayed in any way by the proposals in this resolution. None of these things will be altered in our minds and in our hearts when we support this resolution. We support it as Canadians, because the stand it takes is Canadian and because it marks another stage in the growth of Canada …

I believe that the flag we are submitting in this resolution results not only from our growth but from our diversity, the achievement of peoples with pasts in other countries; but they are now concerned, as we are all concerned, with one future only, and that is the future of Canada. We are all concerned with Canada's future in a world at peace, in freedom and security. So this flag, if it is adopted by parliament, will stand for one Canada; united, strong, independent and equal to her tasks.

MR. NOWLAN: *What about the Union Jack? Are we to adopt that too?*

MR. PEARSON: *I will be delighted to talk about the Union Jack, but when I mentioned it this afternoon I was howled down by my hon. friends opposite ... As I was saying when this interruption occurred, this flag in the resolution, if it is adopted by parliament, will symbolize a Canada united, strong, independent and equal to her task. It will recognize that we cannot be saved or sanctified merely by the valour and devotion of our ancestors. It remains to us in each new generation to do our own duty in changing conditions. Our willingness to do that duty means adaptation and change. It means sacrifice; it means work; it means endurance. And how we meet this challenge in the future under what I hope will be a distinctive Canadian national flag will determine the destiny of our country.*

In these restless and soul-searching days about which Right Honourable Vincent Massey [the governor general] spoke in Charlottetown last week we are being asked particularly to give to the hearts and minds of our children a feeling of national identity, national pride, national loyalty. We are asked to provide for them a symbol of our independent strength and of the bright promise of a future for them. We are asked to help them to be more conscious of our country and more proud of Canadian citizenship. I believe that a distinctive maple leaf Canadian flag will help them in their search of this objective ...

It is for this generation and this parliament to give them and to give us all a common flag; a Canadian flag which, while bringing together but rising above the landmarks and milestones of the past, will say proudly to the world and to the future: "I stand for Canada."

In his peroration, Pearson becomes personal and employs ethos once again. He dwells briefly on his experience in Great Britain during the Second World War. There he saw the Union Jack "flying defiantly over the fires" in bombed-out London. The picture he paints bears some resemblance (probably unintended) to Wilfrid Laurier's speech to the Club Canadien in 1877. Laurier had described "the English flag [floating] from the ancient Citadel of Quebec." The circumstances are different but both men are using the symbolism of the Union Jack to demonstrate their loyalty to Britain and its democratic tradition. Pearson's own wartime experience is important to his credibility. He casts himself as someone who likes and respects the British but who believes it is time that Canada has its own flag. He ends by saying that he stands for Canada, a claim that John Diefenbaker will not allow to go uncontested.

THE IMPACT OF PEARSON'S SPEECH

Pearson made his case and sat down with the applause of his caucus ringing in his ears. Diefenbaker followed Pearson immediately in the debate and he was in no mood to compromise. He described the design of the proposed flag as "innocuous and insipid" and said that it ignored Canada's past. The Maple Leaf design provided no reference to Canada's heritage or the contributions made by either the British or the French in building the nation. He accused Pearson of dividing the country and asked if the flag issue was being used as a diversion from the "confusion and chaos" surrounding the government. He pounced on Pearson's apparent contradictory statements about whether the vote on the flag would be one allowing MPs to vote as they chose rather than being forced to follow the party line. He made passing reference to the pipeline debate of 1956 that preceded the Liberal defeat in 1957, saying that Pearson and the Liberals were showing a similar arrogance in 1964. Once again, he called for a national referendum.

After a parliamentary recess, the debate continued into the hot sultry days of an Ottawa summer. The Conservatives engaged in a filibuster. There were also testy meetings between Pearson and Diefenbaker attended by leaders of the smaller parties. Pearson wanted to have the flag question referred to a parliamentary committee. Diefenbaker was opposed unless Pearson would agree that 80 to 90 per cent of MPs on such a committee must concur on any flag design before it could be sent back to the House for debate. Nor would he agree to any time limitation being placed on that debate. Then in September Léon Balcer, a Quebec MP and deputy leader of the Conservatives, broke with Diefenbaker and asked that the bill be sent to a committee for perusal.

After further meetings, the leaders agreed to set up a committee of fifteen members to consider design options for the flag and to recommend one to the House within six weeks. There was still no agreement about how many committee members would have to agree on the preferred option or what time limit, if any, would be placed on the final debate. Canadians were invited to submit ideas for a flag and amazingly about six thousand designs were forwarded to the committee. In October, after an eye-glazing forty-five meetings, that committee was set to vote. The Conservatives wanted the Red Ensign but they were voted down. Pearson's preferred flag containing three maple leaves was another option, but there was also a new entrant—a single maple leaf on a white background flanked by two vertical red bars. Reluctantly, Pearson had been convinced by John Matheson and others that a single maple leaf was the better option. The Conservatives on the committee believed, mistakenly, that the Liberals would support "Pearson's pennant." So they decided to vote for the single maple leaf with the intent of producing a divided result. It was a fatal mistake. The Liberals, as well as representatives from the NDP and the other parties, crossed them up by voting for the newly proposed design. The Conservatives had been out-manoeuvred and they were both stunned and angry. Diefenbaker believed that there had been collusion between the Liberals and opposition parties and he may have been right.

In late October, the Conservatives changed tactics and focused their attention on a number of scandals involving Liberal cabinet ministers. The intention was to use any available means to discredit the government. In December, however, they returned to their filibuster on the flag. When they did, Léon Balcer broke with Diefenbaker for a second time and urged the government to invoke closure to limit the flag debate. With this political cover from a prominent Conservative, the Liberals did limit the debate. Any member speaking to the flag motion was restricted to twenty minutes. Pearson and Diefenbaker had one final clash in the House late in the evening of December 14. Pearson was to end the debate but the Conservatives demanded that Diefenbaker be heard. That was voted down. Pearson then offered to share his twenty minutes with Diefenbaker who rebuffed him. Their final confrontation occurred a few minutes later, during the dying moments of the debate:

DIEFENBAKER: *The Right Honourable gentleman has done everything to divide this country.*
PEARSON: *Will the Right Honourable gentleman contain himself for two or three minutes longer and then we will vote.*
DIEFENBAKER: *When the Right Honourable gentleman starts giving me advice, I*

say to him, You have done more to divide Canada than any other Prime Minister.
The vote was taken and the committee report to adopt a single maple leaf flag passed easily by a vote of 163 to 78 with 23 abstentions. The French Canadian Conservatives, including Balcer, voted with the government. The debate, which spanned six months, had generated 308 speeches, 210 of them by the Conservatives. Immediately following the vote, most, but not all, MPs rose from their seats and sang both "O Canada" and "God Save the Queen." Two days later the House voted also to adopt the Union Jack as the commonwealth flag. On January 28, 1965, the Queen signed Canada's new flag proclamation in the presence of Pearson, who was in London to attend the funeral of Winston Churchill. The Queen gently teased Pearson by asking him what had become of his original preferred flag design. The new flag was raised above the Peace Tower for the first time on February 16, 1965, on a day that was cold, damp, and grey. There were a reported ten thousand people on hand for the occasion. On the official platform Pearson stood hatless in the cold and said that the day would "always be remembered as a milestone in Canada's national progress." John Diefenbaker was seen using a handkerchief to dab a tear from his eyes.

Pearson got his flag but much of what he hoped it would accomplish was not to be. In his memoirs, completed by others after his death, he writes that he was determined in 1964 to do something to improve national unity and to prevent what he feared was the disintegration of the Canadian federation. He hoped that the flag would blunt the forces of nationalism and separatism. It appears that most Quebecers did not care much one way or the other. Pierre Trudeau, a federalist who was later to be recruited by Pearson, said bluntly that most Quebecers "do not give a tinker's damn about the flag. It's a matter of complete indifference." Quebec nationalists already had a flag to which they related in the blue and white Fleurdelisé, adopted as the province's standard in 1948.

There was much talk during the parliamentary debate about Canada's two founding nations and the symbols appropriate to honour each. There was virtually no mention about Indigenous peoples who surely should count as founding nations. In the flag debate, they were overlooked by parliamentarians of every political stripe.

There is a postscript to the flag debate that casts an added light upon it. Diefenbaker believed there had been collusion among the Liberals and the smaller opposition parties to introduce the Maple Leaf flag. The most damaging collusion, however, came from deep within the Conservative caucus. Southam News journalist Peter Calamai published a story in 1986 based upon sixty-one pages of Liberal cabinet minutes released following an Access to Information request. The flag debate began in the House of Commons on June 15, 1964. Minutes from a cabinet meeting on the following day indicate that Maurice Lamontagne, a minister from Quebec, told his colleagues that all eight Conservative MPs from that province would split from their party and vote for the Maple Leaf flag. According to the same minutes, Lamontagne had received this assurance from none other than Diefenbaker's deputy leader Léon Balcer. It was Balcer who, in September, was to break ranks with Diefenbaker and call for the flag motion to be sent to a committee. The information that Balcer shared would have been invaluable to the Liberals. They knew that he and the others were about to undercut Diefenbaker, who had staked all on the flag debate.

Since Balcer shared that information with Lamontagne, it is possible—even likely—that he would also have given the Liberals notice in December that he would call for closure to limit the flag debate. As promised, Balcer and the eight other Quebec Conservative MPs did vote with the government in favour of the new flag. They may well have tired of hearing from other Conservatives MPs in debate and in the press that the new flag was Pearson's sop to Quebec. Pearson makes brief reference in his memoirs to a late 1964 meeting in his office with Balcer at the latter's request. Pearson writes that Balcer believed Diefenbaker to be a threat to national unity because he was prepared to exploit anti-Quebec feelings. In January 1965, Balcer was among a group of Conservative MPs who called for a leadership convention. A few months before the November 1965 election, he left the party and sat as an independent, claiming that there was no place for a French Canadian in a party led by Diefenbaker. He did not contest the election that occurred later in that year.

In 1965 Pearson won another minority government over Diefenbaker. Pearson chose to vacate the leadership during Canada's centennial year in

1967 to be replaced by Pierre Trudeau. In that same year John Diefenbaker, who had fought to hang on as party chief, was forced out at a leadership convention as he approached his seventy-second birthday. Pearson died in 1972 and when he lay in state his coffin was covered by the red Maple Leaf. Diefenbaker died seven years later and had planned his funeral elaborately. On his instructions, while he lay in state and when he was buried, the Maple Leaf on his coffin was partially overlain with the Red Ensign.

Reduced to its simplicity, Pearson won the flag debate and Diefenbaker lost. Pearson may be accused of playing politics with the issue but his actions and his speeches had a ring of sincerity. He was born at the end of the Victorian era when Canada was still a British colony whose foreign policy was made in London. When Britain went to war with Germany in 1914, Canada was automatically at war as well, her troops at first commanded by British officers. But as the century progressed, the United States replaced Great Britain as the world's great power. Canada was emerging as an independent middle power in its own right, and as a diplomat, Lester Pearson was involved in that transition. He believed, among many other things, that a sovereign Canada should have its own flag and not a hand-me-down from the British merchant marine.

For the literal-minded, flags may appear to be of little importance, but in reality they are steeped in a potent symbolism. One has only to think of their being flown at Olympic or other ceremonies, their use in battles, and their being draped over the coffins of returned soldiers or revered public figures at funerals. Pearson intended to deliberately invent a tradition by creating a new flag signifying a new sense of Canadian independence and purpose. The Liberals would claim, not incidentally, that they were the arbiters of the brave new world. On the other hand, Diefenbaker was adamant about defending and retaining the Red Ensign, which for him and his followers represented Canada's ties to Britain.

Early in 1965, after months of debate and squabbling in Parliament, Canadians were no doubt tired of it all. As the new flag was raised, the acrimonious debate was largely forgotten by all except its partisan combatants. The flag gained a quick acceptance and most people appeared to be pleased with it then as they are now. Pearson had forced the issue and the Maple Leaf was to become both a symbol and a portent of Canada's

PIERRE TRUDEAU
ON QUEBEC SOVEREIGNTY

MAY 14, 1980

*"We are going to say to those who want
us to stop being Canadians, we are going to say
a resounding, an overwhelming No."*

Pierre Trudeau was raised in Quebec at a time when a clerically inspired ethnic nationalism ruled the day. As a youth he absorbed those values but he was well off so he could afford to travel and attend elite schools, and it changed his thinking. When he returned to Quebec, he came to loathe nationalism and to believe that the best choice for Quebeckers lay within the Canadian federal system. Eventually Lester Pearson recruited Trudeau as a Liberal candidate and in 1968 he became prime minister. Trudeau locked horns with René Lévesque, an old political foe who had abandoned the provincial Liberals to create the Parti Québécois (PQ), which won power in 1976. In 1980 the PQ held a referendum to determine whether the Quebec government should press for a sovereignty arrangement with the rest of Canada. Trudeau said it was separatism by another name and he was deeply opposed. Near the campaign's end Trudeau made a dramatic speech in a crowded hockey arena in Montreal.

◆

Pierre Elliott Trudeau was born in 1919 into a bilingual and bicultural family in Montreal. He was the second of three Trudeau children. The ancestors of his father, Charles, had arrived in New France in 1659. Charles Trudeau (or Charlie as he was known) was a lawyer who practised in Montreal's business district. Trudeau's mother, Grace Elliott, was from a prosperous Montreal family whose forebearers had been Protestant United Empire Loyalists, but her father became a Catholic when he married a Québecoise. Grace was raised in the church and remained a devout follower. She was a refined woman who spoke and wrote French and English and both languages were used in the Trudeau home. Charlie Trudeau was a gregarious man who succeeded in a business world dominated by English Quebeckers and largely closed to francophones. He became wealthy as a result of his endeavours. The family, after an earlier modest lifestyle, lived comfortably in the affluent enclave of Outremont and enjoyed the services of a chauffeur and a maid.

Trudeau first attended a bilingual school in his neighbourhood, but in 1932 his parents enrolled him at Collège Jean-de-Brébeuf, a school run by the Jesuits. It was an elite institution for francophone boys that focused on the study of languages, elocution, philosophy, and logic. Trudeau was to receive an education that was in many ways similar to that enjoyed by Wilfrid Laurier and by the young men who were to become prominent public figures in Trudeau's era. He was a brilliant student and recognized as such, although he was also an attention seeker who revelled in contrarian behaviour. He was at times brash and abrasive toward other students. But he was moulded intellectually by his teachers and he dutifully accepted much of what they promoted. There was, for example, a pronounced strain of anti-Semitism at the school and in Quebec, as there was elsewhere in Canada. In 1938, Pierre wrote a play performed at Brébeuf that chided those who purchased goods from Jewish merchants.

The Catholic Church held a powerful and privileged position in Quebec. The church was both an impediment to, and a catalyst for, change. There were Catholic-inspired credit unions, farm organizations, labour unions, and Catholic Action groups in addition to schools and hospitals. The church played a key role in the survival of a French culture in the centuries following the conquest, but it was also arch-conservative in political and social terms. It promoted the belief that francophones in North America were a chosen people in an almost biblical sense and at Brébeuf there was support for a church-inspired, autonomous Quebec state. This was the kind of activity among the clergy that Wilfrid Laurier had warned against in his powerful speech back in 1877. Indeed, there was at Brébeuf both enthusiasm and support for authoritarian and even fascist leaders such as Mussolini in Italy, Salazar in Portugal, and Franco in Spain.

The Jesuits had a reputation for nurturing an elite corps of leaders in politics, academia, law, and journalism. Young Trudeau never doubted that he was destined to become one of them. "I must become a great man," he confided in his diary as a teenager. "I would like so much to be a great politician and guide my nation." The classical curriculum at Brébeuf included both rhetoric and elocution and Trudeau also decided to take extra lessons after school to perfect classical French pronunciation and to shed his street-informed accent. Frail, sensitive, and with an acne condition as a boy, he took up diving, skiing, and canoeing with vigour. He was to remain short in stature but from his teen years onward he had the sculpted body of an athlete and was able to give as well as he received in street fights with other adolescent boys.

Trudeau's final year at Brébeuf was in 1939. He enrolled to study law at the Université de Montréal in 1940. His university years coincided with the Second World War. Students who did not enlist had to join an officers' training corps, which he did without enthusiasm. On one occasion he also engaged in a bizarre stunt by donning an old military uniform and French war helmet and riding off on his motorcycle to the Laurentians. While at university, Trudeau remained in close contact with several of his former Brébeuf professors, who urged him to oppose military conscription, as did most Quebeckers. Trudeau gave fiery speeches during the anti-conscription campaign and in a local by-election. He appeared entirely untroubled by the dire threat posed by European fascism. In fact, he favoured French Marshal Philippe Pétain's puppet and fascist government at Vichy. While a student at the Université de Montréal, he was even for a time involved in a secret revolutionary group committed to violence against the Canadian state. There was a lot of reading and talk but the group was to go nowhere.

Trudeau did not enjoy studying law but finished first in his class in 1943 and applied for graduate work in politics and economics at Harvard University beginning in 1944. His studies there and later in Paris and at the London School of Economics, and perhaps his inveterate travelling, were to challenge and then to surmount much of the earlier education that he had received in Quebec. Some of his most cherished professors at Harvard and later in London were Jewish academics who had been forced to flee fascism in continental Europe. Trudeau came to embrace the political philosophy that informed liberal democracy. He also began to separate the spiritual from the secular in public life, although he was always to remain a practising Catholic. His earlier immersion in nationalism, his anti-Semitism, corporatism, and even his flirtation with fascism were all to fall away after 1944. He never acknowledged this dark side of his past while he lived. It came to light only in academic research and later in a book published after his death by two long-time acquaintances to whom he had granted access to revealing personal papers housed at Library and Archives Canada.

After five years spent studying and travelling, a luxury made possible by his wealth, Trudeau returned home to Montreal in 1949. The province was mired in the long reign of Premier Maurice Duplessis, an authoritarian leader who doled out patronage and relied mostly on the church to provide education and social services. He championed rural Quebec and provincial rights, although not separation. He was fierce in his opposition to communism, trade unions, and liberal tendencies of any kind. His opponents described his years in power as *la grande noirceur*—"the great darkness." Trudeau returned home just as Duplessis was turning the police loose on striking workers at an asbestos mine. Along with his friend Gérard Pelletier, a journalist, and union leader Jean Marchand, Trudeau joined the workers on their picket lines. Although he played only a minor role in the strike, it was his baptism of fire upon his return to Quebec. He began to act as legal counsel for unions and briefly considered becoming the research director of the Canadian Council of Labour. But he surprised all of his friends, and disappointed many, when he took a job with the Privy Council Office in Ottawa later in 1949.

There was a dearth of francophones in the federal civil service and although Trudeau was employed in a junior role, he impressed his superiors and learned much about how the federal government worked. As someone who aspired to a public profile, he did not appreciate the anonymity forced upon public servants. He also found Ottawa to be staid and generally not congenial toward francophones. By 1951 he was back in Montreal. His father had died of a heart attack years earlier at age forty-six and Trudeau had always, while in Montreal, lived with his mother, Grace. He remained her close and devoted companion, often accompanying her to daily mass. He was by then in his early thirties, but despite his brilliance and his own sense of destiny, his accomplishments had been modest. They consisted of an excellent and wide-ranging education, extensive travel, and a honing of his physical prowess. He had gained a reputation in some quarters as a wealthy dilettante. By comparison, at a similar age Wilfrid Laurier had practised law for ten years, edited a newspaper, and won an election to sit in Quebec's assembly.

However, Trudeau was finally prepared to engage. With Gérard Pelletier and others in 1950 he launched *Cité Libre*, a magazine that opposed the Union Nationale government and called for social change and political reform. The publication was never widely read but it was influential in Quebec's intellectual circles. It was to become Trudeau's principal medium of expression throughout the 1950s and early '60s. He criticized Quebec's political elite as being closed and reactionary. He called for the province to reform its politics and modernize its economy, and for its inhabitants to open themselves to the wider world. He was Keynesian in his economics and social democratic in his political outlook. He had come to accept Canadian federalism as the political system that would best promote equality and guarantee the fundamental rights of all Canadians, including Quebeckers. Despite this, he could never quite settle on a political party to which he could offer allegiance. Throughout much of the 1950s, he supported the CCF and had close ties with some of the Montreal-based intellectuals who sustained the party in that city; but he disappointed them by choosing to limit his direct involvement. He distrusted the provincial Liberals, believing the party to be undemocratic, and he would not engage with them either.

Duplessis died in 1959 and the Union Nationale government was replaced by Jean Lesage and the Liberals in 1960. Many of the reformers with whom Trudeau had engaged, including René Lévesque, became involved with Lesage in what came to be called the Quiet Revolution. Lévesque was recruited from his broadcasting career to run as a star Liberal candidate. Trudeau, who had remained aloof, received no such invitation. By 1962 he was attacking the government for what he called the "new treason of the intellectuals" in promoting nationalism. He believed that the wars of the twentieth century had proved it to be a reactionary and destructive force. Many of his former teachers and colleagues, though, were moving toward the idea of an independent Quebec and his split with them became increasingly acrimonious. In 1961 Trudeau became a law professor at the Université de Montréal. He was prominent in intellectual circles within Quebec and increasingly known in English Canada. In Ottawa, the Pearson Liberals were still reeling from political scandals that had forced the resignation of several Quebec ministers and MPs. Pearson was attempting to renew the party. In 1965 he recruited Jean Marchand, Gérard Pelletier, and Trudeau as candidates. All of them won seats in the federal election later that year.

Trudeau was appointed as Pearson's parliamentary secretary and then became minister of justice in 1967. In that portfolio, he quickly reformed divorce laws in a way that would have pleased Agnes Macphail and others who had striven for equality decades earlier. Trudeau also introduced Criminal Code amendments that liberalized laws on abortion and homosexuality. He became known for his quote that the state had no place in the bedrooms of the nation. Pearson retired late in 1967 and Trudeau won the Liberal leadership contest the following year. Among his fans was media guru Marshall McLuhan, who wrote to the new prime minister, saying that his cool demeanour and "man-in-the-mask" face were a perfect fit for a politician in the television age. Trudeau was the first Canadian federal politician to be fully at home in the medium. He called an election in 1968 and rode a wave of adulation to win a majority government, the first for the Liberals since 1953.

He had spent years refining his political philosophy and he brought those ideas with him to Ottawa. He opposed the concept of Quebec's being a nation in its own right. He also opposed any talk of two nations (*deux nations*), which would have granted the province a special status within Confederation. Key to his arguments against the need for Quebec separatism was his promise to enhance the use of French in the federal government and its agencies, and to provide a more central role for francophones in the civil service. He passed legislation in 1969 that made both English and French official languages in Canada and required federal institutions to provide services in either language on request where numbers warranted. These policies created a backlash in English Canada, particularly in the West, and that in turn served as further justification by Quebec separatists to promote their cause.

Then there was constitutional reform. There had been talk among the political classes for decades about changes that would allow Canada to modify the British North America Act of 1867 without having to go cap-in-hand to the Parliament of Great Britain. Trudeau had been involved in reform proposals as a federal civil servant in the early 1950s and more recently as a cabinet minister. He wanted agreement not only on a constitutional amending formula but also on a charter embedded in the constitution that would protect the rights of individuals against encroachments by the state. As prime minister, he thought he had won agreement with the provinces arising from a constitutional conference in Victoria in 1971. However, Premier Robert Bourassa was greeted by a storm of criticism in Quebec for agreeing to sign on. He chose not to present the package to the National Assembly and the deal fell apart. Trudeau was angry about that and never forgave Bourassa.

Trudeaumania did not last long. It was sorely tested in 1970 when British diplomat James Cross and Quebec cabinet minister Pierre Laporte were kidnapped by the Front de Libération du Québec (FLQ), a separatist group prepared to use terror tactics. Laporte, who had been Trudeau's classmate at Brébeuf, was killed by his abductors. Premier Bourassa and Montreal's mayor Jean Drapeau believed that these violent events were part of a wider insurrection and they asked Trudeau for help. He and his cabinet took the unusual, and many said extreme, step of invoking the War Measures Act in peacetime. It gave to police extraordinary powers of arrest and detention. Trudeau also sent the military in to assist and they were omnipresent, particularly on the streets of Montreal. A long list of academics, writers, trade unionists, and activists were arrested, many of them people who had been or were Trudeau's acquaintances. He refused to capitulate to demands of kidnappers. Cross was released in December and Laporte's killers were captured later in the same month.

Most MPs, with the notable exception of the NDP caucus led by Tommy Douglas, supported Trudeau's actions. Polls at the time indicated overwhelming support for the measures by both French- and English-speaking Canadians. However, Trudeau's decision damaged his reputation among civil libertarians and caused an irreparable rift between him and the political and intellectual class in Quebec.

In the 1972 election, he came close to losing office and had to form a minority government with the day-to-day support of the New Democratic Party. The Liberal government was side-swiped by an economic crisis triggered by an Arab oil embargo introduced in retaliation for Western countries siding with Israel in a 1973 war with Egypt and Syria. The result in Canada was both inflation and economic stagnation as a long run of post-war prosperity came to an end. Despite those problems, Trudeau won a majority in 1974, a win attributed in part to the presence in the campaign of his young wife. He had surprised everyone in 1971 by marrying Margaret Sinclair, his junior by twenty-eight years. Trudeau was attractive to women and had numerous relationships going back to his teenage years; but usually he was unable or unwilling to commit. At other times, it was the women who called it off, in one case because the person he was dating refused to convert to Catholicism as he insisted she do. Trudeau had a reputation as a swinging bachelor but he lived at home with his mother until he moved to Ottawa in 1965 at age forty-six. Trudeau and Margaret had three sons. After their marriage disintegrated she was to say that despite his intellectual acuity and hip reputation, Pierre Trudeau had entirely traditional expectations of her in a marriage.

Following his majority victory in 1974, Trudeau's determination to maintain national unity appeared to be more vulnerable than ever. In 1976 the Parti Québécois (PQ) under René Lévesque was elected to office on a promise of achieving Quebec independence. Trudeau and Lévesque had known each other since the mid-1950s when Trudeau returned from his studies and travels and Lévesque was a popular broadcaster. The two clashed almost immediately, long before their politics divided them. Trudeau first met Lévesque in the Radio Canada cafeteria in Montreal to ask him to write a piece for *Cité Libre*. "Hey, Lévesque," he said, "you're a hell of a speaker but I am starting to wonder if you can write." For his part, Lévesque later told an interviewer that Trudeau had an "inborn talent for making you want to slap his face."

Lévesque, as the province's minister of natural resources, merged private hydroelectric companies into the publicly owned Hydro-Québec in 1963. Trudeau opposed that move as well as others taken by the Lesage government in search of becoming, as they described it, masters in their own house. The Union Nationale defeated the Liberals in 1966 and Lévesque left the Liberal Party to sit as an independent. Soon after, he and others created a political movement to pursue Quebec sovereignty. At about the same time, Trudeau became the minister of justice in the federal Liberal government. In 1968 Lévesque created the Parti Québécois. The party won only a smattering of seats in the first two elections it contested in 1970 and 1973. In a Montreal speech in May 1976, Trudeau declared that separatism was dead but just a few months later Lévesque led the PQ to a stunning victory over the Liberals.

Lévesque was born and raised in the Gaspé Peninsula. His father, Dominique, was a lawyer who, like Trudeau's father, had died young. Lévesque was a bright student who also attended a Jesuit school. As had Trudeau, Lévesque decided early on that he was destined to be a leader. He began to study law at Laval University but dropped out to work as a journalist, first with Radio-Canada and later as a foreign correspondent with the Voice of America during the Second World War. He returned home to become a popular and influential host on radio and television. Lévesque arose from more modest circumstances but he and Trudeau had much by way of shared background and experience. Both attended elite Jesuit schools; both felt a sense of personal destiny; and both had been involved in public life during the waning years of the Duplessis regime, Lévesque more prominently than Trudeau. But the two men were also different in many ways. Trudeau was austere, cerebral, and almost patrician in his bearing. Lévesque was a populist who chain-smoked, wore rumpled suits, and relied upon gut instincts and intuition. He was a man about town, someone who kept late nights and was known for his charm and his dalliances with women. He and Trudeau eventually parted company dramatically on their views regarding the best future for Quebec. Although both were committed democrats, Lévesque wanted to lead his province out of Canada while Trudeau was convinced that Quebeckers were better off within it.

Following the 1974 election, Trudeau faced daunting economic challenges. He presided over dramatically increasing government deficits and debt. In 1976 he responded to inflationary pressures by introducing wage and price controls, something that he had campaigned against only months earlier. In Quebec, Lévesque pursued two themes. He wanted to replace a corrupted Liberal regime with good government. But he also proposed sovereignty-association, which he said would preserve an economic arrangement with the rest of Canada, something akin to the European Union. He promised that his government would hold a referendum on the issue during its first term in office. For his part, Trudeau, in a speech to the American Congress in 1977, said that Quebec separation would be a "crime against humanity."

By 1979 fate appeared to be smiling on Lévesque. Trudeau and the Liberals had been defeated by Joe Clark's Conservatives in a May election. Trudeau resigned as Liberal leader. Joe Clark appeared to be comfortable with a more decentralized federation and indicated that he would not attempt to intervene in a Quebec referendum campaign. In the fall, Lévesque presented his plan for sovereignty-association and announced that the vote would be held in May 1980. Then the unexpected happened. Joe Clark had won only enough seats in May 1979 to form a minority government and in December he was defeated in the House of Commons. The Liberals convinced Trudeau to make a political comeback and he won a majority in the election held in February. He appeared at a victory celebration at an Ottawa hotel saying, "Welcome to the 1980s."

In Quebec, Lévesque's polling told him that a majority of people supported sovereignty-association, but the support crumbled when people were asked if Quebec should become its own country. This ambiguity was reflected in the referendum question, which ran to more than one hundred words. Lévesque scribbled it onto a sheet of paper after a long nocturnal meeting with his advisors in an attempt to come up with just the right wording. The question did not talk about separation but rather asked people if they favoured giving the Quebec government a mandate to negotiate sovereignty-association. Embedded in the wording was the promise that if Quebecers said yes to these negotiations there would be a second referendum to decide upon a final parting of the ways with the rest of Canada.

The Parti Québécois was better prepared for the referendum campaign than the Quebec Liberals, now led by Claude Ryan, former editor of the influential newspaper *Le Devoir*. When the televised debate began in the National Assembly in March, the PQ was ready and well-rehearsed. In his speech, Levesque said that "the time has come to choose the path to our future." The PQ focused on a critique of how federalism had failed the province and on the economic arguments in favour of sovereignty-association. In contrast, Ryan and the Liberals looked tired and their arguments were thin. The federalist No side had been comfortably ahead in the polls when the campaign began but by mid-March the lead had shrunk to just a few percentage points. Lévesque was campaigning well and had the momentum. Trudeau believed that Claude Ryan was not up to the job of leading the No forces and that the provincial Liberals lacked communications capacity. He also viewed Ryan as a soft nationalist who believed in a special status for Quebec within Canada, something Trudeau adamantly opposed. He appointed Jean Chrétien, the minister of justice and attorney general, to represent the federal government in the campaign. Ryan nominally led the No side but Chrétien shared the stage with him every night and provided the raw emotion that Ryan lacked.

Ottawa poured federal money into the campaign in barely disguised ways, such as inserting a federalist note into envelopes containing family allowance cheques sent into the province prior to the referendum vote. Chrétien and other federal cabinet ministers attacked the Yes side's claims about economics. They reminded Quebeckers how much federal money was spent in their province. The federalists also threatened that a sovereign Quebec would have to pay a world price for Western oil and natural gas. Premiers from other provinces assisted by saying they would refuse to negotiate sovereignty with Quebec in the event of a Yes vote. The tide began to turn and the weight shifted onto Lévesque's shoulders. For him, a campaign that had begun in a confident and relaxed fashion became stressful and intense. As he watched his lead slipping away, Lévesque drove himself to the point of exhaustion as he spoke to large rallies in crowded halls and arenas night after night.

Trudeau had decided to use his own presence sparingly in the campaign, but he felt the federal Liberals had every right to engage. They had swept seventy-four of seventy-five seats in the federal election held in February 1980 and could argue with justification that they represented Quebec opinion every bit as much as provincially elected politicians. He gave four speeches, one in the House of Commons and three in Quebec. His message to Quebeckers was that Lévesque was trying to fool them with a trick question about sovereignty-association when the real question was a Yes or No to separation. That annoyed Lévesque, who was already under duress. Early in May he snapped back at a heckler in a senior citizens' home, saying that Trudeau's other name was Elliott and that he had "decided to follow the Anglo-Saxon part of his heritage." Trudeau interpreted that remark as a disparaging reference to his Scottish lineage, a slight meaning that he was not a real Quebecker. It fired his passion.

He was scheduled to make his final speech just six days before the vote. The event would occur in Paul Sauvé Arena in Montreal—the very building in which Lévesque had spoken in triumph when the PQ won election in 1976. Trudeau worked hard on his speech, trading increasingly honed drafts with a writer named André Burelle. Trudeau was later to recall in his memoirs that he spoke without any formal text and just used a few notes to remind himself of key points. In reality, he did both—working closely with a speech writer to draft his remarks, then relying on sparse notes so that his speech would be spoken rather than read. The arena was filled to its four thousand seat capacity and the atmosphere was electric. Chrétien and Ryan spoke before Trudeau came forward to grasp the podium. He was greeted by a standing and foot-stomping demonstration that lasted for almost seven minutes.

Trudeau's motto always was reason over passion but on this night he employed both, using some of his favourite rhetorical techniques—Socratic questioning, crisp logic, and a scathing personal attack upon Lévesque and other separatist leaders.

TRUDEAU'S SPEECH

Mr. Chairman, fellow Canadians. First of all, I want to thank you for this warm welcome. I think it is obvious by this immense gathering—it is obvious that these are historic moments. There are very few examples in the history of democracy of one part of a country choosing to decide, for itself and by itself, whether, Yes or No, it wants to be part of the country to which it has always belonged. There are very few occasions when this has happened in the history of democracy. And I believe that all those here this evening, all those who have worked for the No in this province for over a month, will be proud to reply when our children and perhaps, if we are lucky our grandchildren, ask us in twenty or thirty years: "You were there in May 1980. You were there when the people of Québec were asked to decide freely on their future. You were there when Québec had the option to stay in Canada or to leave. What did you do in May 1980—"No, that was our answer."

Trudeau opens by greeting those in the arena as Canadians rather than referring to them as Quebeckers. He acknowledges the boisterous welcome that he has received. Television footage of the event shows him at the podium adopting a shy demeanour as he waits for the cheering and applause to end. He tells his audience that they are attending a dramatically important event. He uses a "you were there" repetition to heighten the drama and underscore the gravitas of both the issue and the evening's event. He invents quotes for children and grandchildren who, in the future, will ask of their elders what they did during the referendum campaign, and he answers his own question. He also introduces a stark Yes-No equation into the speech as it relates to the referendum—a dualism that he will use many times throughout the evening.

I should like to ask you this evening to reflect on the question that is asked of us, and on the consequences of the answers we may give to these questions. Allow me—perhaps for the last time before going to the polls—allow me to remind you of the essence of the question. The first is the sovereignty of Québec, and that is defined in the question itself as: the exclusive power to make its laws, levy its taxes and establish relations abroad… in other words, sovereignty.

And while we in this room answer NO, in other rooms in other parts of the province, there are people who answer YES; who truly and honestly want sovereignty. I share your opinion: this is the false option; an option that means, as Jean Chrétien said, that we will no longer send Québec MPs to govern us in Canada; an option that means independence; an option that means the separation of Québec from the rest of the country. To this our answer is NO.

But it is not to those who are for or against sovereignty that I wish to address my remarks this evening. After the referendum, I hope we will continue to respect one another's differences; that we will respect the option which has been freely chosen by those who are for or against independence for Québec. In this question, therefore, there is sovereignty and there is everything else. Everything else is a new agreement. It is equality of nations. It is at the same time economic association. It is a common currency. It is change through another referendum. It is a mandate to negotiate.

Trudeau then briefly lowers the temperature by becoming professorial in outlining the logos or logic of the issue. He asks his audience to consider both the referendum question and the answer they will give to it. He reminds them that the Yes side is offering to them both sovereignty and "everything else." He employs a drum beat of five "it is" repetitions in describing that everything else. Then after asking people to respect the outcome of the campaign, he moves to a slash-and-burn attack on those behind the Yes vote. He builds momentum by employing the word "Yes" almost a dozen times in describing everything that the PQ has included in the referendum question.

And we know very well what they are doing, these hucksters of the Yes vote. They are trying to appeal to everyone who would say Yes to a new agreement. Yes to equality of nations. Yes at the same time to association. Yes at the same time to a common currency. Yes to a second referendum. Yes to a simple mandate to negotiate.

It is those who say Yes through pride because they do not understand the question, or because they want to increase their bargaining power, and to those among the undecided who are on the brink of voting Yes, to whom I am addressing myself this evening, because what we have to ask ourselves is what would happen in the case of a Yes vote, as in the case of a No vote.

And it is the undecided, those who are on the Yes side through pride, or because they are tired and fed up, who, in these last few days, must be addressed. So let us consider this. The government of Canada and all the provincial governments have made themselves perfectly clear. If the answer to the referendum question is No, we have all said that this No will be interpreted as a mandate to change the Constitution, to renew federalism ...

I know that I can make a most solemn commitment that following a No vote, we will immediately take action to renew the Constitution and we will not stop until we have done that.

And I make a solemn declaration to all Canadians in the other provinces, we, the Québec MPs, are laying ourselves on the line, because we are telling Quebecers to vote No and telling you in the other provinces that we will not agree to your interpreting a No vote as an indication that everything is fine and can remain as it was before. We want change and we are willing to lay our seats in the House on the line to have change. This would be our attitude in the case of a No vote ...

Trudeau is aiming his comments at undecided voters and he says so. They are the people who may vote Yes because, as Trudeau believes, they have been duped or because they want to use the referendum as a bargaining chip to win greater powers for Quebec. Polling commissioned by the federal government showed that soft nationalists, almost exclusively francophones, were leaning toward voting Yes. Trudeau wants to shake them up. He is often accused of arrogance and he exhibits a trace of it here, telling his audience that some among them probably do not understand what is happening. He then promises that if they vote No, his government and the rest of Canada will not interpret that as a vote for the status quo, but rather as a vote for change. This is a promise that will come back to haunt him in later years.

You, the supporters of the No side, you know the divisions this referendum has caused. You have seen the divisions it has caused with families. You have seen the hatred it has created between neighbours. You know it has widened the generation gap. You know that the deep suspicion and mistrust between supporters of the Yes side and those of the No side will last for a long time to come. You know what kind of trial the referendum is. Well, you have been told by the Parti Québécois government that there will be other referendums and you know that the hatred, the differences, the enormous waste of energy in Québec will go on and on. Well, we are saying No to that. No, it will not go on …

Here is a party whose goal was separation, then independence, then sovereignty, then sovereignty-association, and then they even said that sovereignty-association was only for the purposes of negotiation. Here is a party that, in the name of pride, said to Quebecers: Stand up, we are going to move on to the world stage and assert ourselves.

And now, this party, on the point of entering the world stage, gets frightened and stays in the wings. Is that pride? Should we use that as a reason to vote for a party that tells us it will start all over again if the answer is Yes, that there will be another referendum?

Well, that is what we are criticizing the Parti Québécois for—not having the courage to ask a clear question, a question a mature people would have been able to answer, really a simple question: Do you want to leave Canada, Yes or No?
[FROM THE FLOOR]: No …
The answer is No to those who advocate separation rather than sharing, to those who advocate isolation rather than fellowship, to those who, basically, advocate pride rather than love, because love involves challenges coming together and meeting others half-way, and working with them to build a better world. So then, one must say, leaving that whole convoluted question aside, one must say No to ambiguity. One must say No to tricks. One must say No to contempt, because they have come to that.

Trudeau returns to the attack. The referendum has unleashed a tribal battle for hearts and minds in Quebec. Trudeau says it has sown division and even hatred. He uses a series of repetitive "you have seen" and "you know" phrases to drive home his point. He warns that if the Yes side wins, the future will include yet another divisive referendum. That, he says, will extend the hatred, the differences, the waste of energy—and he says No to that. He ridicules the Parti Québécois using an extended set of "here is a party" repetitions. He says that they lack the courage to ask the direct question, which he poses: "Do you want to leave Canada, Yes or No?" The crowd shouts "No." Trudeau is using a device called antithesis, a series of juxtaposed opposites to describe what the Yes side proposes but which the No side rejects. To all of that he says No, No, and No. His intention is to turn the referendum question into a black-and-white choice rather than one that is fuzzy and feel-good.

I was told that no more than two days ago Mr. Lévesque was saying that part of my name was Elliott and, since Elliott was an English name, it was perfectly understandable that I was for the No side, because, really, you see, I was not as much of a Quebecer as those who are going to vote Yes.

That, my dear friends, is what contempt is. It means saying that there are different kinds of Quebecers. It means that saying that the Quebecers on the No side are not as good Quebecers as the others and perhaps they have a drop or two of foreign blood, while the people on the Yes side have pure blood in their veins. That is what contempt is and that is the kind of division which builds up within a people, and that is what we are saying No to.

Of course my name is Pierre Elliott Trudeau. Yes, Elliott was my mother's name. It was the name borne by the Elliotts who came to Canada more than two hundred years ago. It is the name of the Elliotts who, more than one hundred years ago, settled in Saint-Gabriel de Brandon, where you can still see their graves in the cemetery. That is what the Elliotts are. My name is a Québec name, but my name is a Canadian name also, and that's the story of my name.

Trudeau is someone far more likely to engage in logos—exercises in logic—than in ethos, an attempt to win sympathy from his audiences; but here he becomes personal. He turns to Lévesque's comment about Trudeau's showing an "Elliott side" in the referendum campaign. It was an uncharacteristic thing for Lévesque to do and clearly it angers Trudeau. He talks about it years later in his memoirs, describing it as "a slip that demonstrated the intolerant side of separatism." In his speech, he accuses Lévesque of saying that some Quebeckers are more genuine than others. Trudeau lists the Elliott pedigree in Quebec, which dates back more than two hundred years and he accuses Lévesque of showing contempt. To that he predicts, people will say No.

Since Mr. Lévesque has chosen to analyze my name, let me show you how ridiculous it is to use that kind of contemptuous argument. Mr. Pierre-Marc Johnson is a Minister. Now, I ask you, is Johnson an English name or a French name? And Louis O'Neill—a former Minister of Mr. Lévesque's and Robert Burns, and Daniel Johnson, I ask you, are they Quebecers, yes or no?

And, if we are looking at names, I saw in yesterday's newspaper that the leader of Quebec's Inuit, the Eskimos, they are going to vote No. Do you know what the leader's name is? His name is Charlie Watt. Is Charlie Watt not a Quebecer? These people have lived in Quebec since the Stone Age; they have been here since time immemorial. And Mr. Watt is not a Quebecer? And, according to yesterday's newspaper, the chief of the Micmac Band, at Restigouche, the chief of fifteen hundred Indians—what is his name? Ron Maloney. Is he not a Quebecer? The Indians have been there for a good two thousand years. And their chief is not a Quebecer?

My dear friends, Laurier said something in 1889, nearly one hundred years ago now, and it's worth taking the time to read these lines: "My Countrymen," said Laurier, "are not only those in whose veins runs the blood of France. My countrymen are all those people—no matter what their race or language—whom the fortunes of war, the twists and turns of fate, or their own choice, have brought among us."

All Quebecers have the right to vote Yes or No. And all those Nos are as valid as any Yes, regardless of the name of the person voting, or the colour of his skin. My friends, Péquistes [PQ supporters] often tell us: the world is watching us, hold our heads high; the world is watching us, the whole world is watching what is happening in our democracy. Let's show them we are proud ...

Here Trudeau engages in one of his patented rhetorical techniques. He pursues a point to its logical conclusion and beyond to illustrate its absurdity. This is a device that rhetoricians describe as *reductio ad absurdum*. It is something that Trudeau would have learned in logic and rhetoric classes at Brébeuf and he uses it often. Here he cites the names of various other Quebeckers with anglophone names, some in Lévesque's cabinet, and asks rhetorically whether they are Quebeckers. He asks the same question about Charlie Watt and other of Quebec's Indigenous leaders. Trudeau's point is a good one but it is also unintentionally revealing. In this referendum debate about French and English cultures, the existence of Indigenous peoples was largely ignored.

And that world is looking at Canada, the second largest country in the world, one of the richest, perhaps the second richest country in the world ... a country which is composed of the meeting of the two most outstanding cultures of the Western world: the French and the English, added to by all the other cultures coming from every corner of Europe and every corner of the world. And this is what the world is looking at with astonishment, saying: These people think they might split up today when the whole world is interdependent? When Europe is trying to seek some kind of political union? These people in Quebec and in Canada want to split it up?
[FROM THE FLOOR]: No.
They want to take it away from their children.
[FROM THE FLOOR]: No.
They want to break it down? No. That's what I am answering.
[FROM THE FLOOR]: No, No, No.

One can sense Trudeau moving into his peroration. People from all over the world are watching with astonishment, he says, as one of the richest countries contemplates splitting up. He invents a question and places it in the mouths of those unnamed people: "These people in Quebec and Canada want to split it up?" The audience shouts No, then Trudeau continues the hypothetical quote with two more phrases to which, again, the crowd answers No.

I quoted Laurier, and let me quote a father of Confederation who was an illustrious Quebecer: Thomas D'Arcy McGee: The new nationality—he was saying—is thoughtful and true; nationalist in its preference, but universal in its sympathies; a nationality of the spirit, for there is a new duty which especially belongs to Canada to create a state and to originate a history which the world will not willingly let die. Well, we won't let it die. Our answer is: No, to those who would kill it.
  We won't let this country die, this Canada, our home and native land, this Canada

which really is, as our national anthem says, our home and native land. We are going to say to those who want us to stop being Canadians, we are going to say a resounding, an overwhelming No.
[FROM THE FLOOR]: No.

Trudeau uses a final allusion, this one to Thomas D'Arcy McGee, John A. Macdonald's colleague who was sometimes called the poet of Confederation. Trudeau describes him as "an illustrious Quebecker." He then builds on McGee's line about creating a "new nationality" in Canada. "We won't let it die," Trudeau shouts. "No to those who would kill it." The crowd responds with a final No and applauds him as he walks off the stage to be whisked through the darkened hallways of the arena and back to Ottawa.

THE IMPACT OF TRUDEAU'S SPEECH

On May 20 the federalist No side won the referendum by a margin of 60 per cent to 40. Then it was Lévesque's turn to take the podium in the same arena where Trudeau had spoken just a few days earlier. The ovation lasted for as long as Trudeau's had as people chanted, sang, and openly wept. Lévesque promised to abide by the results and to continue governing but he also responded to the ovation by saying, "If I have understood you properly you are saying, 'Wait until next time.'" Trudeau voted in Montreal on referendum day and then returned to Ottawa where in the evening he watched the results on television along with a small group of his close advisors. He was subdued in his response to the victory, saying that everyone had lost something in the referendum—in broken friendships and strained relationships within families. He repeated the promise he had made in his Paul Sauvé speech that this was not a vote for the status quo and that he intended to pursue a renewed federalism.

It is impossible to say whether Trudeau's speech on May 14 turned the tide in the referendum contest; but certainly this speech and three others that he made during the campaign were important to the outcome. When Trudeau entered the fray he imposed a metallic clarity upon what had become a fuzzy issue. He identified it as one of Quebec separatism, Yes or No. That helped to convince a majority of his fellow citizens to step back from the brink.

Trudeau's long-time press secretary Patrick Gossage was in the arena that night and stood among the reporters in a roped-off area while Trudeau spoke. He described the performance as "mythical" and says that even hard-bitten journalists were "awe-struck." Other observers, not on Trudeau's payroll, were impressed as well. Stephen Clarkson and Christina McCall, in their biography of Trudeau, described the Paul Sauvé speech in this way: "It was an inspired performance, probably the crucial act that secured the soft neo-federalist vote, directing it away from the Oui and towards the Non."

L. Ian MacDonald, then a political writer for *The Gazette* in Montreal, was in the arena on May 14. Recalling the speech thirty years later, he wrote that it "was breathtaking to behold." He believes, though, that Trudeau had already turned the tide in his three earlier speeches during the campaign. MacDonald added, "The federalist forces, much in need of a champion, found one in Trudeau, in the role of a lifetime, in truth the role for which he had been preparing his entire life."

Graham Fraser was in 1980 a correspondent working for *The Gazette* in Quebec City and he later wrote a book about René Lévesque and the Parti Québécois. He has written that a facility with language and elevated rhetoric has always been more important for public figures in Quebec than elsewhere in Canada—with the exception of Newfoundland where oratory is also important. Lévesque, Trudeau, and Ryan all had a superb command of the French language, not to mention of English. Fraser says that arose from their education in Quebec's classical college system. He believes that the "emotional turning point" in the referendum campaign came with Trudeau's speech, and in particular his promise that he would interpret a No vote as a mandate for constitutional change in Canada.

On the day following the referendum, Trudeau called Jean Chrétien into his office. He instructed him to travel immediately to speak with each of the premiers about a new effort to amend the constitution. That set off an intense process of negotiation over the next eighteen months. When it ended, Canada had repatriated the constitution and embedded within it was a new Charter of Rights and Freedoms. Most of the premiers had been unhappy about what Trudeau was proposing and the way in which he planned to do it. Eight of them, including Lévesque, created an opposing camp. But at the eleventh hour their solidarity was shattered in a way that isolated Lévesque and the Quebec government. Lévesque and others described it bitterly as "the night of the long knives" and Quebec has never signed on to the constitutional package.

Many in Quebec later accused Trudeau of having deceived them when he promised on May 14 that a No vote would lead to constitutional change. The soft nationalists to whom Trudeau was appealing expected him to decentralize the federation in such a way that more powers would devolve to Quebec. That was not what Trudeau had in mind. The charter in the constitution focuses upon protecting individuals against unreasonable encroachments by the state. In that way, power has shifted away from elected politicians and toward the judiciary as the interpreter and protector of rights. The charter establishes both French and English as the official languages of Canada; and it guarantees protection for both English and French minorities to have their children educated in their own language. Trudeau remained unapologetic about the actions he took following the referendum and says that his critics were disingenuous. He wrote in his memoirs, "I don't know how people can make those claims with a straight face. All my life, even before I entered politics, I always fought against special status for Quebec. I always fought against decentralization in a country that is already among the most decentralized in the world."

The constitution and its accompanying charter were the last great preoccupations in Trudeau's political life. Without them his political legacy would be decidedly modest, although he did bring panache and vitality to the office. Within two years of ceremonies attended by Queen Elizabeth to sign the new constitution in 1982, Trudeau resigned and retired to Montreal. He guarded his privacy closely but emerged on occasion to oppose both the Meech Lake and Charlottetown accords. They were attempts by the Conservative government of Brian Mulroney to have Quebec sign on to the constitution and to devolve powers. Trudeau's

DENNIS GRUENDING

interventions in those campaigns were significant and both of Mulroney's attempts failed. Many accused Trudeau of getting involved in order to protect his legacy in a vision of Canada that was too rigidly centrist. In Quebec the resentment continued to simmer. In 1995 Quebec Premier Jacques Parizeau and Lucien Bouchard, another orator who was equal in prowess to Trudeau and Lévesque, led yet another referendum campaign on Quebec sovereignty. This campaign, too, was hard fought and the results breathtakingly close—50.5 per cent against separation and 49.4 per cent in favour.

Trudeau was not called upon to participate in that campaign and perhaps he would not have wanted to. He had by then retreated into a largely solitary life, living quietly among his children, his friends, and his memories.

JOSEPH GOSNELL ON THE NISGA'A TREATY

DECEMBER 2, 1998

*"Some may have heard us say that a generation of Nisga'a
men and women have grown old at the negotiating table.
Sadly, it is very true. I was a much younger man when
I began, became involved in the tribal council; I was
25 years old. Today I'm 63; today my hair is greying."*

*Joseph Gosnell was one among several generations of Nisga'a leaders who insisted that
their people retained title to lands they had never surrendered to the Crown in what
is now northern British Columbia. For more than a century, Nisga'a representatives
were met with scorn at the provincial level and given no credence in Ottawa when
they pressed their case. Finally, in 1969, under the leadership of hereditary chief
and provincial MLA Frank Calder, the Nisga'a took the BC government to court for
refusing to recognize and act upon their Aboriginal title. They lost in British Columbia
but in 1973 they appealed to the Supreme Court of Canada, which could not quite
make up its mind. However, the court's minority judgment was so persuasive that
Ottawa altered course and agreed to negotiate land claims in any part of Canada
not covered by an existing treaty. After 1973, the Nisga'a spent another fifteen years
negotiating with the BC and federal governments. Joseph Gosnell, another hereditary
chief and normally a quiet man, was to become the Nisga'a face of the struggle in
the public's mind. Negotiators initialled the final agreement in August 1998 and their
people ratified it in November. The BC government drafted a bill to accept and enable
the treaty and it was introduced in late November. On December 2, Gosnell was invited
to address the legislature and he made an historic speech. The Calder legal case and
the subsequent Nisga'a treaty have had an enormous impact in Canada and beyond.*

Joseph Gosnell was born in 1936 near a fish cannery close to the small Nisga'a town of Gingolx in the mountainous, fjord-indented region of northwest coastal British Columbia adjacent to the Alaska panhandle. The fishery had always been a mainstay for the sustenance of the Nisga'a. Eventually, there were several dozen canneries in the area, owned by European settlers but staffed largely by Nisga'a workers and supplied by Nisga'a fishers. Gosnell was one of twelve children in the family of Mary Moore and Eli Gosnell, a hereditary Nisga'a chief. He and his wife were deeply religious and reared their children to embrace both Christianity and the traditional culture of their people. Joseph Gosnell was to say years later that when he was a child his family ate its meals at a long wooden table. The children were expected not to talk but rather to listen and learn about the oral history of the Nisga'a.

The Anglicans were the first to arrive as missionaries in 1862 followed by Methodists and the Salvation Army. They built churches and schools and attempted to undermine the religious and cultural traditions of the Nisga'a. Gosnell recalled playing as a child in the crawl space beneath his grandfather's house. He did not understand why anyone would carve such beautiful figures on the old wooden beams used to shore up the home. It was only years later that he understood the beams had once been lofty totem poles standing along the main street in his village. The totems, seen by the missionaries as competing with the Christian cross, were forcibly abandoned when the Nisga'a were converted to Christianity.

In 1943, when Gosnell was seven years old, the local Indian agent told families that their children must attend a church-run residential school on Vancouver Island, a two-day steamship ride from their home. He was a student there for six years. He lived and studied with others who later became, as he did, leaders of their First Nations. He was to meet them repeatedly at political events and negotiations over the years. Gosnell acknowledged that he learned the English language and about settler ways at the school, but he recalled it as a difficult life: "The discipline was extremely hard. I wouldn't want to put my children through that same thing—never in a thousand years." Yet, decades later, he and other Nisga'a leaders might be found preaching Sunday sermons as lay leaders in Protestant churches in the Nass Valley. Despite his time away at school, Gosnell held his heritage close and returned to the Nass Valley to work as a fisher along with other members of his family. He became a hereditary chief as well and also served as a band councillor and on various committees and task forces related to the fishery. In 1957, he married Audrey Adele Munroe who had attended the residential school with him. They raised a family of seven children.

Gosnell's older brother James, forceful and charismatic, was the politician in the family. Joseph Gosnell, on the other hand, exhibited what one confidant described as a "debilitating sense of shyness" as a young man. Only after his brother's death from cancer in 1988 would he move out of the shadows and into a prominent leadership role. He was elected as president of the Nisga'a Tribal Council in 1990 and became the chief negotiator for treaty deliberations. Despite that public responsibility, he often craved solitude and during negotiating sessions he would usually stay in a hotel separate from others in his party. He proved to be soft-spoken but a focused and tough-minded negotiator, demonstrating an ability to remain above the fray when around him frustrations boiled over. He was a man with broad shoulders and much of the Nisga'a fate rested upon them.

◆

The Nisga'a struggle dated back to the 1870s when the new province of British Columbia entered Confederation. Under the British North America Act, Ottawa retained responsibility for First Nations peoples but the province retained ownership of all public lands. Provincial leaders denied that anything called Aboriginal title had ever existed. In 1881, without being consulted, the Nisga'a had a small amount of land set aside for them, which comprised about half of 1 per cent of what they considered to be their traditional lands. In 1887, a delegation of chiefs travelled to Victoria to meet with Premier William Smithe and press their claim. He rebuked them with a contemptuous comment.

The Europeans who arrived in what is now Canada claimed the land as theirs and over time they dispossessed its original inhabitants. Their actions arose from a sense of superiority but also relied on a peculiar international legal principle known as the doctrine of discovery. Catholic popes in the fifteenth and sixteenth centuries granted permission to Portuguese and Spanish explorers to claim and subjugate on behalf of their monarchs any lands and peoples they "discovered." Protestant nations, including England, France, and Holland, adapted that doctrine to justify similar claims, which rested upon a concept called *terra nullius*. It held that the "discovered" lands were empty and could thus be claimed by the Europeans. The doctrine has been baked into the laws of numerous new world countries, including Canada, the United States, Australia, and New Zealand. It continues to undergird the legal and political approach to Aboriginal rights and title.

The Nisga'a insisted they had never ceded the traditional lands that had been taken from them, nor had they been compensated for their loss. They wanted redress. One day in 1966, Frank Calder and four Nisga'a chiefs climbed the stairs to the Vancouver office of a young lawyer named Thomas Berger. They asked him to take the BC government to court based on the claim that their Aboriginal title had never been extinguished. Frank Calder, also a hereditary chief, was born in the Nass Valley about twenty years before Joseph Gosnell. In 1924, his adoptive parents had sent him to a church-run residential school near Chilliwack in southern British Columbia. The school went only as far as grade ten but Calder spent two more years completing high school in Chilliwack. He later became the first status person ever to attend the University of British Columbia, where he graduated from the Anglican Theological College in 1946. He decided against ordained priesthood and chose to go into politics. In 1949, he ran successfully for the Co-operative Commonwealth Federation (CCF) in his home territory and became the first status person elected to a Canadian legislature. He was a busy man, representing a far-flung northern riding while also founding the Nisga'a Tribal Council and acting as its president from 1955 to 1973.

The concept of Aboriginal title was completely foreign to most Canadians at the time. Prime Minister Pierre Trudeau knew about the claims but was impatient with them. He had long harboured a desire to provide Canada with a charter of rights and freedoms protecting the rights of individuals, but not of collectives. Speaking in Vancouver in August 1968, several months after the Calder case went to trial in the Supreme Court of British Columbia, Trudeau said: "Our answer is no. We can't recognize Aboriginal rights because no society can be built on historical 'might have beens.'" But his plans were to unravel. Trudeau had been elected triumphantly in 1968 and there was a new political energy in the country. The bureaucracy was bulging with plans and position papers and one of those was a white paper on Aboriginal policy. The Liberals' proposed solution to a history of poverty and exclusion was to assimilate Aboriginal peoples as individuals into mainstream society. There would be no collective rights, no Aboriginal title to land, and no treaties beyond those that already existed. There was such an intense and angry reaction from Aboriginal peoples and groups that the paper was withdrawn.

The Calder case was heard before Justice Jay Gould at the Supreme Court of British Columbia beginning on March 31, 1969. As Berger was to describe it years later, "The existence of Aboriginal title would be the sole issue before the court. If we succeeded there would have to be negotiations—and a treaty." Lawyers for the province argued that no such title had existed. Alternatively, if it had existed it was extinguished by the actions of the local colonial government prior to British Columbia's entry into Confederation in 1871. Berger summoned Frank Calder and other Nisga'a leaders as expert witnesses. On the stand, Calder was asked by Berger to identify the Nisga'a lands from a map on exhibit. Calder did so. Berger then had this exchange with Calder:

Q: Does the territory outlined in the map constitute the ancient territory of the Nisga'a people?

A: Yes, it does.

Q: Have the Nisga'a people ever signed any document or treaty surrendering their Aboriginal title to the territory outlined in the map, exhibit 2?

A: The Nisga'a have not signed any treaty or any document that would indicate extinguishment of the title.

Q: Can you tell his lordship whether the Nisga'a today make use of the lands and waters contained in the map, exhibit 2?

A: Put it this way in answer to your question, from time immemorial the Nisga'a have used the Naas River and all of its tributaries within the boundaries so submitted, the lands in Observatory Inlet, the lands in Portland Canal, and part of Portland Inlet. We still hunt within those lands and fish in the waters, streams, and rivers, we still do, as in time past, have our campsites in these areas and we go there periodically, seasonally, according to the game and the fishing season, and we still maintain these sites and as far as we know, they have been there as far back as we can remember. We still roam these territories, we still pitch our homes there whenever it is required according to our livelihood, and we use the land as in time past, we bury our dead within the territory so defined and we still exercise the privilege of free men within the territory so defined ...

The Nisga'a lost their case at the Supreme Court of British Columbia. Justice Gould avoided a decision about whether Aboriginal title had ever existed. He accepted the Crown's argument that, if such title had existed, laws passed before the colony entered Confederation in 1871 had extinguished it. Calder and the other Nisga'a leaders instructed Berger to go to the Court of Appeal on their behalf but they lost there as well. Chief Justice H. W. Davey made the following statement in dismissing the Nisga'a argument: "They were undoubtedly at the time of settlement a very primitive people with few of the institutions of civilized society, and none at all of our notions of private property."

Calder and the others were disappointed but not vanquished. They wanted to appeal to the Supreme Court of Canada but could not afford to do so. They were bolstered by a donation from the Anglican Church of Canada. The case was argued over five days in November 1971. Berger and two other lawyers appeared for the Nisga'a, whose chiefs sat in the room wearing ceremonial sashes while they watched and listened. The court took fourteen months to reach a decision, which was released in February 1973. Three of the justices supported the Nisga'a claim, three opposed, and a seventh hid behind a technicality. It was, in effect, a hung court so the appeal failed. However, the Nisga'a won a moral victory because six of the seven agreed that Aboriginal title had existed. Three of the six then said that such title had been extinguished before the colony became a province.

Justice Emmett Hall, who had earlier led the Royal Commission that recommended Medicare for Canada, wrote for the minority on the court. His judgment ran to seventy-seven pages, but Hall was later to say that the issues were simple: "My view was that the international law accepted Aboriginal rights, secondly that they were extinguishable, but that in this case they had not been extinguished." Hall did not in his judgment quarrel with the doctrine of discovery; nor were the Nisga'a challenging that doctrine. They simply argued, and Hall agreed, that governments must negotiate with them and compensate them for any land they surrendered. Hall went out of his way to answer the statement made by Chief Justice Davey that the Aboriginal peoples at the time of discovery were uncivilized primitives. These qualities attributed to them, Hall wrote, "pale into insignificance when compared to the religious and dynastic wars of 'civilized' Europe in the 16th and 17th centuries."

The court's ambiguous ruling extended the legal uncertainty, but events were moving quickly and the issue was soon tossed back into the public arena where Hall's dissenting judgment bolstered the Nisga'a case. Trudeau had been reelected in 1972, but with a minority government. The Conservatives and the New Democratic Party wanted the government to negotiate outstanding land claims. Within a week of the judgment in 1973, Trudeau had changed his position. Meeting with a delegation of chiefs early in February, he told them the Supreme Court's minority decision had led him to modify his views. He and Jean Chrétien, his Indian Affairs minister, promised to make land settlements a priority. This was a departure from previous government policy. When in 1982 the Constitution was repatriated, existing Aboriginal rights were recognized and entrenched and subsequent court judgments have held that these rights include title. Despite the stated willingness by the Trudeau and subsequent governments to negotiate new treaties, the process was contentious and tortuously slow.

◆

In 1974, Frank Calder, who was still an MLA, lost in the Nisga'a Tribal Council election to Joseph Gosnell's older brother James. The Nisga'a began in 1976 to negotiate with Ottawa for a treaty. Those negotiations were proceeding at a glacial pace when James Gosnell became ill and later died of cancer in 1988. His younger brother Joseph was elected to lead the tribal council and he also became the lead treaty negotiator. It was only in 1990 that the province of British Columbia agreed to participate in the talks. There was an agreement-in-principle in 1996 and Nisga'a leaders initialled a final agreement in August of that year. The treaty then had to await ratification among the Nisga'a communities, which did not occur until November 1998.

Under terms of the treaty, the Nisga'a ceased to be governed by terms of the Indian Act. They achieved self-governing powers on 2,000 square kilometres of their traditional lands in the lower Nass Valley. This was a bitter disappointment to many of them, because the Nisga'a had entered the negotiations claiming more than 24,000 square kilometres of territory, an area three and one-half times the size of Prince Edward Island. However, the treaty also guaranteed more restricted rights for the Nisga'a to harvest forestry, fishery, and wildlife resources in their entire traditional territory. The treaty provided approximately $250 million to the Nisga'a, although they had to repay the federal government $51 million for monies advanced to allow them to conduct the protracted negotiations. The Nisga'a were to begin paying provincial and federal sales taxes, including those on fuel and tobacco, after a transitional period of eight years. The treaty also covered subjects such as Nisga'a citizenship, adoption, language, culture, and heritage, all of which were to be included under Nisga'a self-government. The process had been a long and difficult one but the principle was relatively simple. The courts ruled and governments eventually agreed that the Nisga'a had an Aboriginal title to their traditional lands. There had followed negotiations about how much land was involved and that had been agreed upon as well. The next logical step involved who was to control how that land was used. That was achieved by negotiating for a measure of self-government within the Canadian federation. While the Nisga'a were to create their own self-governing structures, federal and provincial laws, including the Charter of Rights and Freedoms and the Criminal Code, would continue to apply on their land.

◆

Even as it was being negotiated, the treaty was met with a fierce backlash led by BC's Liberal opposition leader, Gordon Campbell, and most of the province's media owners. Campbell said the treaty was "racist" because he claimed it would deny rights to non-Nisga'a people living in the territory. He demanded a referendum. David Black, a press baron who owned many of the community papers in British Columbia, ordered all of them to oppose the treaty. He was quoted as predicting that it would cause a racial divide that could lead to bloodshed, and he cited Northern Ireland as a parallel. "The ultimate goal," Black wrote at the time, "should be the integration of Aboriginal peoples with the rest of society." Influential radio host Rafe Mair used his program on Vancouver-based CKNW Radio to oppose, and he wrote anti-treaty columns for Vancouver newspapers as well. In Eastern Canada, Conrad Black (no relation to David) used his paper, the *National Post*, to attack the treaty. Mike Scott, the Reform-Alliance MP for the northern BC riding of Skeena, predicted that if negotiators concluded the deal there would be "social unrest like we've never seen before ... by non-native people ..."

Gosnell and his Nisga'a colleagues were determined negotiators, but they were out-gunned in the media wars. They hired a variety of consultants to help them in their long campaign and among them were several communications specialists. Alex Rose was one of them. He wrote: "Through it all, Gosnell's high road presentation and on-camera dignity was critical to our success." For the most part, Rose and the others concentrated on a soft message built largely around the integrity of Gosnell and his colleagues and the justness of their cause. But faced with the negative media and political barrage, they also built in a capacity for rapid responses to the many attacks they confronted.

When in August 1998 the Nisga'a held their ceremony to initial the treaty at a village in the Nass Valley, the event received widespread international attention. There were front-page headlines in *The New York Times* and coverage on the BBC World Service, *The Economist*, and *The Guardian*, as well as German and Japanese newspapers. Gosnell was invited to Vancouver to speak to diplomats and consular officers from a variety of countries. Visiting delegations were later to arrive from New Zealand, France, and the United States to learn more about the treaty. In November 1998, when the BC legislature was preparing for a debate to pass legislation enabling the treaty, Gosnell made a speaking tour that included Harvard University in the United States, as well as London, Cambridge, Frankfurt, Vienna, Bonn, and The Hague.

The Nisga'a were the first BC band to sign a modern comprehensive treaty, and the provincial NDP government was ready with enabling legislation. On December 2, 1998, Gosnell was invited to address MLAs assembled in the BC legislature and was welcomed by leaders of the various parties. Gordon Campbell, in his remarks, made reference to the "disagreements amongst us about how to accomplish the goal of coming forward with treaties that will solve the problems and meet the needs of all British Columbians." That was a barely disguised code for his campaign to have the treaty rejected. Then Joseph Gosnell began to speak about the treaty the Nisga'a had been seeking for more than one hundred years.

GOSNELL'S SPEECH

Madam Speaker, today, I believe, marks a turning point in the history of British Columbia. Today Aboriginal and non-Aboriginal people are coming together to decide the future of this province. I am talking about the Nisga'a treaty, a triumph, I believe, for all British Columbians and a beacon of hope for Aboriginal people around the world.

It's a triumph, I believe, which proves to the world that reasonable people can sit down and settle historical wrongs. It proves that a modern society can correct the mistakes of the past. As British Columbians, as Canadians, I believe we should all be very proud. It's a triumph because under the treaty, the Nisga'a people will join

Canada and British Columbia as free citizens, full and equal participants in the
social, economic and political life of this province and, indeed, of this country. It's a
triumph because under the treaty, we will no longer be wards of the state, no longer
beggars in our own land. It's a triumph because under the treaty, we will collectively
own approximately 2,000 square kilometres of land, far exceeding the postage-stamp
reserve set aside for us by colonial governments. We will once again govern ourselves
by our own institutions but within the context of Canadian law. It is a triumph
because under the treaty, we will be allowed to make our own mistakes, to savour
our own victories, to stand on our own feet once again. It's a triumph because, clause
by clause, the Nisga'a treaty emphasizes self-reliance, personal responsibility and
modern education. It also encourages, for the first time, investment in Nisga'a lands
and resources and allows us to pursue meaningful employment for our own people from
the resources of our own territory.

To investors, it provides economic certainty, and it gives us a fighting chance
to establish legitimate economic independence, to prosper in common with our non-
Aboriginal neighbours in a new and, hopefully, proud Canada. It's a triumph, Madam
Speaker and hon. members, because the treaty proves beyond all doubt that negotiations—
not lawsuits, not blockades, not violence— are the most effective, honourable way to
resolve Aboriginal issues in this country. It's a triumph, I believe, that signals the end of
the Indian Act, the end of more than a century of humiliation, degradation and despair
for the Nisga'a nation.

Joseph Gosnell is a political leader and a negotiator who can be either
hard-nosed or conciliatory. He will employ both approaches on this day.
Initially, he strikes a conciliatory tone. He attempts to elevate the treaty
above the tawdry politics that are occurring around it. The treaty is a
turning point, a coming together, a triumph for everyone in the province.
He uses the world "triumph" perhaps too many times in his speech.
Gosnell says the treaty "proves to the world" that historical wrongs can
be righted by well-intentioned people. He is aware, as he says later in his
speech, that the world is watching, which places added pressure upon the
opposing MLAs. The Nisga'a campaign has struck a note internationally,
as evidenced by widespread media coverage and invitations for Gosnell
to speak in Europe and the United States. He describes the treaty as "a

beacon of hope" for Aboriginal peoples everywhere. With the treaty providing for a land base and self-government, he says, the Nisga'a people will join Canada rather than leave it as critics have claimed. This is his response to those who say that the Nisga'a will use the treaty to create a race-based ghetto on their lands.

The Nisga'a will get out from under the Indian Act, Gosnell states. They will no longer be wards of the state or beggars living on the postage-stamp reserves that had been set aside for them in the 19th century. Finally, he makes the point that negotiations rather than blockades or violence are the best way to resolve issues. He is speaking by inference about armed standoffs such as those between police, the army, and Indigenous people at Oka, Quebec, in 1990 and at Gustafsen Lake, BC, in 1995. The Nisga'a have proven to be single-minded and relentless in advocating for their rights, but in more than a century of doing so they have never threatened or resorted to violence. Gosnell's opening words are an appeal to the better angels in the minds and hearts of his audience, an example of his employing the rhetorical device of ethos.

In 1887 my ancestors made an epic journey from the Nass River to here, Victoria's Inner Harbour. Determined to settle the land question, they were met by a Premier who barred them from this Legislature. He was blunt. Premier Smithe rejected all our aspirations to settle the land question. Then he made this pronouncement: "When the white man first came among you, you were little better than wild beasts of the field." Wild beasts of the field. Little wonder, then, that this brutal racism was soon translated into narrow policies which plunged British Columbia into a century of darkness for the Nisga'a and other Aboriginal people.

Like many colonists of the day, Premier Smithe did not know or care to know that the Nisga'a is an old nation—as old as any in Europe. From time immemorial, our oral literature—passed down from generation to generation—records the story of the way the Nisga'a people were placed on earth and trusted with the care and protection of our land. Through the ages, we lived a settled life in villages along the Nass River. We lived in large, cedar-plank houses, fronted with totem poles depicting the great heraldry and the family crests of our nobility. We thrived from the bounty of the sea, the river, the forest and the mountains. We governed ourselves according to ayuuk Nisga'a, the code of our own strict and ancient laws of property ownership, succession and civil order.

Gosnell then engages in a history lesson for his legislative audience. It begins in 1887 when his ancestors made the long journey from the Nass Valley to press their case with Premier Smithe in Victoria. He rejected their plea, describing them as little better than wild beasts. To the modern sensibility of most people this is an astonishing statement. Gosnell describes it as "brutal racism." The premier and other colonists did not know or care, he says, that the Nisga'a at the time were a nation as old as any in Europe. Gosnell is above all a pragmatist but occasionally in his remarks poetry does appear. He speaks about the creation myths and the history of the Nisga'a and how from "time immemorial" they lived a settled life in villages and governed themselves.

Our first encounters with Europeans were friendly. We welcomed these strange visitors—visitors who never left. The Europeans also valued their encounters with us. They thought we were fair and tough entrepreneurs and—no doubt today—negotiators. In 1832 traders from the Hudson's Bay Co. found our people living, in their words, "in two-storey wooden houses the equal of any in Europe." For a time our people prospered, but there were dark days yet to come.

Between the late 1700s and mid-1800s the Nisga'a people, like so many other coastal nations of the time, as well as other tribal groups across this great land, were devastated by European diseases such as smallpox, measles and fevers. Our population, I'm told, was at one time 30,000 strong. We dwindled to about 800 people. Today I am pleased to report that our population is growing. According to our census, we now number approximately 5,500.

We took to heart the promises of King George III, set out in the Royal Proclamation of 1763, that our lands would not be taken away without our permission and that treaty-making was the way the Nisga'a would become part of this new nation. We continued to follow our ayuuk, our code of laws. We vowed to obey the white man's law. And we expected him to obey our laws and also to respect our people.

But unfortunately, the Europeans would not obey their own laws and continued to trespass on our lands. The King's governments continued to take our lands from us, until we were told that all of our land had come to belong to the Crown and that even the tiny bits of land that enclosed our villages were not ours but belonged to the government. Still we kept the faith that the rule of law would prevail one day, that justice would be done, that one day the land question would be settled fairly and honourably.

Madam Speaker, in 1913 the Nisga'a Land Committee drafted the petition to London. The petition contained the declaration of our traditional land ownership and governance, and it contained the critical information that in the new British colony our land ownership would be respected … Sadly, this was not to be the case.

Also in 1913, Duncan Campbell Scott became deputy superintendent of Indian Affairs. His narrow vision of assimilation dominated federal Aboriginal policy for years and years to come and was later codified as the Indian Act. Mr. Scott said: "I want to get rid of the Indian problem. Our objective is to continue until there is not a single Indian in Canada that has not been absorbed into the body politic and there is no Indian question." One of this man's earliest efforts was to undermine the influence of the Nisga'a petition to London and to deflect away from political action. But these men, Smithe and Scott, failed and are now deservedly only dusty footnotes in history.

Still the situation of the Nisga'a worsened. In 1927, Canada passed a law to prevent us from pursuing our land claims, from hiring lawyers to plead our case. At the same time, our central institution of tribal government, our potlatch system we know in Nisga'a as ayuuk, was outlawed by an act of Parliament. It was against the law for us to give presents during our ceremonies, which is central to our tradition; our law instructs us to do that. It was made illegal for us to sing and dance, which again is a requirement of our culture. But still we did not give up, and finally, under the leadership of Dr. Frank Calder, the Nisga'a Land Committee was reborn as the Nisga'a Tribal Council in 1955.

Gosnell runs through the first encounters with the Europeans, employing subtle irony to describe them as "visitors who never left." He refers to the Royal Proclamation of 1763 in which the British king promised Aboriginal peoples that any land surrenders would be negotiated by treaty making. He talks about the trespass by Europeans, the loss of land, the confinement of the Nisga'a to small plots of land, but also of their "moderate and reasonable" struggle to assert their rights. He talks about the "dark days" when infectious diseases reduced the Nisga'a population from thirty thousand at the time of contact to a mere eight hundred people. The death of so many people from diseases that accompanied the Europeans helps to explain why people such as Duncan Campbell Scott believed Indians would one day cease to exist. Happily, Gosnell says, the Nisga'a population has rebounded.

In 1968 we took our land question to the BC Supreme Court. We lost but appealed to the Supreme Court of Canada, where in 1973, in what is now known as the Calder case, the justice ruled that Aboriginal title existed prior to Confederation. This initiated the modern-day process of land claims negotiations. The government of Canada agreed it was best to negotiate modern-day treaties. Canada agreed it was time to build a new relationship based on trust, respect and the rule of law. In time, as you will know, Madam Speaker, the province of British Columbia came to the negotiating table as well. For the past 25 years, in good faith, the Nisga'a struggled to negotiate this treaty, and finally it was initialed in August in our home community of New Aiyansh.

How the world has changed! Two days ago—and 111 years later, after Smithe's rejection—I walked up to the steps of this Legislature as the sound of Nisga'a drumming and singing filled the rotunda. To the Nisga'a people it was a joyous sound—the sound of freedom. Freedom is described in the dictionary as "the state or condition of being free, the condition of not being under another's control, the power to do, say or think as one pleases." Our people have enjoyed the hospitality and the warmth of this Legislature, this capital city, its sights and its people. In churches, schools and malls, streets and public places our people have been embraced, welcomed and congratulated by the people of British Columbia.

People sometimes wonder why we have struggled so long to sign a treaty. Why, we are asked, did our elders and elected officials dedicate their lives to the resolution of the land question? What is it about a treaty?

To us a treaty is a sacred instrument. It represents an understanding between distinct cultures and shows a respect for each other's way of life. We know we are here for a long time together. A treaty stands as a symbol of high idealism in a divided world. That is why we have fought so long and so hard. I have been asked: "Has this been worth it?" I would have to say, with a resounding yes, it has.

The world has changed Gosnell tells the MLAs. He provides a brief description of the Calder case and how it led to negotiations for Nisga'a land claims and to their achievement of self-government. He speaks warmly as he describes the welcome that he and other Nisga'a leaders received at the legislature and in the city of Victoria when they arrived to promote the new treaty. He contrasts that reception to that of Premier Smithe a century earlier. He then uses a novelistic technique, inventing questions from unnamed people about the treaty and its importance. Answering his own questions, Gosnell says that the treaties show respect and understanding. They are sacred. And in what could be a one-line summary of his core message to both Indigenous peoples and settlers, he says: "We know we are here for a long time together."

But believe me and my colleagues; it has been a long, hard-fought battle for those that went before us. Some may have heard us say that a generation of Nisga'a men and women have grown old at the negotiating table. Sadly, it is very true. I was a much younger man when I began, became involved in the tribal council; I was 25 years old. Today I'm 63; today my hair is greying. I've gone through six terms of Prime Ministers … I recall their names—the Rt. Hon. Pierre Trudeau, Joe Clark, John Turner, Brian Mulroney, Kim Campbell and Jean Chrétien—and five British Columbia Premiers— Bill Bennett, William Vander Zalm, Rita Johnston, Mike Harcourt and, yes, Glen Clark. I will spare you the list of deputy ministers, senior bureaucrats and other officials. There are numerous names that we have met across these many years. Their names, I believe, would paper the walls of this chamber at least twice.

Gosnell has not spoken about himself but now he does so briefly. He and other Nisga'a leaders "have grown old at the negotiating table." He is employing ethos, an appeal to listeners to look sympathetically upon the speaker. In making these comments he may well have been thinking of his deceased brother James who, on his deathbed in 1988, apologized to each of his children for having been an absent father because he spent so much time away from home in treaty negotiations.

We are not naïve. We know that some people do not want this treaty. We know that there are naysayers—some sitting here today. We know that there are those who say Canada and

British Columbia are giving us too much, and a few who want to reopen negotiations in order to give us less. Others, still upholding the values of Smithe and Scott, are practising a willful ignorance. This colonial attitude is fanning the flames of fear and ignorance in this province and reigniting a poisonous attitude that we as Aboriginal people are so familiar with.

But these are desperate tactics, doomed to fail. By playing politics with the aspirations of Aboriginal people, these naysayers are blighting the promise of the Nisga'a treaty not only for us but for non-Aboriginal people as well, because this is about people. We're not numbers. The issue that you will deal with over the next weeks ... You will deal with the lives of our people, the future of our people. It is about the legitimate aspirations of our people, no longer willing to step aside or be marginalized. We intend to be free and equal citizens. Witness the flags that have been waved in this chamber over the past two days by the Nisga'a people of British Columbia, the Nisga'a people of Canada.

As he moves toward the end of his speech, Gosnell confronts critics of the treaty directly. In a pointed reference to Liberal leader Gordon Campbell and others, Gosnell says that some of those critics are "sitting here today." He uses juxtaposition to make a point. Some say that Canada and British Columbia "are giving us too much," while others want to reopen the treaty negotiations "in order to give us less." Still others, Gosnell says, are practising "a willful ignorance" reminiscent of former premier Smithe and Duncan Campbell Scott, but he says they are doomed to fail. Speaking directly to the MLAs, Gosnell tells them that in the upcoming treaty debate they will be dealing not with numbers but rather with the lives and aspirations of people who refuse to be shunted aside.

Now, on the eve of the 50th anniversary of the Declaration of Human Rights, this Legislature embarks on a great debate about Aboriginal rights. The Nisga'a people welcome that debate, one of the most important in the modern history of British Columbia. We have every confidence that elected members of this Legislature will look beyond narrow politics to correct the shameful and historic wrong. I ask each and every one of you, hon. members, to search your hearts deeply and to allow the light of our message to guide your decisions.

We have worked for justice for more than 100 years. Now it is time to ratify the Nisga'a treaty, for Aboriginal and non-Aboriginal people to come together and write a new chapter in the history of our nation, our province, our country and indeed the world. The world, I believe, is our witness to the endeavours that we have encountered.

In his peroration, Gosnell again elevates his tone and broadens his reach. He places the Nisga'a struggle within the context of the upcoming fiftieth anniversary of the United Nations Declaration of Human Rights. His striking comment, "the world is our witness," is reminiscent of Pierre Trudeau's remarks in his 1980 Quebec referendum speech about the world watching Canada. In the Nisga'a case, the reminder is even more trenchant because other countries, including their Aboriginal populations, and international bodies such as the United Nations, all watch Canada to see if its rhetoric of fairness and justice is borne out in action.

THE IMPACT OF GOSNELL'S SPEECH

Gosnell was warmly applauded for his speech, but by next morning the amber glow had receded as MLAs began what was to become the longest debate in the BC legislature's history. It was ferocious and continued until April 1999 when Premier Glen Clark used closure to end it. The federal government had also to accept the treaty and a bill was introduced into the House of Commons in October 1999. It was opposed aggressively by the Reform Party whose leader, Preston Manning, attacked the treaty as "based on socialist economics and collective ownership of land and resources." During debate in the House of Commons, the Reform Party introduced 471 amendments to the bill, some of them changing colons to semi-colons. It was a costly and time-consuming attempt to symbolize opposition to the legislation and the principles embedded within it. The bill enshrining the treaty was passed on December 13, 1999, and received Royal Assent on April 13, 2000. Joseph Gosnell was in Ottawa on that day and rushed out of the Senate chambers to celebrate the news.

That euphoria, too, was short-lived. Four days later, Gordon Campbell appeared in the British Columbia Supreme Court to contest the treaty, claiming that it created a "third order" of government and as such was unconstitutional. For decades, the BC government had argued that there was no Aboriginal title to land. Over time, the courts overruled that argument and the modern Nisga'a treaty—the first in British Columbia—was painstakingly negotiated over a period of thirteen years. With the treaty completed, Campbell contended that the Nisga'a had no right to manage the lands, fisheries, and resources on the lands covered by that same agreement. In the words of Thomas Berger, who was once again representing the Nisga'a: "The treaty would be reduced to an empty shell." Justice Paul Williamson dismissed Campbell's claim in July 2000. He upheld the right of the Nisga'a to the limited measure of self-government enshrined in the treaty. Campbell said he would appeal, but in 2001 the Liberals won the provincial election and he became premier. He chose to abandon the lawsuit.

The treaty was also opposed by several other First Nations and even by some of the Nisga'a themselves. In August 1998, the president of the Union of British Columbia Indian Chiefs was caustic in his opposition, calling the treaty a sham that bargained away too much in return for too little. Some individual First Nations, including the neighbouring Gitanyow, Gitksan, and Tsimshian, claimed there was an overlap between their traditional lands and those included in the Nisga'a treaty. The Nisga'a were able to work matters out with the Tsimshian but no such resolution was immediately possible with the other groups. By the time the Nisga'a negotiated their treaty, Frank Calder was eighty-four years old and had been out of provincial politics for more than a decade, although he remained busy in retirement. He voted against ratification as well. He believed the Nisga'a had not received enough land in the negotiations and he did not like the provisions for self-government, preferring a more limited model with municipal-style powers.

In 2001, the Nisga'a government formally came into effect and passed its first laws. Gosnell had indicated that he would retire but either changed his mind or was convinced by others that his leadership was needed. The time for treaty-making had passed and the new challenge was to make self-government work in practical terms. He became the first president of the Nisga'a government although he later left that post. He continued to serve as an alternate member on the influential Council of Elders, which is an important part of Nisga'a self-government as provided for in the treaty.

The Calder case, achieved after more than a century of advocacy and struggle, was tremendously important for the Nisga'a, but Calder's importance goes far beyond one First Nation. The court decision had the effect of suddenly reversing the federal government's policy. Pierre Trudeau changed his mind about Aboriginal title and his government began to negotiate comprehensive modern treaties. They included agreements with the Cree in Northern Quebec, the Inuit in the Eastern Arctic, the Dene and associated Métis in the Northwest Territories, the Council of Yukon Indians, the Inuit in Labrador, and others. Collectively, these modern treaties cover nearly half of Canada's land mass. In legal circles, the Calder case's impact was felt beyond Canada's borders as well. That was especially true in Australia and New Zealand where the courts have drawn on the Calder and subsequent Canadian judgments. In Canada, the courts, which had so often failed Aboriginal peoples, as in the case of Louis Riel, often became their defenders in the post-charter era after 1982.

The Nisga'a treaty was also a singular accomplishment in the manner of its negotiation and in its practical results. The Nisga'a had been spurned for decades by politicians who almost certainly represented the prevailing public mood and opinion. But the tenacity and discipline shown by the Nisga'a leaders allowed them to gain their treaty against all odds. They negotiated for land, although they did not receive as much as they had hoped. But they also made the next logical step in negotiating for self-government to control the destiny of those lands. Gosnell was fond of saying that through their treaty the Nisga'a had negotiated their way into Canada rather than out of it. His leadership and gift for oratory are a big part of the reason that happened. Tom Molloy, a Saskatoon lawyer who served as the chief federal negotiator for the Nisga'a treaty, described Gosnell in this way: "An intensely private, quiet man, he would often prefer to be off on his own than to socialize with the other negotiators during breaks. At the same time, he is a powerful and effective speaker, rational, persuasive, passionate without being bombastic—the type of statesman that beleaguered nations dream of in times of upheaval and change."

The Nisga'a, perhaps fearful of further exciting the ire of treaty opponents, always said that they were negotiating only for themselves, and their treaty should not be seen as a template for others. But it has at the least been a model and an inspiration. Gosnell and the Nisga'a changed the conversation about Aboriginal title, self-government, and the Nisga'a pointed the way toward a new relationship between Indigenous and other Canadians.

NOTES

INTRODUCTION

10 George A. Kennedy, *Aristotle, On Rhetoric*, translation with introduction, notes, and appendices, 2nd ed. (New York: Oxford University Press, 2007).

JOHN A. MACDONALD

15 *John Alexander Macdonald was born:* J. K. Johnson and P. B. Waite, "Macdonald, Sir John Alexander," in *Dictionary of Canadian Biography*, vol. 12 (University of Toronto/Université Laval), 2003, accessed November 18, 2016, http://www.biographi.ca/en/bio/macdonald_john_alexander_12E.html.

16 *never able to attend university:* Peter B. Waite, *Macdonald: His Life and World* (Toronto: McGraw-Hill Ryerson, 1975), 15.

16 *"ugly John Macdonald":* E. B. Biggar, *Anecdotal Life of Sir John Macdonald* (Montreal: Lovell, 1891), 23.

16 *"no beauty":* Waite, *Macdonald*, 8.

16 *time in a sickbed:* Patricia Phenix, *Private Demons: The Tragic Personal Life of John A. Macdonald* (Toronto: McClelland & Stewart Ltd., 2006), 70–71.

17 *Macdonald drank heavily:* Ibid.,160–61; 164–65; 180; 204–05; 234.

17 *"was simply drunk":* Quoted in Marc Bosc ed., *The Broadview Book of Canadian Parliamentary Anecdotes* (Peterborough: Broadview Press Ltd., 1988), 10.

18 *"turgid in style":* Keith Johnson, *Affectionately Yours: The Letters of Sir John A. Macdonald and His Family* (Toronto: Macmillan of Canada, 1969), 62.

18 *more colloquial form of speech:* Kenneth Cmiel, *Democratic Eloquence: The Fight Over Popular Speech in Nineteenth-Century America* (Berkeley, CA: University of California Press), 1990, 20–21.

18 *of being artless and plain:* Garry Wills, *Lincoln at Gettysburg: The Words That Remade America* (New York: Simon & Schuster, 1992), 20; 148–49.

18 *"urbanity, tolerance and sense of humour":* Waite, *Macdonald*, 29.

18 *He seldom drafted text for his speeches:* Joseph Pope, *Memoirs of the Right Honourable Sir John Alexander Macdonald, First Prime Minister of the Dominion of Canada*, vol. 1, (Ottawa: J. Durie & Son, 1894), 284–86.

18 *"some muted legacy":* Ged Martin, "Sir John Eh? Macdonald," *British Journal of Canadian Studies* 17, no. I, (2004): 120.

18 *"He was in tone of voice":* Ibid., 119.

18 *"he took and went":* Ibid.

18 *"the corrupted lingo":* Wallace Stegner, *Wolf Willow: A History, a Story and a Memory of the Last Prairie Frontier* (Toronto: Macmillan of Canada, 1962), 26.

19 *"a little sing song":* Martin, *Sir John Eh?*, 120.

20 *two nations warring in the bosom of a single state:* "Durham Report," Canadian Encyclopedia, accessed March 12, 2017. http://www.thecanadianencyclopedia.ca/en/article/durham-report/.

20 *in his wooing of Galt*: Biggar, *Anecdotal Life*, 220–21.

21 *"a northern nation"*: Dennis Gruending, *Great Canadian Speeches* (Markham, ON: Fitzhenry & Whiteside, 2004), 27–30.

21 *give him any advantage*: Biggar, *Anecdotal Life*, 288–89.

22 *firm hold on power*: Waite, *Macdonald*, 62.

22 *planning to meet in Charlottetown*: For a description of the setting and debates, see Donald Creighton, *John A. Macdonald: The Young Politician* (Toronto: Macmillan of Canada, 1952), 402 ff.

22 *talking to himself for hours*: Biggar, *Anecdotal Life*, 225.

23 *"I have had the honour of being charged"*: Macdonald's speech is to be found in *The Parliamentary Debates on the Subject of the Confederation of the British North American Provinces, 3rd Session, 8th Provincial Parliament of Canada* (Ottawa: King's Printer, 1951), 25–45. Photographic reproduction of the original in 1865.

36 *the most rhetorically polished*: William Safire, ed., *Lend Me Your Ears: Great Speeches in History* (New York: W.W. Norton, 2004), 34.

36 *"a very poor speech"*: Donald Creighton, *The Road to Confederation* (Toronto: Macmillan of Canada, 1954), 236.

36 *not one of Macdonald's best*: Ibid.

36 *longer even than the King James Version*: Ged Martin, "Introduction to the 2006 Edition," in P. B. Waite, *The Confederation Debates in the Province of Canada, 1865*, second edition (Montreal & Kingston: McGill-Queen's Press, 2006), xxiii.

36 *twenty-seven voted for and twenty-one against*: Ibid., liii.

37 *in Halifax alone*: P. B. Waite, *The Life and Times of Confederation, 1864–67: Politics, Newspapers, and the Union of British North America* (Toronto: University of Toronto Press, 1965), 6.

37 *one eventually did:* Waite, *The Confederation Debates*, liii and liv.

37 *its reliance upon elected representatives*: See Janet Ajzenstat, ed., *Canada's Founding Debates* (Toronto: Stoddart, 1999), 458–59.

38 *"the ablest man in the province"*: Creighton, *The Road to Confederation*, 408.

38 *"passed almost without notice"*: Pope, *Memoirs*, vol. I, 312–13.

39 *steeped in their thought*: Ajzenstat, *Canada's Founding Debates*, 2.

WILFRID LAURIER

40 *"the greatest orator"*: Marc Bosc, ed., *The Broadview Book of Canadian Parliamentary Anecdotes* (Peterborough, ON: Broadview Press, 1988), 68.

40 *Wilfrid Laurier was born in 1841*: Réal Bélanger, "Laurier, Sir Wilfred," in *Dictionary of Canadian Biography*, vol. 14, (University of Toronto/Université Laval, 2003), accessed November 21, 2016, http://www.biographi.ca/en/bio/laurier_wilfrid_14E.html.

41 *revolutionary ideas*: Oscar Douglas Skelton, *Life and Letters of Sir Wilfrid Laurier*, vol. I, ed. David M.L. Farr, (Toronto: McClelland and Stewart, 1965), 11.

41 *support of liberalism*: Belanger, *DCB*.

42 *"passionate attachment"*: Ibid.

43 *"noblest and most unselfish man"*: Skelton, *Life and Letters*, Preface.

43 *"as well as Sir Galahad"*: J. W. Dafoe, *Laurier: A Study in Canadian Politics* (Toronto: Thomas Allen Publishers, 1922), 15.

43 *submit to the pope's will*: Laurier L. Lapierre, *Sir Wilfrid Laurier and the Romance of Canada* (Toronto: Stoddart Publishing Company, 1996), 61.

43 *condemned by the Vatican*: H. Blair Neatby, *Laurier and a Liberal Quebec: A Study in Political Management* (Toronto, McClelland & Stewart, 1973), 5.

44 *forced to stop publishing*: Lapierre, *Romance of Canada*, 56–57.

44 *the bishops were going too far*: Neatby, 5.

45 *the rest of his life*: Skelton, 14.

45 *conspicuous by his eloquence*: Belanger, *DCB*.

45 *"our Lord Jesus Christ'"*: Skelton, 37.

45 *Conservatives and Liberals respectively*: Lapierre, 75.

45 *a holy war*: Mason Wade, *The French Canadians 1760–1967*, vol. I (Toronto: Macmillan of Canada, 1968), 356.

46 *to talk discretely*: Neatby, 9.

46 *Conroy's recommendations*: Schull, 115.

46 *could not be a Liberal*: Skelton, p.42–43.

46 *advised Laurier*: Lapierre, 87.

46 *had completed his mission*: Schull, 116.

47 *and they scrutinized him*: For various descriptions of the speech see J. S. Willison, *Sir Wilfrid Laurier and the Liberal Party: A Political History*, vol. I (Toronto: George N. Morang and Company, 1903), 315–16; Ulrich Barthe, ed., *Sir Wilfrid Laurier on the Platform* 1871–1890 (Quebec: Turcotte and Menard, 1890), xv-xvi; see also Lapierre, 89.

47 *"I cannot conceal"*: "Lecture on Political Liberalism delivered by Wilfrid Laurier Esq. MP on the 26th of June, 1877, in the Music Hall, Quebec, under the Auspices of Le Club Canadien," pamphlet printed by *Quebec Morning Chronicle*, 1877.

55 *representing only themselves*: Neatby, 8–9.

57 *the preeminent spokesperson*: Neatby, Ibid.

58 *deafening applause*: See Lapierre, 95; "Lecture on Political Liberalism" pamphlet, vi; Barth, xvi.

58 *proclaimed immutable truths*: See "Lecture on Political Liberalism" pamphlet, 30.

58 *done himself … great harm*: Ibid., 31–32.

58 *a masterpiece of diction*: Ibid., 38.

58 *a new master*: Ibid., 42–43.

58 *with that of Bishop Conroy*: Schull, 122.

58 *what Laurier had said*: Willison, 343–47.

58 *spokesperson for Quebec*: Schull, 122; Skelton, 61.

60 *a majority of seats*: Claude Bélanger, "Quebec and Federal Elections, 1867–2006": Marianopolis College 2008, accessed November 24, 2016. http://faculty.marianopolis. edu/c.belanger/quebechistory/readings/fedelect.htm.

LOUIS RIEL

61 *Louis Riel was born 1844*: Maggie Siggins, *Riel: A Life of Revolution* (Toronto: HarperCollins Publishers Ltd, 1994), 4–45. See also Lewis H. Thomas, "Riel, Louis (1844–85)," in *Dictionary of Canadian Biography*, vol. 11, University of Toronto/Université Laval, 2003, accessed November 5, 2015, http://www.biographi.ca/en/bio/riel_louis_1844_85_11E.html.

62 *the workload was heavy*: Siggins, *Riel*, 49–50.

63 *short of his graduation*: Ibid., 62.

63 *Hugh John Macdonald*: Patricia Phenix, *Private Demons: The Tragic Personal Life of John A. Macdonald* (Toronto: McClelland & Stewart Ltd., 2006), 205–09.

63 *Riel fled to St. Joseph Mission*: Thomas, *DCB*.

64 *Beauport Asylum near Quebec City*: Siggins, *Riel*, 258 ff.

65 *cash in return for their scrip*: "Métis Scrip – The Foundation for a New Beginning," Library and Archives Canada, accessed November 25, 2016. https://www.collectionscanada. gc.ca/Métis-scrip/005005-2000-e.html

65 *defend their rights*: Siggins, 324, 327.

65 *Hugh John Macdonald volunteered*: Phenix, *Private Demons*: 258–60.

66 *brief periods of exercise*: Siggins, *Riel*, 413.

66 *"harsh and unwise"*: Right Honourable Beverley McLachlin, Chief Justice of Canada, "Louis Riel: Patriot Rebel," Keynote to Delloyd J. Guth Visiting Lecture in Legal History, October 28, 2010 (Winnipeg, Manitoba).

67 *a March 1885 meeting*: Siggins, *Riel*, 418.

67 *a mandatory penalty of death*: Ibid., 415.

67 *ill with tuberculosis*: Ibid., 414.

67 *made no further objection*: Desmond Morton, *The Queen v Louis Riel* (Toronto: University of Toronto Press, 1974), 41.

67 *resistance could not be justified*: Paul Groake, "Reconstructing the Substantive Argument in Louis Riel's Address to the Jury," in *Riel's Defence: Perspectives on His Speeches*, ed. Hans Hansen (Montreal-Kingston: McGill-Queens University Press 2014), 206.

68 *not allowed to interfere*: Morton, *The Queen v Louis Riel*, 206.

68 *gone to the jury*: Groake, *Riel's Defence*, 205.

68 *the basis of a later appeal*: Ibid., 209.

68 wanted to enjoy the proceedings: Siggins, *Riel*, 417.

68 *Riel was dressed*: Ibid., 428.

69 *Your Honours, gentlemen of the jury*: Riel's speech is found in Desmond Morton, *The Queen v Louis Riel* (Toronto: University of Toronto Press, 1974), 311–25.

75 *"trapped in a private world"*: Thomas Flanagan, "Louis Riel's Trial Speeches," in Hansen, *Riel's Defence*, 116.

79 *worthy of mercy*: Hans V. Hansen, "Narrative and Logical Orders in Louis Riel's Address to the Jury," in Hansen, *Riel's Defence*, 161.

80 *He lived until 1951*: Siggins, *Riel*, 420.

80 *"He shall hang"*: Ibid., 443.

80 *It was this information*: Ibid., 441–42.

80 *Sixteen of seventeen Quebec MPs*: J. S. Willison, *Sir Wilfrid Laurier and the Liberal Party: A Political History*, vol. I (Toronto: George N. Morang and Company, 1903), 448.

81 *"shouldered my musket"*: Mason Wade, *The French Canadians*, 417.

81 *political calculation*: J. W. Dafoe, *Laurier: A Study in Canadian Politics* (Toronto: Macmillan of Canada, 1978), 19.

81 an egotistical madman: Willison, *Sir Wilfrid Laurier*, 464.

81 *a reward of $5,000*: Siggins, *Riel*, 208.

81 *The Catholic hierarchy*: Wade, *The French Canadians*, 417.

82 *One cannot say without reservation*: H. Blair Neatby, *Laurier and a Liberal Quebec; A Study in Political Management* (Toronto, McClelland and Stewart, 1973), 27.

82 *a galvanizing figure*: Albert Braz, *The False Traitor: Louis Riel in Canadian Culture* (Toronto: University of Toronto Press, 2003), 4–12.

82 *the battle of mythologies*: Desmond Morton, "The Queen vs Louis Riel: The Historical Context," in Hansen, p. 74.

NELLIE MCCLUNG

83 *Nellie Mooney was born in 1873*: Michelle Swann and Veronica Strong-Boag, "Mooney, Helen Letitia (McClung)," in *Dictionary of Canadian Biography*, vol. 18, University of Toronto/ Université Laval, 2003, accessed November 12, 2015. http://www.biographi.ca/en/bio/ mooney_helen_letitia_18E.html

84 *witty and light-hearted*: Veronica Strong-Boag and Michelle Lynn Rosa, *Nellie McClung, The Complete Autobiography* (Peterborough, ON: Broadview Press, 2003), 39. This book contains McClung's two volumes of autobiography: Clearing in the West and The Stream Runs Fast.

84 *"in my grandchildren"*: Ibid., 59.

84 *mother was not pleased*: Ibid., 147–49.

85 *"She had all the sweetness"*: "Nellie McClung, Anecdotal Timeline," accessed January 18, 2017. http://www.ournellie.com/about-nellie/anecdotal-timeline/

86 *"a new world as I talked"*: Ibid.

86 *spoke almost every day*: Ibid.

86 *chicken sandwiches and olives*: Strong-Boag and Lynn Rosa, *Complete Autobiography*, 387.

87 *"dreamed pleasantly of a golden age"*: Randi R. Warne, *Literature as Pulpit: The Christian Social Activism of Nellie L. McClung* (Waterloo, ON, Wilfrid Laurier Press, 1993), 70. Cited from the novel *Painted Fires*.

87 *asked for a meeting*: Strong-Boag and Lynn Rosa, *Complete Autobiography*, 391–93.

87 *for women's suffrage*: Ibid., 394.

88 *Those traits became more established*: W.L. Morton, *Manitoba: A History* (Toronto: University of Toronto Press, 1957), 281.

88 *Roblin was opposed*: Ibid., 283, 334.

89 *"numbered several hundred men and women"*: *Winnipeg Telegram*, January 28, 1914, 53–54.

89 *"standing room on the floor of the house"*: *Winnipeg Free Press*, January 28, 1914, 44–45.

89 *"Straight from the shoulder"*: Ibid.

90 *feminist theatrical parodies*: Kym Bird, "Performing Politics: Propaganda, Parody and a Women's Parliament" in *Theatre Research in Canada / Recherches théâtrales au Canada*, vol. 13, No 1 and 2 (Spring and Fall 1992), accessed January 18, 2017. https://journals.lib.unb.ca/index.php/tric/article/view/7253/8312

90 *The mock parliament would be humorous*: Heather Graves, "The Women's Parliament: Political Oratory, Humor, and Social Change," in *Gender Forum: An Internet Journal for Gender Studies*, 33 (2011), accessed January 18, 2017. http://www.genderforum.org/issues/gender-and-humour/the-womens-parliament/

91 *ingratiatingly friendly*: Strong-Boag and Lynn Rosa, *Complete Autobiography*, 397.

91 *The draft remains*: "Premier's reply to the delegation," Nellie McClung Papers, box 20, file no. 3, Provincial Archives of British Columbia (PABC).

92 *satire and humour*: Heather Graves, "The Women's Parliament."

92 *a name for the device*: Kym Bird, "Performing Politics."

92 *"poll-cats"*: "Urban dictionary," accessed January 18, 2017. http://www.urbandictionary.com/define.php?term=Pollcat

97 *"packed to the roof"*: McClung includes complete stories from the *Winnipeg Telegram* and *Winnipeg Free Press* of January 29, 1914, in Strong-Boag and Lynn Rosa, *Complete Autobiography*, 399–404.

98 *she did not indulge in sarcasm*: Ibid., 399.

98 *"rhetoric of reversal"*: Heather Graves, "The Women's Parliament."

98 *in moving public sentiment*: Strong-Boag and Lynn Rosa, *Complete Autobiography*, 398–99.

98 *addressed one hundred meetings*: Veronica Strong-Boag, "An Introduction" to *In These Times* (Toronto: University of Toronto Press, 1972), xi.

98 *burned in effigy*: Swann and Strong-Boag, *Dictionary of Canadian Biography*.

100 *sentimental and didactic*: Charlotte Gray, *Nellie McClung* (Toronto: Penguin Canada, 2008), 44; 140-41.

ARTHUR MEIGHEN

101 *Arthur Meighen was born in 1874*: Larry A. Glassford, "Meighen, Arthur," in *Dictionary of Canadian Biography*, vol. 18, University of Toronto/Université Laval, 2003, accessed March 4, 2016. http://www.biographi.ca/en/bio/meighen_arthur_18E.htm

102 *"minister of everything"*: Roger Graham, *Arthur Meighen: The Door of Opportunity*, vol. 1, (Toronto: Clarke, Irwin & Company Limited, 1960), 88.

103 *conscription would not be necessary*: Desmond Morton, *A Short History of Canada*, 3rd revised edition (Toronto: McClleland and Stewart, 1997), 167.

103 *Borden was opposed*: Graham, *Arthur Meighen*, 88.

104 *piloted the legislation*: "Conscription," *Canadian Encyclopedia*, accessed March 3, 2016. http://www.thecanadianencyclopedia.ca/en/article/arthur-meighen/

105 *"he was without an equal"*: Introduction to *Arthur Meighen, Unrevised and Unrepented: Debating Speeches and Others* (Toronto: Clarke, Irwin & Company Limited, 1949), xi.

105 *He was … "forensic"*: Graham, *Arthur Meighen*, 44–45.

105 *Laurier spoke at length*: Canada. House of Commons. *Debates*, June 18, 1917 (King's Printer), 2391–2404.

106 *abide by the result*: Ibid., 2403–04.

107 *No one could be present*: *Debates*, June 21, 1917, 2529–38.

115 *would kill the party*: See John English, *The Decline of Politics: The Conservatives and the Party System*, 1901–20 (Toronto: University of Toronto Press, 1993), 129.

116 *riots in Quebec City*: Graham, *Arthur Meighen*, 192.

116 *"imperils national unity"*: Ibid., 126.

116 *"estranged from friends"*: *Debates*, July 24, 1917, 3723.

117 *"I have promoted union"*: Ibid., 3729.

117 *"Nothing was farther from my mind"*: Ibid., 3729.

117 *better left unsaid*: Graham, *Arthur Meighen*, 144.

117 *to the end of the war*: "Military Service Act," *Canadian Encyclopedia*, accessed March 3, 2016. http://www.thecanadianencyclopedia.ca/en/article/military-service-act/

118 *Most French Canadians*: Ibid.

118 *Meighen had recommended*: Graham, *Arthur Meighen*, 164–66.

119 *destroyed Conservative prospects*: "Conscription," *Canadian Encyclopedia*, accessed March 3, 2016. http://www.thecanadianencyclopedia.ca/en/article/conscription/

119 *marched on Ottawa*: Graham, *Arthur Meighen*, 193.

119 *380,000 appealed*: Morton, *A Short History of Canada*, 175.

119 *only 24,000 made it to France*: "Conscription," *Canadian Encyclopedia*.

119 *"amendments to the Criminal Code"*: Glassford, *DCB*.

120 *"unrevised and unrepented"*: Arthur Meighen, *Unrevised and Unrepented*. (Toronto: Clarke, Irwin & Company, 1949). It is worth mentioning that in the Preface to this collection of his parliamentary speeches Meighen says, "there has been no revision in substance and opinion." Actually, he was quite liberal in making changes, including the addition of some things that he had not said in Parliament. He also rearranged some material within the speeches.

AGNES MACPHAIL

121 *Agnes Macphail was born in a log house*: "Agnes, Macphail," *Canadian Encyclopedia*, accessed May 23, 2016. http://www.thecanadianencyclopedia.ca/en/article/agnes-macphail/

122 *economic and political ferment*: "Rise of Rural Power," CBC.ca/history, accessed on May 23, 2016. http://www.cbc.ca/history/episcontentse1ep12ch3pa3le.html

123 *The farm activists*: Terry Crowley, *Agnes Macphail and the Politics of Equality* (Toronto: James Lorimer & Company, Publishers, 1990), 22–25.

124 *came under pressure*: Ibid, 37.

124 *In her first brief speech*: Canada. House of Commons. *Debates*, March 29, 1922 (King's Printer), 479.

125 *"preservation of the home"*: Ibid., June 4, 1925, 3864.

126 *a handsome person*: Doris Pennington, *Agnes Macphail: Reformer* (Toronto: Simon & Pierre, 1989), 32–33.

126 *she lost twenty pounds*: Ibid., 41.

126 *"wish she were a man"*: Ibid., 114.

127 *the Chautauqua lecture circuit*: Pennington, 93–94; Crowley, 160.

128 *the Ginger Group*: Crowley, *Agnes Macphail* , 75–76.

128 *lost power provincially*: Ibid., 69.

129 *"We come again"*: *Debates:* February 28, 1928, 837–44.

134 *cooperative form of government*: Crowley, *Agnes Macphail*, 71.

135 *with the more decorative rhetoric*: Kenneth Cmiel, *Democratic Eloquence: The Fight Over Popular Speech in Nineteenth-Century America* (New York: William Morrow and Company, 1990), 247–49.

138 *"caustic criticism"*: Pennington, *Agnes Macphail*, 74.

138 *"We always enjoy her witticisms"*: *Debates*: February 29, 1928, 893–94.

139 *"occupational group government."*: Ibid., March 2, 1928, 961–63.

139 *she reserved her right to dissent*: Crowley, *Agnes Macphail*, 167.

R. B. BENNETT

141 *Richard Bedford Bennett was born*: P. B. Waite, "Bennett, Richard Bedford,1st Viscount Bennett," in *Dictionary of Canadian Biography*, vol. 17, University of Toronto/Université Laval, 2003, accessed May 3, 2016, http://www.biographi.ca/en/bio/bennett_richard_bedford_17E.html.

144 *bonfire Bennett*: Grattan O'Leary, *Recollections of People, Press, and Politics* (Toronto: Macmillan, 1977), 39.

144 *The Canadian Economy*: "Richard Bedford Bennett," *The Canadian Encyclopedia* (Historica Canada), accessed May 3, 2016. http://www.thecanadianencyclopedia.ca/en/article/richard-bedford-viscount-bennett/

144 *"I would not give a single cent"*: http://www.canadahistory.com/sections/eras/crash%20depression/Bennett.html. Accessed May 16, 2016.

145 *Bennett also attempted*: Blair H. Neatby, *The Politics of Chaos: Canada in the Thirties* (Kemptville, ON: Golden Dog Press, 2003), 56 ff.

145 *"the iron heel of capitalism"*: Ibid., p. 65.

145 *"a wet nurse to every derelict"*: Pierre Berton, *The Great Depression: 1929–1939*, (Toronto: McClelland & Stewart Inc., 1990), 223.

145 *"the only thing we have to fear"*: John Grafton, ed., *Franklin Delano Roosevelt–Great Speeches* (Mineoloa, New York: Dover Publications Inc. 1999), 29.

146 *listening to the same speech*: J. R. H. (Richard) Wilbur, *The Bennett Administration 1930–1935* (Ottawa: Canadian Historical Association, 1969), 14.

146 *He asked for calm*: Grafton, *Franklin Delano Roosevelt*, 35.

146 *familiar with each word*: Samuel Irving Rosenman, *Working with Roosevelt* (London, Hart-Davis, 1952), 26.

146 *"[Roosevelt] looked for words"*: "Fireside chats," *Wikipedia, The Free Encyclopedia*, accessed May 4, 2016. https://en.wikipedia.org/w/index.php?title=Fireside_chats&oldid=717426162.

147 *"bumper on his car"*: P. B. Waite, *The Loner: Three Sketches of the Personal Life and Ideas of R. B. Bennett, 1870–1947* (Toronto: University of Toronto Press, 1992), 70.

147 *"one of the ablest diplomats:"* Dean Acheson, *Morning and Noon* (Boston: Houghton Mifflin, 1965), 178–80.

147 *"we simply prime the engine"*: J. R. H. Wilbur, ed., *The Bennett New Deal: Fraud Or Portent?* (Toronto: Copp Clark Publishing Company, 1968), 67 ff.

148 *"Government is now in business"*: Ibid., 71.

148 *responded in kind*: Ibid., 121–23.

148 *the lens of a cartoon capitalist*: Larry A. Glassford, *Reaction and Reform: The Politics of the Conservative Party under R.B. Bennett, 1927–1938* (Toronto: University of Toronto Press, 1992), 153.

149 *he had spoken well*: Roderick K. Finlayson, "Life with R.B.: That Man Bennett," personal memoirs, unpublished manuscript, 60–63, accessed May 4, 2016. http://heritage.canadiana.ca/view/oocihm.lac_mikan_102041. Original documentation found at Library and Archives Canada, Roderick K. Finlayson fonds: H-1310.

149 *hand them over to Bennett*: Ibid., 253-56.

149 *Bennett could do the same*: Glassford, *Reaction and Reform*, 153.

150 *to get maximum coverage*: Ibid., 154–55.

150 *"The time has come"*: *The Premier speaks to the people: the first address delivered from Ottawa on Wednesday, January 2nd, 1935, between 9:00 and 9:30 p.m.* (Ottawa: Dominion Conservative Headquarters, 1935). 20 pp, accessed May 4, 2016. Archived at: https://www.collectionscanada.gc.ca/primeministers/h4-4049-e.html.

153 *"perish in the attempt"*: Berton, *The Great Depression*, 64.

154 *"The policy of laissez-faire must be abandoned"*: Wilbur, *The Bennett New Deal*, 76.

157 *sermons from the mount*: Wilbur, *The Bennett Administration*, 14.

157 *eight million Canadians*: *The Premier Speaks to the People*, 3.

157 *"quickened the spirit of the country."*: Ibid., 5.

157 *join the democratic socialists*: Berton, *The Great Depression*, 284.

158 *oppose Bennett's proposals*: Glassford, *Reaction and Reform*, 155–57.

158 *plans were failing*: Wilbur, *The Bennett New Deal*, 100–01.

158 *just around the corner*: Ibid., 102–04.

158 *In a January 4 memo*: For *Free Press* exchanges see Wilbur, *The Bennett New Deal*, 94–99.

159 *Mackenzie King raged*: Berton, *The Great Depression*, 285.

159 *a toned-down synopsis*: Glassford, *Reaction and Reform*, 159.

159 *He did introduce several bills*: Wilbur, *The Bennett Administration*, 15. See also Berton, *The Great Depression*, 286.

160 *pieces of new deal legislation*: Glassford, *Reaction and Reform*, 162.

160 *threatened to drain votes*: Ibid., 170.

TOMMY DOUGLAS

162 *Thomas Clement (Tommy) Douglas was born*: Thomas H. McLeod and Ian McLeod, *Tommy Douglas: The Road to Jerusalem* (Edmonton: Hurtig, 1987), 5–15. See also "Tommy Douglas," *Canadian Encyclopedia*, accessed July 6, 2016. http://www.thecanadianencyclopedia.ca/en/article/tommy-douglas/

163 *a title he defended*: McLeod, 19–45.

164 *enamoured with eugenics*: Walter Stewart, *The Life and Political Times of Tommy Douglas* (Toronto: McArthur & Company, 2003), 76–81.

164 *Nellie McClung was a prominent advocate*: Charlotte Gray, *Nellie McClung* (Toronto: Penguin Canada, 2008), 125-28. See also "Eugenics: Keeping Canada Sane," *Canadian Encyclopedia*, accessed March 11, 2017. http://www.thecanadianencyclopedia.ca/en/article/eugenics-keeping-canada-sane-feature/

165 *stayed away from such policies*: McLeod, 40–41; Stewart, 81.

165 *a demanding task master*: L. D. Lovick, ed., *Tommy Douglas Speaks: Till Power is Brought to Pooling* (Lantzville, British Columbia: Oolichan Books, 1979), 11–42.

166 *speaking at three public meetings*: McLeod, 107–17.

166 *physical gestures and postures*: Lovick, 14–15.

167 *ambitious reform agenda*: A. W. Johnson and Rosemary Proctor, *Dream No Little Dreams: A Biography of the Douglas Government of Saskatchewan, 1944–1961* (Toronto: University of Toronto Press 2004), 59–93. See also McLeod, *Road to Jerusalem*, chapters 12 to 21.

167 *endorsed public health insurance in 1933*: Dennis Gruending, *Emmett Hall: Establishment Radical* (Toronto: Macmillan of Canada, 1985), 85–87.

168 *"civil conscription" of doctors*: Ibid., 88.

168 *dedicated more money*: Dennis Gruending, *Promises to Keep: A Political Biography of Allan Blakeney* (Saskatoon: Western Producer Prairie Books, 1990), 32. See also McLeod, 198.

168 *an even bigger battle to come*: See Johnson, *Dream No Little Dreams*, 259–271.

168 *"flatly opposed"*: Ibid., 263.

169 *"this session of the legislature"*: *Legislative Assembly of Saskatchewan Debates*, October 13, 1961 (Throne Speech Debate), pp: 2-27. Accessed, July 6, 201. http://docs.legassembly.sk.ca/legdocs/Legislative%20Assembly/Hansard/14L2S/611013Debates.pdf

180 *"legal training and judicial bearing"*: Gruending, *Emmett Hall*, 80–102.

180 *"take some satisfaction"*: Ibid., 80.

180 *Medicare has served Canadians well*: See *Building on Values: the Future of Health Care in Canada*, Commission on the Future of Health Care in Canada, 2002. Roy J. Romanow, commissioner, accessed March 11, 2017. http://publications.gc.ca/collections/Collection/CP32-85-2002E.pdf.

LESTER PEARSON

182 *Lester Bowles Pearson was born in 1897*: See John English, "Pearson, Lester Bowles," in *Dictionary of Canadian Biography*, vol. 20, University of Toronto/Université Laval, 2003, accessed July 29, 2016, http://www.biographi.ca/en/bio/pearson_lester_bowles_20E.html.

184 *sent him home to Canada*: Ibid.

185 *"artfully concealed ambition"*: Ibid.

186 *Diefenbaker's family migrated*: See Denis Smith, *Rogue Tory: The Life and Legend of John G. Diefenbaker* (Toronto: Macfarlane Walter & Ross, 1995), 1–33

187 *suffered from fear and anxiety*: Ibid., 30–31.

188 *"sixty days of derision"*: Thomas Van Dusen, *The Chief* (Toronto: McGraw-Hill, 1968), 55.

188 *still smarting from his losses*: Peter C. Newman, *The Distemper of our Times* (Toronto: McClelland and Stewart, Carleton Library Edition, 1978), 255.

188 *a mix of reasons*: Gregory A. Johnston, "The Last Gasp of Empire: The 1964 Flag Debate Revisited," in Phillip Buckner, ed., *Canada and the End of Empire* (Vancouver: UBC Press, 2004), 241 ff.

189 *spoke to the Canadian Legion*: Johnston, *Last Gasp*: 233.

189 *eight Parliamentary Press Gallery reporters*: Ibid., 256.

189 *his first dramatic pitch*: John Ross Matheson, *Canada's Flag* (Belleville, ON: Mika Publishing Company, 1986), 68–69.

190 *talking about the flag*: The text of Winnipeg speech can be found in Lester B. Pearson, *Words and Occasions* (Toronto: University of Toronto Press, 1970), 228–32.

190 *"drop dead"*: Johnston, *Last Gasp*, 234.

190 *As Harry Truman used to say*: Matheson, *Canada's Flag*, 73. See also *Chicago Tribune*, "Pearson's flag plan jeered," May 18, 1964, accessed, September 22, 2016. http://archives. chicagotribune.com/1964/05/18/page/49/article/pearson-flag-plan-jeered-hes-cheered.

190 *"selling Canada to the pea-soupers"*: Newman, *Distemper*, 257.

190 *"I would like to ask"*: Canada. House of Commons. *Debates*, May 19, 1964 (Queen's Printer), 3336.

191 *he changed his mind*: Newman, *Distemper*, 257.

191 *Diefenbaker had his own reasons*: See Johnston, *Last Gasp*, 244–47.

192 *it could work again*: "Flag Debate," *Canadian Encyclopedia*, accessed September 22, 2016. http://www.thecanadianencyclopedia.ca/en/article/flag-debate/

192 *I would remind the house: Debates,* June 15, 1964, 4306 ff.

197 *he was humiliated:* John English, *The Worldly Years: The Life of Lester Pearson*, vol. II (Toronto: Alfred A Knopf Canada, 1992), 140–41. See also Johnston, *Last Gasp*, 242.

199 *who had served at the front*: C. P. Champion, "A Very British Coup: Canadianism, Quebec, and Ethnicity in the Flag Debate," in *Journal of Canadian Studies*, vol. 40, No. 3 (Fall 2006), 74.

202 *Diefenbaker followed Pearson: Debates,* June 15, 1964, 4326–32.

202 *one final clash: Debates*, December 14, 1964, 11135–36.

204 *spanned six months*: Matheson, *Canada's Flag*, 171.

204 *hatless in the cold*: Ibid., 180.

204 *In his memoirs*: J.A. Munro and A.I. Inglis, eds., *Mike, The Memoirs of the Right Honourable Lester B. Pearson*, Vol 3 (Toronto: University of Toronto Press, 1975), 270.

204 *"a tinker's damn"*: Champion, "A Very British Coup," 79.

205 *journalist Peter Calamai*: "Did Grits have 'mole' inside Tory caucus during flag debate?" *The Ottawa Citizen*, February 15, 1986, B9.

205 *vote with the government*: Ibid.

205 *threat to national unity*: Munro and Inglis, *Mike*, 270.

205 *no place for a French Canadian*: Smith, *Rogue Tory*, 524.

206 *overlain with the Red Ensign*: Ibid., 575–76.

PIERRE TRUDEAU

207 *Pierre Elliott Trudeau was born in 1919*: See John English, "Trudeau, Pierre Elliott," in *Dictionary of Canadian Biography*, vol. 22, University of Toronto/Université Laval, 2003, accessed October 3, 2016, http://www.biographi.ca/en/bio/trudeau_pierre_elliott_22E.html.

208 *the study of languages*: Michael Higgins, "Defined by Spirituality?" in John English, Richard Gwyn, P. Whitney Lackenbauer, eds., *The Hidden Pierre Elliott Trudeau: The Faith Behind the Politics* (Ottawa: Novalis, 2004), 27.

208 *a catalyst for change*: Solange Lefebvre, "Politics and Religion in Quebec: Theological Issues and the Generation Factor," in *The Hidden Pierre Trudeau*, 57.

209 *"guide my nation"*: Andrew Cohen, "I must become a great man," *The Globe and Mail*, October 14, 2006, D12. Cohen is reviewing the John English biography, *Citizen of the World: A Life of Pierre Trudeau*.

209 *shed his street-informed accent*: Stephen Clarkson and Christina McCall, *Trudeau and Our Times: The Magnificent Obsession* (Toronto: McClelland & Stewart, 1990), 37.

209 *body of an athlete*: Ibid., 36.

209 *donning an old military uniform*: Max and Monique Nemni, *Young Trudeau: Son of Quebec, Father of Canada 1919–1944* (Toronto: McClelland & Stewart, 2006), 19.

209 *the group was to go nowhere*: Ibid., 212.

210 *revealing personal papers*: Ibid., 3

212 *"man-in-the-mask"*: John English, *Just Watch Me: The Life of Pierre Elliott Trudeau, 1968–2000* (Toronto, Vintage Canada, 2009), 16.

212 *legislation in 1969*: "Pierre Elliott Trudeau," *Canadian Encyclopedia*, accessed November 16, 2016. http://www.thecanadianencyclopedia.ca/en/article/pierre-elliott-trudeau/

214 *traditional expectations*: Nino Ricci, *Pierre Elliott Trudeau* (Toronto: Penguin Canada, 2009), 145.

215 *"if you can write"*: English, *Just Watch Me*, 449.

215 *"you want to slap his face"*: Ibid.

215 *stunning victory:* Graham Fraser, *René Lévesque and the Parti Québécois in Power* (Toronto: Macmillan of Canada, 1984), 362 ff.

216 *a "crime against humanity"*: Ibid.

216 *"Welcome to the 1980s"*: John English, *DCB*.

217 *become its own country*: Fraser, *René Lévesque*, 198–99.

217 *parting of the ways*: Ibid., 201.

217 *"the path to our future"*: Dennis Gruending, ed., *Great Canadian Speeches* (Markham, ON: Fitzhenry & Whiteside, 2004), 201.

217 *Lévesque was campaigning well*: English, *Just Watch Me*, 448.

217 *family allowance cheques*: Clarkson and McCall, *Trudeau and Our Times*, 228.

218 *spoke to large rallies*: Fraser, *René Lévesque*: 231–34.

218 *not a real Quebecker*: Pierre Elliott Trudeau, *Memoirs* (Toronto: McClelland & Stewart, 1993), 273 ff. See also Fraser, 227 ff, and Clarkson and McCall, 236.

218 *a writer named André Burelle*: Patrick Gossage, *Close to Charisma: My Years Between the Press and Pierre Elliott Trudeau* (Halifax: Formac Publishing Company Limited, 1986), 196.

218 *remind himself of key points*: Trudeau, *Memoirs*, 278.

219 *foot-stomping demonstration*: Gossage, *Close to Charisma*, 197–98.

219 *fellow Canadians*: Library and Archives Canada, "The Right Honourable Pierre Elliott Trudeau, Speech at the Paul Sauvé Arena, Montreal, Quebec, May 14, 1980," accessed, November 12, 2016. http://www.collectionscanada.ca/primeministers/h4-4083-e.html

223 *"the intolerant side of separatism"*: Trudeau, *Memoirs*, 281.

226 *back to Ottawa*: English, *Just Watch Me*, 457.

226 *'Wait until next time'*: Graham Fraser, *René Lévesque*, 235.

226 *a renewed federalism*: John English, *Just Watch Me*, 458–59.

227 *journalists were "awe-struck."*: Gossage, *Close to Charisma*, 197.

227 *"towards the Non"*: Clarkson and McCall, *Trudeau and Our Times*, 239.

227 *"preparing his entire life"*: L. Ian MacDonald, "Trudeau's speeches 30 years ago were his finest hours," *The Gazette*, May 8, 2010, accessed November 12, 2016. http://www. lianmacdonald.ca/columns/gazette/20100508.html

227 *mandate for constitutional change*: Fraser, *René Lévesque*, 227.

228 *"the most decentralized"*: Trudeau, *Memoirs*, 283.

JOSEPH GOSNELL

231 *Joseph Gosnell was born in 1936:* Alex Rose, *Spirit Dance at Meziadin: Chief Joseph Gosnell and the Nisga'a Treaty* (Madeira Park, BC: Harbour Publishing, 2001), 152–74.

231 *The children were expected not to talk:* Kevin Griffin, "Canada 150: Joseph Gosnell helped negotiate historic treaty for the Nisga'a," *Vancouver Sun*, May 12, 2017. http://vancouversun. com/news/local-news/canada-150/canada-150-joseph-gosnell-helped-negotiate-historic-treaty-for-the-nisgaa. Accessed July 11, 2017.

231 *The Anglicans were the first to arrive:* Rose, *Spirit Dance*, 56–75.

231 *The totems … were forcibly abandoned*: Ibid., 156.

232 *"never in a thousand years"*: Ibid., 158 ff.

232 *lay leaders in Protestant churches*: Ibid., 64-65.

232 *"debilitating sense of shyness"*: Ibid., 155.

232 *He rebuked them with a contemptuous comment*: Ibid., 13.

233 *to undergird … Aboriginal rights and title*: Joe Gunn, "Revoke 15th century 'doctrine' which approved the Conquest," *Western Catholic Reporter*, March 9, 2015.

233 *a young lawyer named Thomas Berger*: Thomas R. Berger, *One Man's Justice: A Life in the Law* (Vancouver/Toronto: Douglas & McIntrye, 2002), 112.

233 *Frank Calder … was born in the Nass Valley*: "Frank Calder," *The Canadian Encyclopedia*. http://www.thecanadianencyclopedia.ca/en/article/frank-calder/. Accessed July 11, 2017. See also Joan Harper, *He Moved a Mountain: The Life of Frank Calder and the Nisga'a Land Claims Accord* (Vancouver: Rosedale Press, 2013).

234 *"historical 'might have beens'"*: Berger, *One Man's Justice*, 114.

234 *"there would have to be negotiations—and a treaty"*: Ibid., 113.

234 *"The Nisga'a have never ceded or extinguished"*: Quoted in Rose, *Spirit Dance*, 91–92.

235 *"few of the institutions of civilized society"*: Quoted in Dennis Gruending: *Emmett Hall: Establishment Radical* (Markham, ON, Fitzhenry & Whiteside, 2005), 203.

236 *"My view was that the international law accepted Aboriginal rights"*: Ibid., 204.

236 *"pale into insignificance"*: Ibid., 206.

237 *Under terms of the treaty*: See "Financial Arrangements," Indigenous and Northern Affairs Canada. https://www.aadnc-aandc.gc.ca/eng/1100100031313/1100100031314. Accessed July 11, 2017. See also Berger, *One Man's Justice*, 135.

237 *three and one-half times the size of Prince Edward Island*: Rose, *Spirit Dance*, 38.

238 *the treaty was met with a fierce backlash*: Rose, *Spirit Dance*, 175–200. See also Berger, *One Man's Justice*, 130 ff.

238 *"critical to our success"*: Rose, *Spirit Dance*, 115.

239 *Gosnell made a speaking tour*: Stewart Bell, "Nisga'a Negotiation Gets Global Attention," *National Post*, October 30, 1998.

239 *"Campbell … made reference to the "disagreements amongst us"*: British Columbia, Legislative Assembly. *Debates*, December 2, 1998, 10859. https://www.leg.bc.ca/documents-data/debate-transcripts/36th-parliament/3rd-session/H1202PM. Accessed July 11, 2017.

239 *Joseph Gosnell began to speak*: Ibid.

248 *"reduced to an empty shell"*: Berger, *One Man's Justice*, 135.

248 *He chose to abandon the lawsuit*: Ibid., 137.

248 *The treaty was also opposed*: Rose, *Spirit Dance*, 200–12.

248 *with municipal-style powers*: Ibid., 158–60.

249 *modern treaties cover nearly half of Canada's land mass*: Hamar Foster, Heather Raven, and Jeremy Webber, eds., *Let Right Be Done: Aboriginal Title, the Calder Case, and the Future of Indigenous Rights* (Vancouver: UBC Press, 2007), 1–33. See also, Julie Jai, "The Journey of Reconciliation: Understanding our Treaty Past, Present and Future" (The Caledon Institute of Social Policy, 2014).

249 *"the type of statesman that beleaguered nations dream of"*: Tom Molloy with Donald Ward, *The World Is Our Witness* (Calgary: Fifth House Ltd., 2000), 147.

INDEX

ABOUT THE AUTHOR

Dennis Gruending is an Ottawa-based writer, a former member of Parliament, and author of the blog Pulpit and Politics. He has worked as a print, radio, and television journalist, as a radio host, and has written or edited seven previous books. His anthology *Great Canadian Speeches* was a best seller. *The Ottawa Citizen* described the book as a history of Canada as seen from the podium. He has also written biographies of Emmett Hall, whose Royal Commission recommended Medicare for Canada, and of former Saskatchewan premier Allan Blakeney.

Gruending holds an Honours degree in English literature from the University of Saskatchewan and a Masters degree in journalism from Carleton University in Ottawa. He writes a blog for the United Church Observer and his pieces also appear regularly on Rabble.ca.